Mixed News

The
Public/Civic/Communitarian
Journalism
Debate

Jay Black, Editor

LEA LAWRENCE ERLBAUM ASSOCIATES, PUBLISHERS
1997   Mahwah, New Jersey

Lawrence Erlbaum Associates, Inc., Publishers
10 Industrial Avenue
Mahwah, New Jersey 07430

Library of Congress Cataloging-in-Publication Data

Mixed news : the public/civic/communitarian journalism debate / Jay
    Black, editor
       p.   cm. -- (LEA's communication series)
    Includes bibliographical references and index.
    ISBN 0-8058-2542-8 (cloth : alk. paper). -- ISBN 0-8058-2543-6
  (pbk. : alk. paper)
    1. Journalistic ethics. 2. Journalism--Social aspects.
  I. Black, Jay. II. Series.
  PN4756.M59 1997
  174'.9097--dc21   96-48127
                                    CIP

Books published by Lawrence Erlbaum Associates are printed
on acid-free paper, and their bindings are chosen
for strength and durability.

Printed in the United States of America

10 9 8 7 6 5 4 3 2

Table of Contents

Preface

This project originated in 1994, with a request to the Ethics and Excellence in Journalism Foundation in Oklahoma City, to support a series of public lectures on a controversial topic that was starting to emerge within daily journalism. The grant request was somewhat narrow; the grant proposal sought support to explore:

> . . . one of the central ethical issues of journalism today: To what extent is the ethical journalist an isolated "individualist," and to what extent is he/she a "communitarian" or a committed member of the wider community? This issue has generated a great deal of discussion and debate within newsrooms and classrooms, and much confusion in the general community. Traditional journalists advocate avoiding any real or apparent conflicts of interest, which many take to mean journalists should refrain from membership in community groups and even refrain from voting. Contemporary (often market-driven) journalists approve closer involvement in their communities, often as an "image building" technique. Some philosophers advocate the ethics of independence and individualism for "professional" journalists, and others insist upon "communitarianism" and commitment to local and generalized "communities" as a prerequisite for citizenship. Some say involvement is fine for publishers and editors, but not for reporters; others say everyone is and should be a stakeholder. There's been a lot of shouting about the issue. Is it any wonder there is confusion?

Fortunately, the Ethics and Excellence in Journalism Foundation board agreed that this narrow issue should be systematically examined in a series of public lectures and, later, in published form. Even more fortunately, the speakers invited to the University of South Florida's St. Petersburg campus had the good sense to broaden the subject matter to cover the expansive territory found within these pages. All of them—and a couple of others, who were drafted into service for contributions to the book but missed out on the chance to visit sunny St. Petersburg (a situation that shortly will be rectified)—addressed the independence/interdependence issue. However, they all had the professional and academic insight to identify the issues much more fully.

Individually and collectively, the contributors to this project addressed such topics as the nature and needs of the individual vs. the nature and needs of the broader society; theories of communitarianism vs. Enlightenment liberalism; independence vs. interdependence (vs. co-dependency); negative vs. positive freedoms; Constitutional mandates vs. marketplace mandates; universal ethical values vs. situational and/or professional values; traditional values vs. information age values; ethics of management vs. ethics of worker bees; commitment and compassion vs. detachment and professional "distance;" conflicts of interest vs. conflicted disinterest; and "talking to" vs. "talking with."

All of the former topics are interesting in their own right, but become much more fascinating when applied to the frenetic field of daily journalism. As more than one of the authors herein maintains, journalism operates at a pace and under a set of professional standards that all but preclude the careful, systematic examination of its own rituals and practices. (That isn't just academic talk; look at chapters 8, 10, and 11 for evidence that three veteran journalists, with a century of practical experience among them, share the concern that all too often the journalistic life is left unexamined.) The examination herein should advance the enterprise, and help student and professional observers to work through some of the most perplexing dilemmas to have faced the news media and public in recent times.

To a person, the contributors to this project recognize that journalism is important to democracy, that things are not going as well as they should be, that some new techniques and theories are being tried out, that some of them are better than others, and that along the way we'd better not lose sight of journalism's fundamental missions and mandates. Beyond that, they differ enormously in their assessment of how serious the problems are and how valid are the industry's responses to them.

With all due respect to our valued colleagues Clifford Christians, John Ferré, and Mark Fackler, whose seminal work on communitarian journalism was titled *Good News: Social Ethics & the Press* (New York: Oxford University Press, 1993), the title chosen for the present volume and lecture series was *Mixed News: The Public/Civic/Communitarian Journalism Debate*. That title was selected not only because the jury was still out on whether the current ferment in journalism is good news or bad news or something in between, but also because there seems to be little agreement on what the movement "is." As we see in the following chapters, and in the massive annotated bibliography, the nascent movement has gone by various names: public journalism, civic journalism, communitarian journalism, community journalism, even good-journalism-done-the-way-it-ought-to-have-been-done-all-along. (A couple of our contributors debate why the "thing" needs a name at all; editor Buzz Merritt and academic Jay Rosen once agreed that they ought to just call it "banana" and get on with it.)

Semantics notwithstanding, *Mixed News* attempts to bring some cutting edge voices to bear on a significant contemporary issue in public life. Unlike previous books and monographs, which have tended toward unbridled enthusiasm about public journalism, and trade press articles, which have tended toward pessimism, *Mixed News* offers strong voices on several sides of the complex debate. Better yet—if it works as anticipated—it will help professional and lay readers reach common ground on the issue.

The Book's Chapters

Jim Carey, one of our most thoughtful commentators on journalism and public life, argues that community, public, and journalism are inextricably linked. He explores the dilemma of community that has always disbelieved Americans, whom he describes as people who are always building a city on a hill and then promptly trying to figure out a way to get out of town. He asks us to consider what values we try to articulate and express through the word *community* that seem to be available to us nowhere else, and what the place of journalism should be in establishing and maintaining community.

Clifford Christians, a noted scholar whose works on media ethics are passionate and theologically informed, explores journalists' need to understand the "common good" in these days of rampant individualism. He urges public spirited journalists to recognize that they and their communities may gravitate toward self-interest; therefore, to be truly ethical, they should take universal values into account, and do their utmost to facilitate discourse that mitigates against isolationism.

Lou Hodges, an interdisciplinary ethicist, analyzes several fractures in contemporary society, and journalism's role in fomenting and cementing them. He proposes relying on communitarian/liberal democratic frameworks and the biblical notion of the "kingdom of God" as a general guide for journalists who have not resolved the question of how humanity can be simultaneously individual and social.

John Merrill, author of more than thirty books on journalism, ethics, and international communication, maintains that the communitarianism espoused by press critics is a vague rhetorical—but dangerous—war against Enlightenment liberalism and the fundamental foundations of a free press. Long a spokesperson for individualism, Merrill argues that pleas for a responsible press are in reality pleas for a weak, monolithic, and eviscerated press.

Ralph Barney, whose chapter titled "A Dangerous Drift? The Sirens'

Call to Collectivism" leaves little doubt as to his thinking on the matter, joins Merrill in a serious critique of communitarianism and the public journalism movement. Barney, who has worked extensively in media ethics and in communication of developing countries, worries that collective thinking is eliminating self-determination in journalism, at a serious cost to truth, First Amendment freedoms, and democracy.

Rob Anderson, Bob Dardenne, and Mike Killenberg, co-authors of the 1994 book *The Conversation of Journalism: Communication, Community, and News*, take a pragmatic middle ground, showing how the public journalism movement is a natural response to the communications crises wrought by out-of-touch media. The three authors wonder why most political theorists overlook the newspaper's potential as the most natural vehicle for reestablishing connections among a community's stakeholders; they propose numerous examples of how to enable a "conversational commons."

Ted Glasser, director of Stanford University's graduate program in journalism, and Stephanie Craft, a veteran journalist and PhD candidate at Stanford, ponder the irony of a public journalism movement in an industry that, despite its Constitutional protections, remains "private, closed, and generally unexamined." A good overview of the public journalism movement is followed by an examination of the newspaper's editorial voice and a plea for the sort of openness and public accountability the press demands of other democratic institutions.

Herbert Altschull, who toiled in the vineyards of newspaper, radio, television, wire service, and magazine journalism before joining the academy, analyzes the news industry's "crises of conscience," and asks whether community journalism provides an answer. Altschull wonders whether some of the illusions that have accompanied journalism to this point in history ought to be tossed overboard; among those he questions are unbiased and objective news media whose reporters and editors are supposed to maintain a non-political stance in their own communities. The motive of "Big Money" perplexes Altschull, who says one vehicle to consider is good, old-fashioned, low budget talk radio.

Bob Steele, who directs the ethics programs at the Poynter Institute for Media Studies, brings his academic and media insights to bear on the ethics of the civic journalism movement. Rather than polarize such issues as detachment and involvement, he suggests placing the "buzz words" on a continuum and seeing whether debates over public journalism can be based on common ground. The ethical principle of journalistic independence becomes problematic, but if carefully considered should help news media serve society as intended, Steele maintains.

"Buzz" Merritt, the Wichita, Kansas editor who more than any other working journalist has led the public journalism bandwagon, insists that public journalism, independence, and civic capital are three ideas in complete harmony. The author of *Public Journalism & Public Life* worries that many critics and some practitioners of public journalism have not taken the philosophic journey necessary to understand the movement; weakly articulated and badly executed practices have added fuel to the critics' fires. Merritt's base line: Journalism should be done in ways calculated to help public life go well; it should engage citizens in public life.

Paul McMasters, First Amendment Ombudsman for the Freedom Forum and, like Merritt and Altschull a working journalist for three decades, suggests we all take a closer look at history before tossing in the towel and giving up on our Constitutional heritage. He sees public journalism as a natural outgrowth of contemporary concerns over slippage in press credibility and influence. He says journalism should not voluntarily relinquish its First Amendment rights, but it should also never forget that the press garners its support by exercising its responsibilities, not its freedoms. In some of the book's most poignant passages, he offers eight "cautions" to those who would embrace public journalism.

Lee Wilkins of the University of Missouri combines her research and teaching interests in media ethics and environmental communications in an essay that demonstrates how the communitarian philosophy is a natural fit for journalists interested in the broadest community—the environment. Environmental journalism calls on a different set of values than is routinely employed by news reporters, Wilkins says. She notes that those values tend to be nurturing and feminist in nature, so a "woman's moral universe" is applied to significant issues of public concern. Why, she asks, should not the same be true of other forms of journalism?

Deni Elliott, of the University of Montana, draws from her work in the ethics of journalism, health care, and other professions to make a strong argument against what she calls "compassionate journalism." In an essay whose theoretical focus bridges those of Merrill, Barney, Steele, and McMasters, she notes that journalists have unique professional duties that are too readily compromised by public claims for attention and support. The best journalism, she maintains, tells people what they need to know so they can participate in self-governance. That means news media should not participate in institutional unfairness such as occurs when they use their influence to advance the cause of one needy or sick individual while ignoring others in similar situations.

In other words...

Other voices inform the debate. A series of "Voices," journalistic interviews with practitioners and critics of public journalism, is interspersed throughout the text. (It might be noted that some of the practitioners are among the movement's most strident critics.)

At the conclusion to each essay is found a series of quotes from a wide variety of sources; "In other words..." augments each chapter by adding ideas and insights that support and contradict the points raised by each chapter author.

Finally, we offer an extended annotated bibliography of books, monographs, academic and trade articles, and reports and speeches on public/civic/communitarian journalism.

Acknowledgments

The primary benefactor of this project has already been singled out. Again, however, a special thanks goes to the Ethics and Excellence in Journalism Foundation for its willingness to support the lecture series and book preparation.

University of South Florida graduate students in journalism deserve special recognition, particularly Lee Peck, Rick Kenney, Lynn Waddell, and Eric Eyre. All four are veteran newspaper reporters who returned to graduate school to answer some of their vexing questions about their chosen profession. All received prestigious Poynter Fellowships to support their graduate studies.

Lee Peck, who has gone on to join the faculty at Colorado State University, did a masterful job wading through thousands of pages of materials to prepare the annotated bibliography. When she left campus in the summer of 1995, Lynn Waddell picked up the task, and updated the bibliography until the spring of 1996, when the deadline overtook us all. Meanwhile, Lynn conducted several interviews and drafted the "Voices" segments to which her byline is attached.

Rick Kenney, who completed his masters degree studies and moved on to doctoral work at the University of Georgia, also contributed to the "Voices" segments. His major task, which he assumed with talent and energy, was tracking down elusive references and changing the many creative citation styles offered by our contributors into a more consistent APA style. Eric Eyre did likewise.

Credit for the design and layout of *Mixed News* goes to Molli Gamelin, who has worked with talent, grace, and good humor under a heavy deadline.

Appreciation is expressed to Jennings Bryant of the University of Alabama, communications series editor for Lawrence Erlbaum Associates, for convincing Kathleen O'Malley, LEA's acquisitions editor, that this project was worthy of publication, and to Ms. O'Malley for helping see it through to completion.

Finally, a thanks to The Ethics Center and the community of scholarship and civility that attracts many voices and many citizens to public lectures on the University of South Florida's St. Petersburg campus.

Jay Black

p.s.: An irony that cannot be ignored: Despite all the talk of interdependence and community, this manuscript has been prepared on a portable laptop computer in a cedar-lined study at an isolated log cabin nestled deep in the scenic mountains of northern Utah, linked to the outside world by an 80-year-old single-wire telephone line that is grounded by four million trees and that shorts out whenever the wind blows . . . the only place this particular writer seems to be able to escape from humanity long enough to commit to the craft. Quirks of style and oversights or mistakes of substance may be attributed to the folly of believing oneself to be independent. My wife, Leslie, and English Setter, Ginger, constitute an ideal nurturing community, and deserve public thanks for their tolerance and support.

Contributors

J. Herbert Altschull is a visiting professor in The Writing Seminars at Johns Hopkins University. He has served as a reporter and editor in Washington and Western Europe for *The Associated Press, The New York Times, Newsweek,* and NBC, winning numerous awards in both newspaper and television. Dr. Altschull is the author of *Agents of Power: The Media and Public Policy* and *From Milton to McLuhan.*

Rob Anderson is professor and director of graduate studies in the Department of Communication at St. Louis University. He is widely published in speech and communication theory; among his books is co-authorship of *The Conversation of Journalism: Communication, Community, and News* and *Before The Story: Interviewing and Communication Skills for Journalists.*

Ralph Barney is professor of communications at Brigham Young University and co-editor of the *Journal of Mass Media Ethics.* A former newspaperman and university public relations officer, he has written widely about press ethics and communications in developing nations. He is a co-author of the Society of Professional Journalists' *Doing Ethics in Journalism: A Handbook With Case Studies,* and co-editor of *Ethics and the Press: Readings in Mass Media Morality.*

Jay Black is Poynter-Jamison chair in media ethics and press policy at the University of South Florida St. Petersburg and co-editor of the *Journal of Mass Media Ethics.* He is a co-author of the Society of Professional Journalists' *Doing Ethics in Journalism: A Handbook With Case Studies* and *Introduction to Media Communication,* now in its fourth edition.

James Carey is professor in the Graduate School of Journalism, Columbia University. He served for thirteen years as Dean of the College of Communications at the University of Illinois. He has published over 100 essays, monographs and reviews and two books, *Communication as Culture and Media, Myth* and *Narrative: Television and the Press.*

Clifford G. Christians is director of the Institute of Communications Research at the University of Illinois. He is co-author of *Good News: Social Ethics and the Press* and of *Media Ethics: Cases and Moral Reasoning.* He serves on editorial boards of several communications journals, and is published widely in communications ethics.

Stephanie Craft is a doctoral student in communications at Stanford University. She is a former newspaper journalist who worked in California, Washington, and Arkansas. Her research interests include how history is evoked in journalistic writing and the press' role in shaping collective memory.

Robert Dardenne is associate professor of mass communications at the University of South Florida St. Petersburg. A former reporter, editor, and feature writer in Louisiana, Mexico City, New York, and Washington, D.C., he is co-author of *The Conversation of Journalism: Communication, Community, and News.* His doctoral dissertation from the University of Iowa was titled *Newstelling: Story and Themes in "The Courant" of Hartford.*

Deni Elliott is Mansfield professor of ethics and public affairs at the University of Montana; previously she directed the Ethics Center at Dartmouth College. Her doctoral degree from Harvard University was interdisciplinary, with work in policy, law, philosophy, and education. Editor of *Responsible Journalism* and book review editor of the *Journal of Mass Media Ethics,* she writes and consults widely in professional ethics.

Theodore L. Glasser is associate professor of communication and director of Stanford University's graduate program in journalism. He is co-editor of Guilford Publications' Communication Series and recently co-edited *Public Opinion and the Communication of Consent.* His research focuses on the norms of practice in American journalism, with emphasis on questions of press responsibility and accountability.

Louis W. Hodges is Fletcher Otey Thomas professor of Bible and director, Society and the Professions program in applied ethics (medicine, law, journalism, and business) at Washington and Lee University. He is editor of *Social Responsibility,* is the "Cases and Commentaries" editor for the *Journal of Mass Media Ethics,* and is a frequent lecturer and writer on issues of professional ethics.

George M. Killenberg is professor of mass communications at the University of South Florida, St. Petersburg. He has been a reporter and editor for the *Alton Telegraph, St. Louis Globe-Democrat,* and *Los Angeles Times.* He is author of *Public Affairs Reporting: News Coverage in the Information Age,* co-author of *Before The Story: Interviewing and Communication Skills for Journalists,* and co-author of *The Conversation of Journalism: Communication, Community, and News.*

Paul McMasters is First Amendment Ombudsman at the Freedom Forum. A thirty-year veteran journalist, he spent nineteen years at Springfield, Missouri, newspapers before joining the newly-founded *USA Today,* where he ran the day-to-day operations of the editorial pages for eleven years. He has written and spoken extensively on the First Amendment and Freedom of Information issues, including a 50-state tour in 1994-1995 while national president of the Society of Professional Journalists.

John C. Merrill is professor-emeritus at the University of Missouri School of Journalism. One of the world's leading writers on journalism ethics and international mass communication, he has authored some thirty books, including *The Imperative of Freedom: A Philosophy of Journalistic Autonomy; The Dialectic in Journalism: Toward a Responsible Use of Press Freedom; Existential Journalism; Ethics and the Press: Readings in Mass Media Morality;* and *Legacy of Wisdom: Great Thinkers and Journalism.*

Davis "Buzz" Merritt is editor and senior vice president of the *Wichita (KS) Eagle.* A graduate of the University of North Carolina, he spent thirteen years at the *Charlotte Observer* as a reporter, city desk editor, copy desk chief, and national editor. He was also news editor of the Knight-Ridder Newspapers' *Washington Bureau.* In 1993 he won the Knight-Ridder Excellence Award for Community Service. In 1994 he took a one-year leave of absence to write *Public Journalism & Public Life: Why Telling the News is Not Enough.*

Robert M. Steele is director of the ethics programs at the Poynter Institute for Media Studies in St. Petersburg, Florida. A former broadcast reporter and editor, he is co-author of the Society of Professional Journalists' *Doing Ethics in Journalism: A Handbook With Case Studies.* His doctoral dissertation at the University of Iowa dealt with values and ethical decision making in television news. He consults widely with media clients on issues of ethics.

Lee Wilkins is professor of journalism at the University of Missouri and co-author of *Media Ethics: Issues and Cases.* A former newspaper reporter and editor in Michigan, Oregon, and Colorado, she has done extensive research on environmental disasters and environmental risks. Her PhD in political science was earned at the University of Oregon.

Community, Public, and Journalism

James W. Carey
Columbia University

Community is one of the most difficult, complex, and ambiguous words in our language. It is a contested concept, one that represents or gathers to it contradictory, mutually exclusive images, meanings sacred and profane by turn. For many, community has a positive image—blessed community: the restoration or creation of an ideal way of life and a redemptive form of social relations. Community names a way of life where something more and other than the values of the market—"the almighty dollar," in common expression—holds sway. However, while community is for many a beacon of hope, it is for others, perhaps many more, a sign of despair, desperation, and despondency.

To some, and not only economic conservatives and libertarians, community is the nightmare word of the twentieth century. Press the word very hard and it yields images of communism, collectivism, and the oppressive power of the state—all the totalitarianisms of our time. However well intentioned and noble, the invocation of community yields a vector that runs from its utterance to Orwell's (1949) Airstrip One, a world of total surveillance, the pitiless diremption of all forms of privacy and individuality, a world of total conformity. At the opening of *1984*, Winston Smith struggles to find a space out of eyeshot and earshot of Big Brother and the omnipresent two-way television screen where "the last man in Europe" might escape the community and hold on to his dignity by making entries into that most personal thing, a written diary. All he wants is private space and a notebook, yet he finally discovers that even at such moments he is under observation from the state. At the end of the novel a transformed Winston sits mindlessly staring at the television screen in the Chestnut Tree Cafe, shorn of every defense by which the self might ward off the invasive power of the state. The Last Man in Europe, the last figure of European civilization before it was ground out in a wave of state sponsored domination, is without love, honor, reason, or conscience, the virtues that must give way to the total community. The architect of that community is O'Brien, the *intellectual* apparachik, who is

1

clearminded concerning the final destination of the "quest for community."

In Orwell's world of socially sanctioned cruelty, the only recognizable life is lived in the pubs among the proletariat, a group now rendered harmless. It is only in the pub that Winston hears anything resembling conversation, the only place it is possible to talk to anyone without surveillance. Even in the upper room, the site of Winston's idyll with Julia, he is unknowingly under the gaze of the state. In Airstrip One, there is no private life, but there is no public life, either.

Community has another image in our time, equally satanic, though more benign in its typical rendition: the oppressive suffocating enclosure of the small town, Main Street, the babbitry of everything we have spent a lifetime trying to escape. This is the small town of peeping ears and peeping Toms, a world of gossip, innuendo, and ostracism for all who resist its strict mandate of conformity. Such small worlds may exist even within the largest city, for they represent everything that suppresses and suffocates us, keeps us under the perpetual surveillance of our neighbors. This suffocating image of community is brought forward each time nostalgia for the world we have lost, for the world before our fall and loss of innocence, is held out as an ideal. Community is made to represent the provincial life we have been trying to exit and to which, paradoxically, we are romantically, magnetically drawn. We are, as I have put it on other occasions, a people who are forever creating new communities and then promptly trying to figure a way to get out of town. The City on the Hill that names the national aspiration also names the national nightmare.

> **We apparently want a virtual community rather than a real one . . . one that simulates or imitates qualities of a common life and a common culture without the physical or emotional geography of the small town, the centralized power of the state, or the exclusive dominion of the market.**

Given these dominant images of community in the twentieth century, why does the word hang on in the language as a hope and aspiration, a national romance? Presumably none of us aspires to the world of Orwell or Sinclair Lewis (1920), but they are the inevitable endpoints, or so it seems, to which we are dragged against our will by the invocation of community. If it is the case that none of us are looking for community, what is it we do want? We apparently want a virtual community rather than a real one, something less than a community as it has been historically understood but containing remnants of community life. A virtual community is one that simulates or imitates qualities of a common life and a common culture without the physical or emotional geography of the small town, the centralized power of the state, or the exclusive dominion of the market. And, a virtual community is one based on certain virtues, the virtues identified with the long tradition of civic humanism: tolerance, fellow-feeling, reason, public engagement existing alongside genuine privacy. But is it possible to pursue this image of a virtual community and still escape the fate of Winston Smith and Babbitt? That is the minefield we have to navigate.

Defining "Community"

As Robert Fowler (1991) has deftly outlined, there are a number of concepts of community currently at work among us. We inherited from the politics of the 1960s a image of the *participatory* community, a life of endless democracy in which we are fully devoted to the engagements of citizenship, participating not only in politics but in economics and all the institutions of social life. Others are searching for a community of *roots*, something that will withstand the blinding obsolescence that infects all objects and social relations. Today, the metaphor for roots is the family, though new "families" based on race, gender, and ethnicity are represented as symbols of new rooted communities. The ideal of a *religious* community, formally united in sanctified and shared belief, has, if anything, gained in adherents in recent decades, although it has always played a major part in the American imagining of the very meaning of the country. In recent years, at least since we have grown accustomed to seeing "spaceship earth" photographed via satellite from "out there," a new conception of an *ecological* community, a global community uniting everyone in shared fate of survival on a unitary planet, has taken up residence in popular imagination. Finally, and paradoxically the most potent vision of community among us is the anti-communal image of the independent self, the community of *one*. The self who has absorbed all the necessary resources of living into private capital is perhaps the most viscous and illusory of the dreams of reason that animate the nation.

I do not have much truck with any of these conceptions of community, for they all pretty much are based on a utopian vision shorn of history.

The dreams of a community of one or a community of endless participation, a fully private or fully public life, must have a common ending in totalitarianism. An ecological community is too broad and devoid of solidarity to be useful, and a religious community to narrow and exclusive to do much other than damage. A virtual community models, then, a middle way, a balance point where we can avoid the tyranny of extremes toward which we are pulled as in a gravitational field in which one pole is anchored in the market and the self and the other in the state and the social. To give this image a name, if only to provide a stick with which others can beat it, let us call it the image of a republican community.

The Republican Community

If the notion of a republican community is to avoid the nightmare world for which many would find it predestined, what meanings does it have to recover? Put differently, what does the notion of a republican community attempt, however artlessly, to express?

First, "community" attempts to hold on to and express the truism that, however disguised by the conditions of modern living, we live fully interdependent lives. The notion of the self-sufficient individual, the self that contains within his or her own person the resources necessary to a full life, is the single most pervasive image and myth of our time. The interdependency of the self is masked by virtually all the facts and images of modern life. Put differently, modern life disguises our interdependence. It cultivates quite systematically the notion that we can live by our possessions and that our possessions include our opinions, our values, our language, our capacity to deal with trauma and tragedy, our economic means, and our political existence.

> The word "community" attempts to make vivid the interdependency of all life, in war and peace, and the fact that we inevitably share a common life boat and, therefore, owe one another the terrible loyalty of passengers on a fragile craft.

To live in a community is to be aware that one's life depends on the uncoordinated decencies and actions of others; that life would constantly fail without the invisible contributions of others who with us inhabit the polity and the economy. In modern life interdependency only becomes apparent when the technology fails, the electric power goes off, the garbage workers go on strike and we are threatened by suffocation in our own filth, or, interestingly enough, in times of war, those anti-modern interludes such as World Wars I and II, when our mutual dependencies are rendered transparent by the need to consciously work toward common goals. The word "community" attempts to make vivid the interdependency of all life, in war and peace, and the fact that we inevitably share a common life boat and, therefore, owe one another the terrible loyalty of passengers on a fragile craft.

A Flawed Economic Model

In addition to this "fact" concerning our common life, the word community attempts to recover a philosophical point as well concerning the limits of individualism. Perhaps those limits can be explored indirectly through a brief but common example from economics. Classes in elementary economics almost inevitably begin by illustrating the laws of supply and demand. The teacher dutifully demonstrates how the demand curve slopes down to the left (more is demanded as the price goes down) and the supply curve upward to the right (more is supplied as the price goes up). Equilibrium between supply and demand occurs at the price where the two curves intersect. The teacher then summarizes the analysis using the two most elementary equations of the discipline: the demand equation stating that the quantity demanded of any commodity is inversely proportional to its price, and the supply equation stating that the quantity supplied of any commodity is directly proportional to its price. What is sometimes, but not always, mentioned by the teacher is that truth of these equations depends on certain assumptions that precede and support the analysis of supply and demand. The two crucial assumptions are, first of all, that, in the language of my student days, all of us are rational and, second, that tastes and preferences are given or exogenous. So stated the assumptions sound innocent enough—but what do they mean?

The assumption that all of us are rational makes a largely technical point. It states that individuals are rational in the sense that they are adept at figuring out the most efficient, economical, or costless means of getting what they want. The assumption says nothing about the rationality of ends, of what people desire; in fact, it allows that people desire the most harebrained and thoughtless sorts of things—power, prestige, emotional satisfactions of all kinds—that we rarely think of as rational. Again, the assumption merely says that once people have found an object of desire they are quite capable of calculating the most efficient, least costly way of getting what it is they want. All people can calculate to their own advantage, and so rationality means little more than observing a contest over whose ox will be gored.

The second assumption completes the groundwork of the analysis, for it tells us that not only are people's desires, the objects of their wants, beyond the scope of reason, but every person's desires are independent of every other person's. This is what it means to state that tastes and preferences are given or exogenous to the system: To analyze the conditions of supply and demand you simply have to assume there is no logic or reason to people's tastes and preferences and each individual's desire is independent of that of every other. I like poetry, you like baseball. We will both figure out how to get what we want in the most efficient manner, at the lowest cost in terms of time, effort, and dollars. But we are otherwise unrelated to one another: You may be a means to my end and I may be a means to your end, but there is otherwise no presumed membership in a community—no desires in common, no cooperation necessary, no shared rationality except that of calculation.

Economics achieves its precision, then, at a very high price, for it paints a picture of a society without community, unless one chooses to call the market a community. It assumes people have no need for community and, furthermore, they have nothing in common with which to form a community: no common needs, no common values, no common investments in the future. When Margaret Thatcher (Rankin, 1996, p. 154) remarked a few years back at the height of her reign that "we have no need for society," she was testifying to the power of elementary economics: We only have need for individuals aggressively pursuing their own self-interest. And, if we have no need for society or, for that matter, government, we certainly have no need for that more intense and conscious form of society represented in the word community. The only necessary institution is the invisible hand of the market which, in coordinating all our disconnected needs and desires, supplies whatever community is necessary.

Insights From Social Theory

Virtually all of the major figures in the classical tradition of social theory revolted against this economic outlook. The arguments of Marx are well known. Emile Durkheim (1965) in one book, *The Division of Labor in Society*, pointed out that you could not have any economic activity without formal contracts. However, a contract presumes a common culture. In other words, without elementary particles of trust and mutual understanding, loyalty, and mutual regard, it would prove impossible to efficiently operate economic institutions in which individuals entered into contracts with one another. Why would I enter a contract unless I presume you will fulfill your obligations without the omnipresent enforcement of the law? In a later work, *The Elementary Forms of the Religious Life,* Durkheim (1995) emphasized the necessary role that collective representations—shared beliefs and their manifestation in common symbolic forms—were to all social order. Like Durkheim, Max Weber (1974) emphasized the role religion played in providing the substratum of meanings, motivations, and mutual outlooks—the so-called Protestant ethic—on which rational economic activity was based. And even more disturbingly, he characterized a world in which instrumental reason—the kind celebrated in the economics of calculation and exchange—held sway as the iron cage of rationality: a world of Kafka rather than Adam Smith. This nightmare version of economics and politics without community has reappeared again and again in our literature most tellingly, as mentioned earlier, in Orwell's *1984.* For us, for we Americans, that is, the last word on the sustainability of economics without community, individuality without a common culture, goes to De Tocqueville (1961):

> As social conditions become more equal, the number of persons increases who, although they are neither rich enough nor powerful enough to exercise any great influence over their fellow-creatures, have nevertheless acquired or retained sufficient education and fortune to satisfy their own wants. They owe nothing to any man, they expect nothing from any man; they acquire the habit of always considering themselves as standing alone, and they are apt to imagine that their whole destiny is in their own hands. Thus not only does democracy make every man forget his ancestors, but it hides his descendants, and separates his contemporaries, from him; it throws him back for ever upon himself alone, and threatens in the end to confine him entirely within the solitude of his own heart. (p. 120)

De Tocqueville's emphasis on democracy and equality ought not to mislead us. The habits of the heart of which he speaks were cultivated by an entire culture which had at its base the assumptions of individuality, rationality, and desire outlined earlier. Therefore, opposing the view of individualism embedded in economic theory and, through economics, the culture as a whole, is but a prelude to asserting an alternative and hopefully more humane view of culture and community which might contain the divisive force of individualism and technical reason. In this alternative view, reason is more than a property of the means we calculate to arrive at our ends—it is a capacity we humans possesses to determine the shared ends of action. Rather than emphasizing the "giveness" of our tastes and preferences, it emphasizes how such tastes and desires are formed within, though not determined by, the structure of community life. It asserts that from the outset we are born into human communities; that we are made human by those with whom we share common membership. The figure of Robinson Crusoe, which inspires so much of economics, the figure of a person wholly self-sufficient and complete unto himself, a self who has need for the labor but not the companionship of Friday, is a literary myth and a social monstrosity. All that we are, good and bad, is created, actively created, within the structures of community, which means within the structures of culture. The playwright Eugene O'Neill caught this in just about the right tones when he remarked in "The Great God Brown" that far from being self-sufficient individuals "Man is born broken. He lives by mending. The grace of God is glue!" (O'Neill, 1959, p. 370).

> The figure of Robinson Crusoe, which inspires so much of economics, the figure of a person wholly self-sufficient and complete unto himself, a self who has need for the labor but not the companionship of Friday, is a literary myth and a social monstrosity.

I take this to summarize, however obliquely, the outlook of John Dewey (1954) on which I here so much depend, an outlook Oliver Sacks (1985) has renamed "Romantic Science." Outside of culture we are not rationally calculating creatures but characters from *Lord of the Flies* (Golding, 1964). Our most important resource in living, language, is wholly a social and collective product, and even our brains, which assumed their present biological form within culture, are incapable of functioning without the input from that culture.

Highlighting the Ordinary

The word community then, beyond its sheer romance, does some heavy-duty conceptual work. It highlights the necessary interdependence of all human living and action and, philosophically, calls into question the spiritual individualism on which American culture is based while juxtaposing that individualism to the human need for community and culture as the ground conditions for our functioning as a species.

The word community, with its linguistic roots in the common, the ordinary, the vernacular, the vulgate, the vulgar, also has the social task of cultivating respect for the intelligence and capacity of ordinary men and women.

When the émigré historian John Lukacs (1984) came to the United States following World War II, he was struck, like earlier European observers, by the tendency of Americans to overestimate the ability of ordinary men and women. He stood in a long line of European intellectuals who criticized the country because it expected ordinary people to have political capacities as citizens, moral capacities as neighbors, and intellectual capacities as students and learners that were simply beyond them. He concluded, fifty years later, that American institutions in the interim reversed themselves and now systematically underestimated the capacity of ordinary men and women whether in education or politics or cooperative work. While it is perhaps always unwise to mis-estimate the ability of people, it is far better to overestimate their abilities than to underestimate them. The word community calls us to this overestimation; it assumes that inevitably there is more wisdom in a community of tradition, in the shared and pooled intelligence of people, than there ever can be in any individual or small group, however elite.

> The notion of community ... must express and value interdependence without sacrificing individuality; it must militate against the bias of individualism; it must cultivate respect for the capacity of ordinary people and create the institutions which call forth and nurture these capacities.

These, then, are the criteria the notion of community must satisfy: it must express and value interdependence without sacrificing individuality; it must militate against the bias of individualism; it must cultivate respect for the capacity of ordinary people and create the institutions which call forth and nurture these capacities. This is the political work of a republican conception of community and, not so incidentally, a republican conception of the press.

Social and Political Dimensions

In contrast to other conceptions of community, a republican community does not presume common roots or a common religion; it does not use the metaphor of the family and familial relations to conceive of community; it does not demand universal, incessant and obligatory participation; and, finally, it does not await a realization of the unity of man and nature or a universal brotherhood to realize its goals. The republican community is no more than the name of our desire, but that desire has two dimensions, one social and one political.

Socially, a republican community is organized around the principle of common social space in which people mingle and become aware of one another as inhabiting a common place. On the social side, a republican community opposes segregation, the artificial separation of people by class and function, and an exclusive emphasis on private life and the provision of all human needs, including sociability, within that private life. In itself this notion of community is hard to create and satisfy within American life, which is organized around the private dwelling and the provision of services, electronically and otherwise, to that private space.

We have witnessed over the last century a decline in public space, in space easily and freely accessible for common activity, including that most important activity, idling. The "malling of America," the corporatization of space, is perhaps the most important example of this phenomenon. Similarly, we have witnessed a widespread revolt of families against the city, to use Richard Sennett's (1970) phrase, a withdrawal of people into private space as protection against what they see as the disorder, moral as well as physical, of public space. The crucial importance of this lies in the withdrawal from public life by those with the power and income to support the provision of private luxury and services. It is best symbolized, technologically and architecturally, by those high-rise dwellers of the city whose connection to public life is mediated by glass: smoked windows through which they gaze out at the city below, smoked automobile windows through which they are simultaneously present and absent from the life of the city, smoked cathode ray tubes through which they connect to public life and keep it safely imprisoned, at a distance, beyond physical contact.

But for the purposes of this essay, the most important aspect of a republican community is on its political side. When Benjamin Franklin told the Philadelphia citizens awaiting news of the completion of the Constitution that they had a new form of government, a "republic if you can keep it," he was testifying to the both the fragility and suprisingness of what the convention had created. Republican forms of government were and still are odd and aberrant occurrences in history. The natural state of humankind is domination; submission is the natural, our natural, condition. Political communities founded on civic ties rather than blood relations or bureaucratic rule are rare creatures of history; they have a definite beginning, a point of origin in historical time and, therefore, they presumably have an end. After all, there had been few republics in history, and they had been short-lived. To create such a political form was to act against history and experience and it was to place demands on citizens that were both new and extraordinary.

The foundation of a political society, a republic, unites it in space and time. The art of political creation is to lay a foundation that will make citizens into patriots and patriots into citizens. Only when that is achieved will it be possible to deliver republican government, public life, against all the vicissitudes of history down unchangeable to posterity.

First Amendment Considerations

The way we think about politics, public life, has been deeply shaped by the economic assumptions previously outlined. Similarly, our understanding of the press has been shaped by these same assumptions. We think of both the press and politics as a marketplace in which we and others possess rights against one another but in which we longer have a social relation within a republican community. Politics is a market in which we satisfy our individual desires through the purchases negotiated with a vote. When our purchase goes awry, when the product is defective, we want to return it for full satisfaction, for the fault is not in ourselves but in the state which exists to coordinate desire and satisfy wants. Similarly we understand the First Amendment as a bundle of rights we possess in the same way we possess a body. We are a people who have rights. We do not constitute a people in any other sense. So, the press constitutes a marketplace of ideas from which we buy what we need. We have the rights of buyers, the press has the rights of sellers. When the market fails, when our needs are unsatisfied, we turn to the

> **We think of both the press and politics as a marketplace in which we and others possess rights against one another but in which we longer have a social relation within a republican community.**

courts to adjudicate disputes. The courts in turn decide whose rights should prevail in given cases.

However, if we think of the Constitution not as the granting of a set of rights and immunities possessed by persons against the community but as a document that constitutes the community, that brings it into existence and lays out its form, the nature of a republican community becomes clearer. Read this way the First Amendment, for example, says that people are free to assemble without the intrusion of the state, that once assembled they are free to talk to one another about issues of mutual concern and they are free as well to write down, publish and circulate what they have said and any conclusions they have reached. Finally, it claims that persons cannot be excluded from public space, from participation in talk and writing on the basis of their religion, which for us means on the basis of any ascriptive criteria of membership. Assembling, speaking, and writing here are activities in which the community lives, in which the public becomes visible to itself, visible to one another, and visible to the state. Assembling, speaking, and writing are neither duties nor responsibilities; they are activities which describe a concrete way of life, the way a republic community lives.

> **The press ... must support the maintenance of public space and public life; it must find ways in which the public can address one another, and it must enhance those qualities of discourse such as decent manners and formal social equality that allow public space to develop and to be maintained.**

This sense of a political community, a republican community, is deep within in American jurisprudence, within the work of Louis Brandeis (1953) and Alexander Meiklejohn (1948) for example, and should provide our basic understanding of the press. The press exists not as the surrogate holder of the rights of the public but as an instrument which both expresses the public and helps it form and find its identity. The press, then, as an institution must support the maintenance of public space and public life; it must find ways in which the public can address one another, and it must enhance those qualities of discourse such as decent manners and formal social equality that allow public space to develop and to be maintained.

Conclusion: Cyberspace Community?

Perhaps one way of capturing the republican conception of community is to contrast it with a theory of community, one both more globalized and individualized emerging within the rhetoric of computer technology. We hear much these days concerning new forms of community emerging in cyberspace, community without propinquity. One of the spokesman and defenders of these new communities is John Perry Barlow who in 1992 expressed his fears as follows:

> . . . we could shortly find ourselves under a government that would have the automated ability to log the time origin, and recipient of every call we made . . . read our e-mail. . . . Hey, I've never been paranoid before . . . most governments are too incompetent to keep a good plot strung together all the way to quitting time. [We have] a last ditch attempt to establish imperial control over cyberspace. If they win, the most liberating development in the history of humankind could become, instead, the surveillance system that will monitor our grandchildren's morality.[1]

It is not Barlow's fears that are in question; his Orwellian world contains much to fear from government, but it is, after all, our government. Cyberspace is not some free range that has miraculously appeared or some unoccupied space we discovered through exploration but something that has been built, created with public money through the Defense Department, the national science institutes, and universities. That is, it has been created with our tax funds, even though it is now imagined, by equivalents of cattle and sheep ranchers, as either free range or enclosed commercial space. Here Barlow recreates the myth of the existentially independent self, free and unfettered on the open range, freely choosing with whom he might talk, if anyone there is interesting enough to qualify as a conversational partner.

But even if we accept cyberspace on Barlow's terms, such space still depends on the safety and security provided within space-based communities. We can only figuratively live in cyberspace, and there are few of us with the resources to do even that. But until we transcend our biology, we will by necessity live in real neighborhoods with real neighbors, real buildings with real tenants, with whom our lives are structurally intertwined. The imagined ecological community of cyberspace parasitically lives off the geographical communities which sustain and protect it.

These new images of cyber-communities end up as denials of the republican community of shared space, mutual dependence, and human potential. Cyber-space is something we build as a playground for the elite or a commercial resource to be exploited for profit, but not as an instrument of a common life. We are now busy adjudicating the disputes which arise in this new space, attempting to redetermine the meaning of the First Amendment. The press in this new configuration would redesign journalism to exploit such opportunities for profit by creating the newspaper for the

> **The press in this new configuration would redesign journalism . . . by creating the newspaper for the individual—the "Daily Me" for those whose needs and desires are now totally disconnected from a wider polity.**

individual—the "Daily Me" for those whose needs and desires are now totally disconnected from a wider polity.

What we need in this circumstance is to revive notions of a republican community: a public realm in which a free people can assemble, speak their minds, and then write or tape or otherwise record their extended conversation so that others out of sight might see it. If cyberspace can help us, fine. But if not, we will simply have to create a space for citizens and patriots on our own, using the simple resources of the foot and the hand and the tongue that provided all the inspiration necessary in Philadelphia two hundred plus years ago.

Notes

[1] Barlow has made this argument in several places. See, for instance, "Decripting the Puzzle Palace" in *Communications of the ACM*, 35, 7, July 1992, 27-33.

References

Brandeis, L. (1953). *The words of Justice Brandeis*. Soloman Goldman (Ed.). New York: H. Schuman.

De Tocqueville, A. (1961). *Democracy in America*, Vol. 2. New York: Schocken Books.

Dewey, J. (1954). *The public and its problems*. Chicago: Swallow Press.

Durkheim, E. (1965). *The division of labor in society*. New York: The Free Press.

Durkheim, E. (1965). *The elementary forms of the religious life*. New York: The Free Press.

Fowler, R. (1991). *The dance with community*. Lawrence, KS: University of Kansas Press.

Golding, W. (1964). *Lord of the flies*. New York: Harcourt Brace.

Lewis, S. (1920). *Main street*. New York: Harcourt Brace.

Lukacs, J. (1984). *Outgrowing democracy*. New York: Doubleday.

Meiklejohn, A. (1948). *Free speech and its relation to self government*. New York: Harper.

O'Neill, E. (1925, 1959). The great god Brown. In *Nine plays by Eugene O'Neill*. New York: Modern Library.

Orwell, G. (1949). *Nineteen eighty-four*. New York: Harcourt Brace.

Rankin, A. (1996). Christopher Lasch and the moral agony of the left. *New Left Review*, No. 215.

Sacks, O. (1985). *The man who mistook his wife for a hat*. New York: Summit Books.

Sennett, R. (1970). *Families against the city*. Cambridge, MA: Harvard University Press.

Weber, M. (1974). *The protestant ethic and the spirit of capitalism*. New York: Scribner's.

In other words...

We need to see people not as readers, nonreaders, or endangered readers; not as customers to be wooed or an audience to be entertained; not as spectators at an event, but as a public, as citizens capable of action.

Davis "Buzz" Merritt. (1995, July 1). The misconception about public journalism. *Editor & Publisher, 128*(26): 80.

The real problem of journalism is that the term which grounds it—the public—has been dissolved, dissolved in part by journalism. Journalism only makes sense in relation to the public and public life. Therefore, the fundamental problem in journalism is to reconstitute the public, to bring it back into existence.

James W. Carey. (1987, March/April). The press and public discourse. *The Center Magazine, 20,* **p. 14.**

Acts of citizenship (besides voting) are unnecessarily hard for ordinary Americans to perform, and so, just as one ought to expect, they don't perform them often or well. They don't find common ground, draft clear messages, or act in concert to solve their problems. Journalists should always be on the lookout for ways to make those acts easier . . . there are indeed lines that newspapers can draw—still well this side of bias, advocacy, and subjectivity—within which public journalists can do much more to help citizens act.

Arthur Charity. (1995). *Doing public journalism.* **New York: Guilford, p. 126.**

In committing an act of public journalism, you know you have succeeded when you have left behind something people continue to use, some added ability the community now possesses. The power of the press thus empowers others besides the press.

Jay Rosen, quoted by Arthur Charity. (1995). *Doing public journalism.* **New York: Guilford, p. 160.**

The god term of journalism—the be-all and end-all, the term without which the entire enterprise fails to make sense—is the public. Insofar as journalism has a client, the client is the public. The press justifies itself in the name of the public: It exists—or so it is regularly said—to inform the public, to serve as the extended eyes and ears of the public, to protect the public's right to know, to serve the public interest. The canons of journalism originate in and flow from the relationship of the press to the public. The public is totem and talisman, and an object of ritual homage.

James W. Carey. (1992, Winter). The press and the public discourse. *Kettering Review,* p. 11.

The Common Good and Universal Values

Clifford G. Christians
University of Illinois, Urbana

In preparing a special issue of *Philosophy and Social Criticism*, David Rasmussen (1990) noted that "the two principal orientations in contemporary ethics" (pp. 1-2) these days are communitarianism and universalism. Observing that ethics is once again at the center of philosophical discussion and dominates the public sphere, he considers the debate between community and the universal supremely urgent at present.[1]

One of the participants in this controversy, Alessandro Ferrara (1990) of the Universita Degli Studi de Roma, put the argument this way:

> Critical theory and communitarianism . . . are the only approaches that offer a way to overcome the opposition of a context-insensitive, "objectivistic" universalism . . . on the one hand, and a sophisticated relativism aware of the "local" cogency of rules, norms and standards, but incapable of overcoming a particularist perspective or even of questioning it on the other hand. (p. 13)

Seyla Benhabib (1992) drew a similar conclusion; she contended that in this watershed age our primary task in ethics is reconstructing a post-Enlightenment universalism "without metaphysical props and historical conceits" (p. 3). In her view, a defensible universalism at present must learn from and engage the communitarian critique (along with feminism and postmodernism). Her interactive universalism makes participatory communities non-negotiable (cf. Benhabib, 1992, pp. 68-88).

Important debates over democratic political theory will continue as the underpinnings of community journalism are deepened and clarified. Given the intellectual leadership of Michael Sandel (1992), Carole Pateman (1970), Charles Taylor (1989), and Michael Walzer (1983), scholarly attention to date has focused on communitarianism as a philosophical alternative to individualistic liberalism. This chapter concentrates on one section of this larger terrain while recognizing that often the issues from one domain overlap with and intersect the other.

Within a metaethics of universalism, one particular problem is crucial—the issue of the common good and its definition. Communitarian democracy emphasizes goods instead of rights. Therefore, if we shift our thinking in community journalism from individual rights to the public good, the long-term validity of our approach hinges on the integrity of this concept. In community journalism, news becomes an agent of community formation.

> Good journalism requires more than good journalists—more even than enlightened ownership, First Amendment protections, and a strong economic base. For without an engaged and concerned public, even the most public-minded press cannot do its job. . . . This is precisely the predicament of the American press today. It addresses a "public" it does little to help create. . . . Rather than assuming that a vibrant civic culture exists—or simply lamenting its absence—the public journalist takes responsibility for helping to support and even create it. (Rosen, 1994b, pp. 6-7) [2]

Contrary to an egoistic rationalism, which says individuals make up their minds based on objective data, public journalism assumes that the community is ontologically (in terms of its being) and axiologically (in terms of values) prior to persons. What then does its root word entail? *Communis,* the communal, a common good?

Public journalism will continue to thrive as a revolutionary idea to the extent that it can make believable claims about *communis.*[3] Because civic journalism aims for a public that is politically and morally literate, working on the concept of community in ethical terms—that is, the common good—is especially provocative theoretically.

From Tribalism to Universals

Freud (1952) argued that every society has taboo structures that distinguish it from others. To maintain their identity, all people groups refuse to permit certain practices, but Freud claimed that every society also raises up totems, ideas, a vision of what makes life worth living. These totems are not fashioned out of thin air. They come into being when communities agree on some kind of common commitment. They survive through engagement with others. Through social interaction, which is primary and irreducible, societies draw conclusions that are beyond individual self-interest, on behalf of their identity as a distinct entity.

But Freud's typology considers only goods that order societies locally. When the community is considered ontologically and axiologically prior to persons, one could argue that we are really unleashing a wave of tribalism. Ethnicity as a matter of fact has replaced Marxist class struggle as the most powerful force of the twentieth century. The patriarchal Eurocentric majority is under siege in North America. In the United States, for example, 1.5 million people from across the globe become new citizens every year, and debates over immigration policy are acrimonious and irresolute. More than 50 percent of the school children in New York State will belong to non-Caucasian ethnic groups by the end of the decade. In cultural terms, south central Los Angeles is a continent away from residential Hollywood. A subculture of Chaldean Christians with Iraqi roots owns 1,500 small stores in Detroit, Michigan. Residents of the neighborhood called Robert Taylor Homes in Chicago's public housing live in constant threat to their safety. Amish farmers in Pennsylvania and Amana Colonies in Iowa struggle to maintain their identity. Consensus under the melting-pot thesis holds little salience. Charles Taylor (1992) identifies the conundrum for democratic politics: Can a democratic society treat all members as individually equal and yet recognize specific cultural identities as essential to someone's dignity?

On a global scale, according to anthropologists, nearly 20,000 culture groups are locked away from the social mainstream. For the most part these hidden peoples exist without recognition or adequate representation. Urdu-speaking Muslims are aliens within the Punjab of India. Since winning independence in 1989, the Belorussians have had little success in creating a sovereign state; for 70 years their history and language have not been taught. Their identity crisis reaches even to the parliament in Minsk (Applebaum, 1995). Only the remnants of Mayan culture survive in the Yucatan peninsula of Mexico, obscured under the government's official commitment to the Spanish language and to nationalism. Anthony Cortese (1990) documents how deeply moral commitments are embedded in social relations—

> **If the task of community journalism is to enable local communities to speak in their own language and to participate actively in public life, what glue is left to hold us together?**

his cross-cultural evidence including among others an Israeli kibbutz, Kenyan village leaders, Tibetan monks, and folk societies in Papua, New Guinea, and India.[4]

If the task of community journalism is to enable local communities to speak in their own language and to participate actively in public life, what glue is left to hold us together? Daniel Moynihan's (1993) recent book on ethnicity and international politics is appropriately called *Pandemonium*. With cultural identity coming into its own from Miami to east Asia, is ethnic conflict inevitable? The Hutu and Tutsi massacres in Burundi, Russian soldiers shooting people in the streets of a Chechen village, and brutal warfare in Bosnia are not stories about tribal disputes only, but also about ethnic cleansing. Is anarchy likely?[5]

Therefore, the question is whether in a communitarian view of public life and the press, we are referring to local cultures only. Is a cultural unit the trump card, the substitute for individual rights in classical democracy? Does the common good refer to whatever an ethnic, religious, or linguistic subculture values? We tend to conflate the common good with indigenous values. But without a commitment to the common *human* good, we will not avoid a cacophony of tribalism. The issue for communitarian journalism is not communal values per se, but universal ones—not the common good understood as the communal good, but common in its richest universal meaning.

> **The issue for communitarian journalism is not communal values per se, but universal ones**

If individual rights are the axis around which mainstream media revolve, the most radical alternative to individual rights would be universal human solidarity. Instead of a society conceived by Enlightenment thinkers based on John Locke—that is, discrete individuals who only by contract agree to live communally—the radical opposite is obviously the entire human race. The ultimate trump of all individualism is global oneness. Universalism contradicts individualism at its root, and the focus of communitarian ethics is not the community per se, but human solidarity as a whole.

What could that possibly mean? What is human solidarity? What are some universal principles on which we could all agree? Whether we belong to one of the 20,000 marginalized groups or not, are there common goods in spite of the splendid variety of human ingenuity? If we are to foster community journalism, we need a vocabulary of master norms and of universal values, not lame appeals to community standards only. In its theorizing and everyday practice, civic journalism must advocate protonorms, principles that hold true universally. Rather than universalism *versus* communitarianism, they need to feed from one another. If adjudicating among individual rights is often impossible, we confront the same issue among competing communities: Which one is normative?

Universal values provide a framework for bringing our community conventions under judgment as necessary. Obviously not every community ought to be celebrated. Through a moral order we raise questions about those communal values that are exclusionary and oppressive. Dietrich Bonhoeffer (1955), in his social ethics, distinguished penultimate values from ultimate ends.[6] The point is that humans tend to take a penultimate value like excellence in work and make it ultimate, destroying people or violating other obligations in the process. Penultimate values matter, in the same sense that a slash on the second-to-the-last syllable matters in the ancient Greek language. But when they become ultimate in themselves, our behavior is immoral. Universal values are a way of keeping our common human solidarity as ultimate and of restricting particular conventions on the local level to secondary status.

Contradicting Jean-Francois Lyotard's direct line from Enlightenment thought to modern atrocities, Julia Kristeva (1991) wrote:

> The Nazis did not lose their humanity because of the "abstraction" that may have existed in their notion of "man." . . . On the contrary, it is because they had lost the lofty, abstract, fully symbolic notion of humanity and replaced it with a local, national, or ideological membership, that savageness materialized in them and could be practiced against those who did not share such membership. . . . In that so-called "abstraction" there was a symbolic value that went against the desire to dominate and possess others under the aegis of a national, racial, or ideological membership that was considered superior.[7] (p. 13)

Cultures need norms beyond their own totems in order to be self-critical. "Only an 'outside' lets us know that we are limited, and defined by those limitations; only an 'outside' shapes us and recalls us to our 'internal principles'" (Fleischacker, 1992, p. 223). Without norms that are more-than-contingent, dehumanization cannot finally be condemned except on the grounds of personal preference or emotional makeup. Without a commitment to norms, an emancipatory intention is radically jeopardized and the byproduct is moral agnosticism. George Orwell underscored this truth in his classic essay *Revenge is Sour* (Greenberg, 1990).[8] Revolutions born of revenge are futile, even self-destructive. Machine-gunning a tyrant destroys the revenger's legitimacy. Successful revolts are normed by conciliation and peace. Without distinctive protonorms, history is but a contest of arbitrary power. That is why the French Revolution proved to be a new birth not of freedom but of tyranny.

Establishing Universal Principles

Should we grant the desirability of universal norms to orient community values? Are there global principles or common goods or a moral order that belongs to our humanness as human beings? For metaethics, as Benhabib (1992) reminded us, the challenge is a universalism that is not modernist, formal, or static. Habermas' (e.g., 1990) reconstructions have made us recognize that we cannot credibly repeat Kant's categorical imperative and its universalizability criterion in a postmodern age.[9] In the same way that the practice of civic journalism moves beyond mainstream traditions of classical democracy, appeal to universals must be done without presuming traditional versions of foundationalism.[10]

Several approaches to universal norms do not presume the Enlightenment's dichotomies and its Newtonian cosmology. One such master norm is human dignity, reflecting a humanitarian world view[11] and most widely known as the Universal Declaration of Human Rights (1988, pp. 1-2), established in 1948 by UNESCO.

> • Recognition of the inherent dignity and of the equal and inalienable rights of all members of the human family is the foundation of freedom, justice and peace in the world. (Preamble)
> • All human beings are born free and equal in dignity and rights. . . . (Article 1)
> • Everyone is entitled to all the rights and freedoms set forth in this Declaration, without distinction of any kind, such as race, color, sex, language, religion, political or other opinion, national or social origin, property, birth or other status. . . . (Article 2)

Every child, woman and man has sacred status without exception.[12] Inspired in large part by the atrocities of World War II (the Preamble refers to "barbarous acts which . . . outraged the conscience of mankind"), the Declaration "is the most universal expression of the moral aspirations of the civilized world" (Hamelink, 1988, p. 6).

Humans are a unique species. No society has open hunting season on people: "In October you can shoot three as long as you have a license." On the principle of our unassailable dignity as human beings without exception, we begin to articulate notions of justice and public policy. During Jimmy Carter's presidency, at least, there were brief attempts to make human rights across the board the centerpiece of the State Department—regardless of the trouble it caused at that time with the Soviet Union or South Africa. That is the master norm or protonorm of human dignity at work.

Another strategy for establishing the idea of a common good across cultures is rooted in philosophical anthropology. German philosopher Hans Jonas (1984) argued that when giving birth to others, humans do not begin with a neutral calculus trying to decide whether to take responsibility for that new life. Rather our primal instinct is toward preserving life, protecting it, giving unquestioned commitment to it. Parental duty to children is an archetype of human responsibility for animate beings as a whole that is "independent of prior assent or choice; irrevocable, and not given to alteration of its terms by the participants" (Jonas, 1984, p. 95). And out of that notion emerge ethical theories about not harming the innocent as an obligation that is cosmic, primordial, and irrespective of our roles or contracts.

Truth telling also can be cited as a universal norm. In his research on human values among indigenous peoples, Tom Cooper (1994) has identified truthfulness as one of their primary principles.[13] Truth telling is a central ethical principle among the Shuswap bands in Western Canada. Deception destroys social order. Living with others is impossible if we cannot tacitly assume that people are speaking truthfully. Lying, in fact, is so unnatural that it induces a bodily reaction that can be measured by lie detectors. In those instances where we "depart from the truth," the imperative itself "is recognized in advance—otherwise there would be no need to justify such exceptions as special cases." Those who relativize truthfulness as a protonorm are actually justifying it by indirectly recognizing it as generally valid (Mieth, 1995, p. 89).

Nonviolence, a commitment to peace, is likewise an example of a nonnegotiable imperative. In fact, Gandhi's work and that of Martin Luther King developed this principle beyond a political strategy into a philosophy of life. In Emmanuel Levinas' *Ethics and Infinity* (1985), for example, flesh and blood encounters with the Other anchor, our moral convictions, including this one: "The first word of the Other's face is 'Thou shalt not kill.' It is an order. There is a commandment in the appearance of the face, as if a master spoke to me" (p. 89). In the face-to-face encounter, the infinite is revealed. "The Other's presence is one of height and majesty; it involves an obligation . . . to which I owe allegiance and my assistance" (Chase, 1994, p. 8). Darrell Fasching's (1995) comparative study of religions identifies hospitality to strangers as a common commitment, "giving birth to a cross-cultural ethic of nonviolent and civil disobedience . . . through movements of liberation which seek to protect the dignity of those who were treated as strangers" (p. 15).[14] The public's general revulsion against physical abuse in intimate settings and our consternation over brutal crimes and savage wars are glimmers of hope reflecting the validity of the principle.

These formulations illustrate the manner in which certain norms have a taken-for-granted character. Our human identity is seen as rooted in the nonrelativistic principle that "human beings have certain inescapable claims on one another which cannot be renounced except at the cost of their humanity" (Peukert, 1981, p. 10). Given the oneness of the human species, "universal solidarity is thus the basic principle of ethics, and can be shown to be the normative core of all human communication" (p. 11). Our common humanness we share intersubjectively as a moral demand across cultural, racial, and historical boundaries. Instead of constructing a purely rational foundation for morality, our mutual human existence is the touchstone of ethics.[15] Ethics is rooted fundamentally in the creaturely and corporeal rather than in the conceptual. "In this view, ethics . . . is as old as creation. Being ethical is a primordial movement in the beckoning force of life itself" (Olthuis, n.d., p. 9).

Implications for Community Journalism

Craig Calhoun (1993) rejected forms of communitarianism that postulate an abstract good and uncritically lump together diverse constituencies into a uniform whole. He walks with communitarians "through the valley of utilitarian despair" and agrees that "their challenge to atomistic, interest-based individualism is powerful" (p. 10). But rather than philosophical declarations about discovering and serving the good, Calhoun insists on

> building the conditions of public life so that publics always in the process of making themselves might also make themselves good. . . . Positing *a* community as the basis of *the* public good is apt to obscure contests over collective identity and disempower those whose projects are not in accord with those of dominant groups. (pp. 6, 10)

In his view, communitarian discourse "obscures the extent to which social collectivities are forged rather than found" (p. 17).

Community journalism meets this critique head on. Through public vehicles of communication—redesigned with a communitarian mission—people "are able to reconstitute their social and cultural lives together through their conscious action and communication with each other" (Calhoun, p. 17). "The press plays a vitally important role in the process of self-governance not as the provider of information but the facilitator of public opinion . . . . A journalism of conversation views public opinion as the consequence of a social and public inquiry into common goods" (Glasser & Salmon, 1995, pp. 452-453). Instead of a static and impoverished communitarianism that "treats citizens' goods as existing in advance of public life" (Calhoun, 1993, p. 24), civic journalism activates it toward multiplex social relations, various local constructions, and a mixture of contending identities.

Language is the marrow of community; therefore, the peculiar task of the public media is empowering the common good. Relations between the self and others opens up discourse. Persons are displayed, made accessible, nurtured, and integrated into social units through symbol, myth, and metaphor. Such symbolic forms as words are concrete to life; their meaning derives from an interpretive, historical context humans themselves supply. Our constitutive relations as human beings are linguistic.

In Ernst Cassirer's (1962) terms, in their creatureliness humans are *animal symbolicum*.[16] Human environments are not coded genetically (as with animal instinct) but are created symbolically, that is, open-endedly in terms of an organizing principle. We do not merely exist in a vast museum, but are curators of our own. Instincts produce perennially identical beaver dams and ant hills; cultures are developed and imagined, always transcending biological necessity. Humans readily displace both time and space; animals act only when stimuli are in fact present. Humankind alone possesses creative imagination, the unusual capacity to describe experience, evaluate action, and transmit such to public discussion. Communication, in this view, is the creative process of building and reaffirming through symbols, and culture signifies the constructions that result.[17] The ancient differences among human symbolic systems—music, art, philosophical essays, mathematics, news, religious language, and Bacon's scientific method—are placed on a level playing floor.

Given the social nature of language, the community's "lifestory is the space of ethics and its authorizing structure" (Olthuis, n.d., p. 9). The specific humanness of human beings is that they interact linguistically with others. Therefore, the protonorm for all cultures identified earlier, "Thou shalt not lie." Society is inconceivable without an overriding commitment to telling the truth. As a primary agent of the symbolic theater in which we live, the public press has no choice but to honor this master norm as well.

When human solidarity is understood as a universal common good, civic journalism operates with a richer epistemology than minimalist notions of accurate representation. Instead of objectivist ways of knowing separated from human consciousness and social formation, truth telling is located in the moral sphere. It is understood as a problem of axiology rather than cognition per se. A truthful account lays hold of context, motives, and presuppositions (Bonhoeffer, 1955). Truth is not "a mirror of nature" and "privileged contact with reality," but "what is better for us to believe" (Rorty, 1979, p. 10). Truth means to strike gold, to get at "the core, the essence, the nub, the heart of the matter" (Pippert, 1989, p. 11). The assumption is that our common humanity is not inscribed first of all in politics or economics, but in our universal human bond as a moral commitment. Therefore, solidarity, covenant, and an obligation to the whole needs to be nurtured in the public arena rather than overweening preoccupation with the political domain, business, and technique. It does not merely mean that we expand international reporting, though thinking globally is a necessary condition of adequately understanding the common good.

But universal solidarity as the common good is not a deductivist program. A commitment to universals does not eliminate all differences in what we think and believe. Normative ethics grounded in universals is a complex architecture and in a post-Enlightenment era of global communications, it inevitably involves a particular form of pluralism.[18] The issue is whether a community's values affirm the human good. As our ideologies, philosophies of life, and beliefs are lobbied within the public sphere, some agreements will emerge that form a common good. Because we hold our worldviews not as isolated individuals but socially, we have a responsibility to make public the course we favor and to demonstrate in what manner it advances our common citizenship. The press monitors these worldview debates and assesses them in terms of their contribution to universal human solidarity. The issue is whether they help build a civic philosophy and thereby demonstrate a transformative intent. Arthur Holmes (1983) indicated that clashes over world views at their deepest level do not preclude their frequent similarity at crucial points as well. Worldview pluralism allows us to hold our beliefs in good faith and debate them openly rather than search for a phony consensus, all the while recognizing that our worldviews must contribute in the long run to human solidarity.

Communities tend to be hidebound and turned inward. To better shape civic journalism by universal criteria, more experiments are needed that come to grips with community life in global terms. Some glimmers of that consciousness are emerging over the environment; overusing our share of

> "Because we hold our world views not as isolated individuals but socially, we have a responsibility to make public the course we favor and to demonstrate in what manner it advances our common citizenship."

the world's resources has now taken on moral resonance. But statecraft, demands for health care, educational strategies, styles of transportation—all should be brought to judgment in terms of the ultimate test. Do they sustain life, enhance it long-term, contribute to human well-being as a whole?

James Fishkin (1992, 1995) developed a successful experiment in England in what he called democratic deliberation. After cultivating British citizens around Manchester for seven months, he brought 100 of them together into a local television studio. Instead of giving simplistic, off-the-cuff remarks about the problems in England, they spent the entire weekend from Friday afternoon until Sunday night going over the issues, arguing among themselves, televising it on Channel 4. One of the leading newspapers in London, *The Independent*, promoted the event, participated in it, trying to get more in-depth policy position papers based on informed and systematic debate. This was deliberative democracy, replacing sound bites and phantom opinions, an attempt for the citizenry to come alive and identify what the public problems were in Manchester as they saw them. The press energized the community's discourse—not just informing an abstract audience but actively nurturing the public mind. However, regarding the concerns of this chapter, did any universal principles enter the debates? Was it a *dialogue of justice* that reached beyond Manchester and Britain to our global oneness? If not, how can such appeals be meaningfully made? Three examples might be suggestive.

One illustration of public communication in terms of human solidarity is the historic four-day rebellion in the Philippines.[19] Ferdinand Marcos controlled the media system. As the possible election of Corazon Aquino was coming to a head, he kept predicting a landslide election for himself as always and censored other messages at every turn. He refused to acknowledge contrary voices and exaggerated his own promises to the people. In fact, radio and television orchestrated a campaign of defamation against Aquino. They called her a housewife with no experience in politics and a dirty communist.

Meanwhile, Cory Aquino's speeches were being passed around secretly on audio cassettes. She talked in living rooms, and people made notes and they handed them out on the streets. Posters went up, and graffiti appeared on the walls, and socially conscious theater was performed in the countryside, away from the police force of metro Manila. Then on February 22, 1986, at the station Radio Veritas—a small Catholic radio outlet just outside of Manila, used for education and religious instruction—a priest went on the air and began stirring up the audience. He did not speak in terms of particular policies—that Marcos was selling off their fishing rights to the Japanese and ruining people in the marketplace and squandering public money, not caring about workers' safety, and so forth.

Some of these political complaints were a subtext or appeared later. When people heard that voice on the radio station, they perceived it first of all in terms of universal human dignity. They knew they ought to walk tall. Marcos was violating elementary justice. Filipinos did not deserve their abuse and poverty. The priest put their story in terms of human unique-ness. Spurred on by the radio station, hundreds of thousands began pour-ing into the streets of Manila. Wall-to-wall human beings, jamming the city, put a stop to a military power that had been considered impossible to contradict.

How do you explain this phenomenon in ordinary political analysis? Was it just a rebellion of General Ramos and the minister of defense, Enrile? Was it intervention by the United States or maybe the Communists? What happened illustrates people's radio, community journalism, and the public voice, but through the priest the issues were phrased in terms of a protonorm. He appealed on a primal level to ordi-nary listeners about the question of human justice, and out of it he acti-vated their conscience and helped develop a political change of sweeping proportions known since as the February Revolution.

One also can note briefly an example from India, after communications from Delhi covered the country with monologues about nutrition, educa-tion, and medicine.

In this context, the group in the southern State of Kerala decided to take the issue of medicine into their own hands and put it in terms that the people themselves could understand. By the time they finished with their new medical system, they had not one sophisticated, technological bo-nanza that could do every kind of surgery possible, and which needed surgeons from the Royal College of London to operate. Instead, they chose to have a hundred small clinics staffed by nurses, native to the community themselves, accessible to the people, so that patients could walk for medical attention and return home during the same day. They chose a populist kind of democracy in which the communications system was put in the hands of the people, and they devised a medical plan that to this day has a better infant mortality rate than the United States or England.

Walt Harrington (1987) of the *Washington Post* understood the larger common good also in his classic "In Ricky's Wake." His suicide coverage embraces human solidarity and in the process irrigates the public sphere. Harrington weaves together with finesse and psychological savvy the story of Ruth and Bucky Jenkins after their son killed himself at 22. The result is an equivalent in news to Hemingway in literature. As readers sit-uate themselves in the family pathos, their preoccupation is not belea-guered parents or a contrary kid, but the universal human struggle with guilt in the deepest recesses of our being. As we reach into the mysteries and the power of intimacy, Harrington asks, when ought we like Ricky's parents accept responsibility but not the blame? Harrington crafts Ricky into Sartre's universal singular. Readers wrestle through the drama not as a remote suicide but with their own version of coming to peace with guilt.

Conclusion

These three examples are discourse that irrigates public debate, refusing simply to focus on communities isolated by themselves. In these cases, the news media as agents of community formation stitch the issues into a universal norm, engrafting ordinary questions about communal life into our human oneness. As a result, cultural diversity does not become tribalism in the extreme, but an opportunity for reaching into the moral imagination and helping communities work constructively from our own backyard and from the bottom up. In the process, local groups still make decisions for themselves, while resonating in principle with other human beings across the globe who are also struggling with human values of a similar sort. Universal solidarity and our home territories are all rooted in the same human spirit and revolve around the same axis. At least it is possible to escape the excesses of individual rights and to avoid tribalism, but only if the common good is understood correctly and implemented.

Notes

[1] Philips (1994) introduces the concept of "social artifacts" as an alternative to both skepticism and universalism. While this notion stresses contextuality, as does communitarianism, it is not politically complex; therefore, this chapter prefers Rasmussen's formulation.

[2] For an extensive review essay on the literature of community journalism—both theory and practice—see Rosen (1994a). For written descriptions of various experiments in public journalism (Columbus, Georgia; Wichita, Kansas; Charlotte, North Carolina, for example), see the list in Rosen (1994b, p. 10). Charity (1995) describes in detail the reporting and writing process from a public journalism perspective.

[3] Three terms are used interchangeably in this chapter: community journalism, public journalism, and civic journalism. The first connects the enterprise most directly to communitarian political philosophy, and to the importance of community in social theory and communication studies. Public journalism, preferred by Jay Rosen, underscores its legacy in pragmatism (Dewey's *The Public and Its Problems*, for example) and makes a direct lingual connection to current debates about the public sphere initiated by Jurgen Habermas and others. Given the mission of the press and his own background in political theory, Edmund Lambeth prefers civic journalism; he is spearheading an interest group by that name within the Association for Education in Journalism and Mass Communication.

[4] Cortese (1990) insists on the ethnic and cultural context of moral values as an alternative to the cognitive development models of Piaget and Kohlberg, the latter presuming universal moral stages toward autonomous rationality.

[5] Joel Kotkin (1993) makes a different, less worrisome argument about ethnicity—that various tribes across the globe are linked together by their common culture for purposes of commerce. The Chinese Diaspora, for example, drive economic growth among themselves.

[6] Bonhoeffer's (1955) terminology comes from the Greek language in which the second to the last syllable, if it has an accent, periodically makes a difference in the meaning of the word. But the penultimate is always trumped by the final accent in any ambiguous cases.

[7] For an analysis of the debate, see Michael Payne (1993, pp. 162-211).

[8] Greenberg (1990) elaborates on Orwell (1968) and on Edmund Burke's *Reflections on the revolution in France* (London: Dent, 1910).

[9] For debate on the issues raised by Habermas' strategy, see Benhabib and Dalmayr (1990).

[10] Enlightenment epistemology, inspired by Descartes, presumed clear and distinct axioms unencumbered by context. Often labeled *objectivism*, because this epistemological system achieved its greatest success among physicists and mathematicians; Rorty (1979, pp. 365-94) uses the more descriptive *foundationalism*.

[11] For elaboration on appeals to humanitarian universalism, see Fleischacker 1992 (ch. 8, pp. 181-226). Hamelink (1988, p. 7) notes that a humanitarian commitment cannot mean one homogeneous interpretation. "There are presently three leading concepts of human rights: the bourgeois/capitalist, the Marxist, and the Islamic." Viable notions of universality recognize "the concurrent existence" of different connotations and motivations.

[12] Berger (1979, pp. 18-19) argues for a broader view of universal rights. Rather than reducing them to the "specifically Western values of [civil] liberty and [economic] equality," he insists that we regard as universal, the right to life (that is, against terror, enslavement, mass expulsion, and separation from families). On the other hand, "accepting a minimal level of universalism" provides a "greater possibility of intervening" by the international community (cf. Hamelink, 1988, p. 7).

[13] From his cross-cultural content analysis of journalism codes of ethics, truth emerged as one of three (also freedom of expression and social responsibility) overarching themes (Cooper, 1989).

[14] Fasching develops hospitality to strangers as the centerpiece of ethics in his *Narrative theology after Auschwitz* (1992). For a summary paragraph linking Gandhi, King, nonviolence, and the stranger, see his "Prologue," p. 3.

[15] This model is actually closer to the way the moral imagination operates in everyday life, refusing as it does to separate moral agents from their situatedness. It benefits from recent philosophical efforts to develop an epistemology that reflects the actual process of making moral decisions: For example, Michael Polanyi, *The Tacit Dimension* (Garden City, NY: Doubleday, 1966); Stephen Toulmin, *Human Understanding* (Oxford, England: Oxford University Press, 1972); Morton G. White, *What Is and What Ought to Be Done* (New York: Oxford University Press, 1981); and Hilary Putnam, *Philosophical Papers. Volume 1: Mind, Language and Reality* (Cambridge, England: Cambridge University Press, 1975).

[16] For Cassirer (1953-1957), symbolization is not merely the hallmark of human cognition; this capacity defines us anthropologically. His (1962) summary monograph, *An Essay on Man*, identifies our unique capacity to generate symbolic structures as a radical alternative to *animale rationale* since classical Greece and to the biological being of evolutionary naturalism.

[17] Carey (1989) defines this as the *ritual view*—rituals being ceremonies or sacraments in which we define meaning and purpose, events of celebration (graduation, weddings, birthdays, worship)—in contrast to the mainstream view that communication is the transmission of information.

[18] For a book-length demonstration of this type of confessional pluralism which respects the diversity of narrative traditions and simultaneously insists on a cross-cultural protonorm of human dignity, see Fasching (1993). In this construction, he defies our ordinary academic conventions; no fair-minded reader can label him either an absolutist or a relativist.

[19] For elaboration, see "Communication and Liberation in the Philippines" in the special issue of *Media Development* (1986): 33(4); cf. Maggay (1994).

References

Applebaum, A. (1995, April 18). Ethnic cleansing: A dirty business that works. *London Daily Telegraph*, p. 18.

Benhabib, S. 1992). *Situating the self: Gender, community, and postmodernism in contemporary ethics*. Cambridge, UK: Polity Press.

Benhabib, S. & Dalmayr, F. (Eds.). (1990). *The communicative ethics controversy*. Cambridge, MA: MIT Press.

Berger, P. (1979). Are human rights universal? In B. Rubin & E. Spiro (Eds.), *Human rights and U.S. foreign policy*. Boulder, CO: Westview Press.

Bonhoeffer, D. (1955). Truth. In his *Ethics* (Trans., N. H. Smith). New York: Macmillan.

Burke, E. (1910). *Reflections on the revolution in France* London: Dent.

Calhoun, C. (1993, November). *The public good as a social and cultural product*. Keynote address to Lilly Foundation Conference, Indianapolis.

Carey, J. W. (1989). *Communication as culture*. Boston: Unwin Hyman.

Cassirer, E. (1953-57). *Philosophy of symbolic forms* (3 Vols.) (Trans., R. Manheim). New Haven, CT: Yale University Press.

Cassirer, E. (1962). *Essay on man*. New Haven, CT: Yale University Press.

Charity, A. (1995). *Doing public journalism*. New York: The Guilford Press.

Chase, K. R. (1994, May 14). *Rethinking rhetoric in the face of the other*. Paper presented at the National Communication Ethics Conference, Gull Lake, MI.

Cooper, T. W. (1989). *Communication ethics and global change*. New York: Longman.

Cooper, T. W. (1994). Communion and communication: Learning from the Shuswap. *Critical Studies in Mass Communication*, 11(4): 327-345.

Cortese, A. J. (1990). *Ethnic ethics: The restructuring of moral theory*. Albany: State University of New York Press.

Fasching, D. (1992). *Narrative theology after Auschwitz: From alienation to ethics*. Minneapolis, MN: Fortress Press.

Fasching, D. (1993). *The ethical challenge of Auschwitz and Hiroshima*. Albany: State University of New York Press.

Fasching, D. (1995, January). Response to Peter Haas. *The Ellul forum*, No. 14, p. 15.

Ferrara, A. (1990). Universalisms: Procedural, contextualist and prudential. In D. Rasmussen (Ed.), *Universalism versus communitarianism: Contemporary debates in ethics*. Cambridge, MA: MIT Press.

Fishkin, J. (1992). *Democracy and deliberation: New directions for democratic reform*. New Haven, CT: Yale University Press.

Fishkin, J. (1995). *The voice of the people: Public opinion and democracy*. New Haven, CT: Yale University Press.

Fleischacker, S. (1992). *Integrity and moral relativism*. Leiden, Netherlands: E. J. Brill.

Freud, S. (1952). *Totem and taboo* (Trans., J. Strachey). New York: Norton.

Glasser, T. L. & Salmon, C. T. (1995). *Public opinion and the communication of consent*. New York: The Guilford Press.

Greenberg, P. (1990, January 3). Revenge is sour. *Chicago Tribune*, sec. 1, p. 11.

Habermas, J. (1990). *Moral consciousness and communicative action*. (Trans., C. Lenhardt & S. W. Nicholsen). Cambridge, MA: MIT Press.

Hamelink, C. J. (1988). Communication and human rights: The international dimension. *Media Development*, 35(4): 6-8.

Harrington, W. (1987, June 7). In Ricky's wake. *The Washington Post Magazine*, pp. 15-21, 42-45.

Holmes, A. F. (1983). *Contours of a worldview*. Grand Rapids, MI: Eerdmans.

Jonas, H. (1984). *The imperative of responsibility: In search of an ethics for the technological age*. Chicago: University of Chicago Press.

Kotkin, J. (1993). *Tribes: How race, religion and identity determine success in the new global economy*. New York: Random House.

Kristeva, J. (1991). *Strangers to ourselves*. (Trans., L. S. Roudiez). Hemel Hempstead, UK: Harvester-Wheatsheaf.

Levinas, E. (1985). *Ethics and infinity: Conversations with Philippe Nemo* (Trans., R. A. Cohen). Pittsburgh, PA: Duquesne University Press.

Maggay, M. (1986). Communication and liberation in the Philippines. *Media Development,* 33 (4).

Maggay, M. (1994). *Transforming society.* Oxford, UK: Regnum Books.

Mieth, D. (1995). The basic norm of truthfulness: Its ethical justification and universality. In C. Christians (Ed.), *Communication ethics and universal values* (ch. 5). Thousand Oaks, CA: Sage Publications.

Moynihan, D. P. (1993). *Pandemonium: Ethnicity in international politics.* New York: Oxford University Press.

Olthuis, J. H. (n.d.). *An ethics of co-responsibility and compassion.* Unpublished paper.

Orwell, G. (1968). Revenge is sour. In his *In front of your nose* (vol. 4) (pp. 3-6). London: Secker & Warburg.

Pateman, C. (1970). *Participation and democratic theory.* Cambridge, UK: Cambridge University Press.

Payne, M. (1993). *Reading theory: An introduction to Lacan, Derrida and Kristeva.* Oxford, UK: Basil Blackwell.

Peukert, H. (1981). Universal solidarity as goal of communication. *Media Development,* 28(4): 11.

Philips, M. (1994). *Between universalism and skepticism: Ethics as social artifact.* New York: Oxford University Press.

Pippert, W. (1989). *An ethics of news: A reporter's search for truth.* Washington, D.C.: Georgetown University Press.

Polanyi, M. (1966). *The tacit dimension.* Garden City, NY: Doubleday.

Putnam, H. (1975). *Philosophical papers. Volume 1: Mind, language and reality.* Cambridge, England: Cambridge University Press.

Rasmussen, D. (1990). Philosophy and social criticism, 14(3-4). Published with two additional essays in D. Rasmussen (Ed.), *Universalism versus communitarianism: Contemporary debates in ethics.* Cambridge, MA: The MIT Press.

Rorty, R. (1979). *Philosophy and the mirror of nature.* Princeton, NJ: Princeton University Press.

Rosen, J. (1994a). Making things more public: On the political responsibility of the media intellectual. *Critical Studies in Mass Communication,* 11(4): 363-388.

Rosen, J. (1994b). Public journalism: First principles. *Public journalism: Theory and practice.* Dayton, OH: Kettering Foundation Occasional Paper, pp. 6-18.

Sandel, M. (1992). *Liberalism and the limits of justice.* Cambridge, UK: Cambridge University Press.

Taylor, C. (1989). *Sources of the self: The making of the modern identity.* Cambridge, MA: Harvard University Press.

Taylor, C. (1992). *Multiculturalism and the politics of recognition.* Princeton, NJ: Princeton University Press.

Toulmin, S. (1972). *Human understanding.* Oxford, England: Oxford University Press.

Universal declaration of human rights. (1988). *Human rights: A complication of international instruments* (pp. 1-7). Geneva, Switzerland: Centre for Human Rights.

Walzer, M. (1983). *Spheres of justice.* New York: Basic Books.

White, M. G. (1981). *What is and what ought to be done.* New York: Oxford University Press.

—— In other words... ——

Public journalism is thus a confrontation with a long-suppressed fact: the press is a participant in our national life. It suffers when the quality of public life erodes. And when the performance of the press deteriorates—as it has in recent years—then public life suffers as well. This means there are limits to the stance of the observer in journalism; but the American press has no philosophy that takes over when those limits are reached. Public journalism provides one.

Jay Rosen. (1996). *Getting the connections right: Public journalism and the troubles in the press.* **New York: The Twentieth Century Fund Press, p. 2.**

Conventional journalists see the people who buy their newspapers as readers; public journalists see them as citizens. . . . Public journalism doesn't only aim to treat readers as citizens, it assumes that readers want to be citizens. By and large they're sufficiently serious about making their cities, states, and country work better that they would hammer out a smart agenda, ask experts and candidates smart questions, and strive for a smart set of solutions, if only they had the time, money, access, and professional expertise of journalists. The reporter's and editor's task, therefore, isn't to report facts in a vacuum (as in the *New York Times'* front-page boast, "All The News That's Fit to Print") but to make up for the public's shortfall: to figure out (as only a good journalist can) how to round up a whole community's agenda and questions, and then to put out (as only a good journalist can) a readable newspaper with just the answers citizens are looking for. Public journalists aim to print "all the news that citizens want to know." Consequently the mortal sin for a public journalist is falling out of touch.

Arthur Charity. (1995). *Doing public journalism.* **New York: Guilford, pp. 12, 19.**

(T)oo many in the press prefer to claim that they have no view of citizenship, no image of political life embedded in their routines, no particular understanding of democracy to question and perhaps revise in the face of the widening disconnect. Public journalism steers clear of this abuse of neutrality. It argues openly for citizens as participants, politics as problem solving, democracy as thoughtful deliberation. These, it says, are sound beliefs on which to base a revitalized press. They have a neutral core to them, but they are values nonetheless—choices journalists might make—and they can be defended as intelligent choices.

Jay Rosen. (1996). *Getting the connections right: Public journalism and the troubles in the press.* **New York: The Twentieth Century Fund Press, p. 16.**

Try to engage a roomful of journalists in a discussion about values and the discomfort is palpable; you can see the necks stiffening, hear the teeth grinding in emotional overload. . . . The tradition that says journalists should not deal in the realm of values blinds us to the central fact that other people do. It is another of those "trained incapacities" that our culture foists on us.

The people we seek to inform filter virtually everything they learn through their own value systems. By reporting and writing as if that does not happen, we create yet another major disconnection between us (and our product) and citizens at large.

Davis "Buzz" Merritt. (1995). *Public journalism & public life: Why telling the news is not enough.* **Hillsdale, NJ: Lawrence Erlbaum Associates, pp. 93, 95.**

I can't imagine . . . any group of investigative journalists sitting down and talking about what it is that they'd like to write about without dealing with the basic questions of good and bad and right and wrong. In fact that is at the heart of investigative journalism: exposing wrongdoing.

Now, you don't know what's wrong without having made a moral judgment. As much as journalists like to deny making moral judgments, they are embedded in their language and they are embedded in the decision making that we call "news judgment." (We call it news judgment, not moral judgment; and I think that tells us something about the language that we, in journalism, use.) . . . I think the . . . hard-hitting stories, the investigative stories, lack a morally sensitive vocabulary. They don't talk about moral issues in moral terms. They go to great lengths to do what, in a more technical language, might be called "objectifying morality"—by taking moral claims and making them appear to be editorial claims.

Ted Glasser. (1992, Winter). Squaring with the reader: A seminar on journalism. *Kettering Review,* **p. 44.**

Voices

Lynn Waddell
University of South Florida

A Different Way of Covering Crime

After two Charlotte, North Carolina, policemen were shot and killed apprehending a suspect, the local media reacted with more than the usual follow-up crime stories.

The *Charlotte Observer*, along with WSOC-TV, embarked on a public journalism project that garnered the attention of the community and the Pulitzer Prize board.

"Taking Back our Neighborhoods" involved computer analysis, months of interviews, polling, and town meetings.

Although the newspaper had completed in-depth projects before, this project was different. The *Observer* committed more time and resources to the project than normal. It pushed to give a voice to residents, not just public officials. It held town meetings. It hired a community coordinator to write a community "needs list" for each troubled neighborhood.

"We wanted to get at the roots of crime," said Liz Chandler, a reporter on the project.

In their attempts, the reporters also reconnected with the residents.

"It just reminded me about the real value of listening to people on the street, part of what old-time journalism is all about," Chandler said. "We tend to get away from it with all the deadlines and technology."

The canvassing of neighborhoods with the highest crime statistics taught the reporters and readers that crimes were not always committed by "bad people." There were other problems in these neighborhoods that bred crime.

"I'm sure I had as many stereotypes as anybody else, and now they are gone," said Chandler, who was a political reporter. "I realize what a small number of people are involved in crime and how complex it is."

The series, however, didn't overlook repeat offenders. The *Observer* wrote about how these criminals were released soon after their arrests.

"It made the prosecutors answer some questions as to why," Chandler said. "If you shine the light long enough, they squirm."

And squirm people did—initially inside, and then outside the newsroom.

Televised town meetings held in the targeted neighborhoods sometimes put politicians and police on the defensive as residents questioned their lack of response.

At first, some of the *Observer* staff also squirmed at the introduction of a non-journalist into the news pages. But their fears soon dissolved.

"The things she came up with were almost unarguable," Chandler said of the community consultant. "You wouldn't want a reporter to do that—making judgments about what people need."

The community coordinator constructed a needs list, which was printed along with the articles. It was an important part of the project, for it served as sort of a community bulletin board. For example, if one neighborhood was listed as needing playground equipment, it might prompt a reader to donate a basketball hoop. The specifics of the needs list was one of the keys to the project's success, Chandler said.

"If we had written about it in generalities it would have been so overwhelming that people wouldn't know where to begin," Chandler said.

With the exception of the town meetings and hiring an outside person to make the "needs list," the project revived some traditional journalistic practices such as the wearing out of shoe leather. Reporters, who mostly lived in the suburbs, spent six weeks interviewing and getting to know the people in each targeted inner-city neighborhood.

Chandler said she believes the new elements were needed because the crime-ridden neighborhoods had become frustrated with the lack of response to previous complaints to public officials.

"Historically, they have gotten little attention. Finally they give up and stop asking. After awhile everybody is doing their own thing," she said. "They feel like they don't have clout. When a newspaper asked politicians to come, they knew there was the power to spotlight them or to point out commitments and contradictions."

As a result of the *Observer's* and WSOC-TV's efforts, things did begin to change within the troubled neighborhoods. The city committed to building a $1 million recreation center in one of the neighborhoods. A church and bank got together and created a day-care center. More than 600 calls came in offering to help fill a need.

The success, however, doesn't mean that Chandler is ready to embrace public journalism as the sole type of reporting.

"You need to make sure it's not just a public interest type thing at the cost to investigative journalism," Chandler said. "It's just one of the many complimentary tools we have been missing over the years."

Ruminations About the Communitarian Debate

Louis W. Hodges
Washington and Lee University

The world is a fractured place. Community is broken. Journalists are in transition, trying to find their way in dealing with a fragmented society, a diverse audience.

Among the experiments journalists and news organizations are undertaking is a re-examination of the traditional ideal of maintaining distance between themselves and the communities they serve, distance that is required if journalists are to report the news, not make it. The ideal of journalist as "detached observer," watching at arm's length what goes on, is being questioned.

Hence, in a number of cities around the country journalists and other employees are being encouraged by news organizations, chiefly newspapers, to become more involved in the affairs of their communities. They are taking on more leadership roles in community organizations and are even stimulating community examination of local needs by sponsoring forums for public discourse. The experiment is called "community" or "civic" or "public" journalism.

Serious doubt has been raised in the journalistic community about the wisdom of and the motive for the sudden wave of "communitarian" spirit. Ralph Barney, in his article found elsewhere on these pages, "A dangerous drift? The sirens' call to collectivism," worries about the dangers we face if journalists abandon their traditional function of observer. Barney's concerns are well-founded. Who will ride herd on the centers of power in communities if journalists are part of those centers of power? What is the force behind community journalism? Is it a genuine desire to serve the public in new and better ways, as some have claimed? Or is this just a public relations effort on the part of owners to boost lagging sales?

I am going to look generally into the notion of *community* by examining ways human beings relate to each other, especially the way we conceive relations between the individual human being and the group (community) of which that individual is a part.

Hence, I begin by looking at some of the marks of fracture in society.

Second, I present a footnote about communitarian thinking. Third, I briefly sketch some of the main moral bases of the liberal democratic ideal. Fourth, I propose the biblical notion of the "Kingdom of God" as a conceptual foundation for a way of thinking about the individual in community. Finally, I close with a note about the future.

The Fractured, Disoriented World

"Fracture" in society manifests itself in many ways. For example, journalists have given Paula Jones more attention than they have given Stephen Breyer. Jones was in the news because she has accused President Clinton of sexual misconduct, her complaint surfacing four years after the alleged events; Breyer was a nominee for appointment to the U.S. Supreme Court. Why was she a bigger item in the news than he? Something is fractured here.

Members of the Associated Press Managing Editors and the Society of Professional Journalists debated three years apiece about simple, nonbinding moral guidelines. That reflects the absence of even a common sense consensus. Something is fractured.

In Lake County, Florida, the school board mandated that all teachers include a message of American superiority in every lesson. Once more, arrogant ethnocentrism reared its ugly head to reveal transcultural fracture. Something is amiss.

But can we move beyond these anecdotal notes to find some general characteristics of the society we have created? Let me illustrate five rather common attributes, issues—or maybe problems:

1. Reason out; feeling in. We live in a time when feeling has largely replaced thinking as the primary mode of facing the world. Reaction supplants reflection. This is reflected in the language where the verb "to feel" has virtually replaced the verb "to think." People ask, "How do you *feel* about crime and gun control?" Others say, "I *feel* that abortion is wrong." Ask them why they feel that way and they say, "I just do." That is consistent because feelings and emotions are not subject to rational control or reasoned discourse. In a world of feeling, one opinion is as solid as another. In a world of thinking, however, one conclusion may not be as solid as another.

It is not clear where this change comes from. Psychologically it may make some sense because feeling is both easier and less threatening than thinking. Thoughts can be challenged as wrong and therefore can be rejected. Feelings cannot. If those whose thoughts are rejected equate that rejection with rejection of themselves, they are uncomfortable. Hence, the insecure personality retreats into some group of like-minded companions where all can *feel* secure. Reason is out, feeling is in, and no society can survive that move—except through dictatorship.

2. Polarized special interests. We live in a world that is not only constituted of feeling groups but polarized by them as well. Examples of interests that show polarization: homosexuality, gun control, feminism, and abortion. That is fracture.

In their monumental study of a few years ago, Robert Bellah (1985) and his fellow scholars found a serious erosion of the centripetal forces that draw us together as a whole people. The nation, they found, seems to have lost the "habits of the heart," a core of moral virtues that make us one nation and civilize us. We are increasingly polarized.

Abortion is a perfect example of polarization and of the way feeling has supplanted reason. There is no rational debate: Special-interest groups are merely shouting at each other in a partisan political struggle. On the one hand we have one group that calls itself "pro-life," and on the other hand we have a group that calls itself "pro-choice." They scream at each other and seldom debate or sit down to think together. Doctors are shot, clinics are stormed, and women with unwanted pregnancy are spat on. In the shouting match no one seems to want to recognize that everybody is, in principle, for life *and* for choice.

Their language, in which symbol trumps thought, reflects polarization. Pro-lifers talk about killing babies; pro-choicers talk about the rights of women to their own bodies. That language would change if we were to introduce a modicum of thought into the issue. On the one hand, every thinking person agrees that we ought to respect human life, including its fetal stage. On the other hand, we agree also that it is a terrible thing for a woman to have to give birth to a child who is unwanted, deformed, or whom she can not feed. For that reason, there are some circumstances, tragically, under which we should terminate pregnancies. And, equally tragically, there are times when pregnant women should go to term, even against their will.

But that is not the modern idiom. Reasoned discourse having given way to emotive reaction, we find ourselves polarized, i.e., fractured.

3. Rights, not responsibilities. We live in a world wherein assertion of individual rights supplants recognition of duties to others. That is true despite the fact that minimum thought demonstrates that the whole notion of an individual's rights is meaningless in the absence of another's duty to respect those rights. Nevertheless, in our time rights have become symbols in the struggle, not concepts that might reasonably guide the struggle. As I have suggested, it is simply easier to feel than it is to think, and in so doing, to feel victimized so as to blame others for one's plight.

Everybody these days, even White males, seems to feel like a victim whose rights have been trodden underfoot. Hence, we have the cacophony of rights talk and the dearth of duties talk.

4. Messianism and zealotry. We have a messiah on every corner, a savior in every garage. Rush Limbaugh trumps Walter Cronkite. G. Gordon Liddy's audience is said to rival Peter Jennings', or at least Dan Rather's. Jerry Falwell and Jimmy Swaggart have followings that may outnumber Christians, and the messianic zeal they arouse rivals that of Nazis chasing Hitler. In my home state of Virginia, one of the major contenders for the United States Senate was Colonel Ollie North, a confessed liar. But, his followers say, he is a patriot, and his heart is in the right place. Nobody has said much about where his mind is. At least I have not heard much about what he thinks on how specifically we might achieve important common goals.

> "Journalists love zealotry. Extremes become grist for the journalistic mill. "Balance" seems now to be journalistically defined as quoting idiots on at least two extremes. Zealots and messiahs thrive on media events, and journalists are happy to accommodate them."

Zealotry is a close corollary to messianism. Many people seem to have their whole being wrapped up in some cause or another. People take a legitimate but narrow interest, for instance reducing damage to the environment, and ignore equally legitimate but competing interests. Tree huggers and fern fondlers, for example, pay little attention to the need for 2-by-4s to build houses. Entrepreneurs who sell 2-by-4s are willing to rape the wilderness with no thought to the environment.

Journalists love zealotry. Extremes become grist for the journalistic mill. "Balance" seems now to be journalistically defined as quoting idiots on at least two extremes. Zealots and messiahs thrive on media events, and journalists are happy to accommodate them.

5. Individualism versus collectivism. This one may lead to something. It seems clear that the fragmented shouting match in which the nation is engaged turns in part on the language of "-isms": individualism/collectivism/communism/libertarianism/capitalism/socialism. The problem with -ism language is that it denotes ideologies, not concepts, and it attracts ideologues, not thinkers. It is intriguing to note that the communitarian quest was barely born when objectors began speaking of communitarianism. This twist on language is both a symptom and a cause of the intellectual paralysis.

It has not always been so. But earlier political battles, as in the several that surrounded the writing of the U.S. Constitution, were waged in light of a widely shared conceptual framework, that of the Enlightenment, from which emerged the liberal democratic ideal.

Before examining some issues related to Enlightenment thought and democracy, I must mention a new line of philosophical thought that is emerging as one response to the fractured society I have just sketched. These thinkers generally call themselves communitarians.

The Communitarians

Clifford G. Christians, research professor in communications at the University of Illinois, is the leading exponent of communitarian thinking among scholars in communication. Christians and colleagues John P. Ferré and P. Mark Fackler (1993) have published a book titled *Good News: Social Ethics and the Press*, a work that sets the agenda for scholarship in this field. A frontal assault on rampant individualism and libertarianism, their work seeks to recast the function of journalism and mass communications in light of a communitarian understanding of the human condition. The focus is on the relationships between the individual and the community, the one and the many.

The centerpiece of the communitarian ideal, Christians says, is the notion that the community both ontologically and axiologically precedes the individual. I cannot fully unload that assertion here, but the basic thrust is clear. To say that community ontologically precedes the individual is to acknowledge that the *ontos*, being, of the individual is totally dependent on the group. The group is the organism and individuals are the organs. (This is my own metaphor.) Communities outlast individuals, and individuals working together for the common good perpetuate communities. Individuals are born into communities; they do not create them.

This view contrasts sharply with the Enlightenment idea that assumes the reverse. Hobbes, Locke, and others believed that in the state of nature there are individuals who, to survive, must find ways of living together in peace and harmony. To do that, they come together and form a "social contract" to regulate relations with one another. Hence, they create social systems and give birth to governments that they design. That is what was going on in the 1770s among the colonies when "a nation was born."

Given that ontological priority of community over individuality, it follows axiologically that the community, not the individual, is the center of value. The community has priority over the individual in terms of *axios*, value. Individuals must act morally in ways that strengthen and perpetuate community. At a more mundane level, that means that journalists must function to sustain and build community—hence, "communitarian journalism." My own view is that journalists historically have done precisely that, not by promoting the United Way but by reporting on the community and revealing its shortcomings.

How the communitarian ideal will work itself out philosophically and in practice is not clear. What is clear is that we have before us a fresh way, potentially redemptive and potentially

> "Journalists must function to sustain and build community—hence, "communitarian journalism." My own view is that journalists historically have done precisely that, not by promoting the United Way but by reporting on the community and revealing its shortcomings."

dangerous, to look not only at the human condition but also at the function of the press in the modern world. It is just possible that Christians *et al.* are closer to the liberal democratic ideal than at first might appear, and perhaps they are closer than the libertarians are. At least communitarian thought sets the stage for a brief look at liberal democratic thought.

The Liberal Democratic Ideal

The term *liberal* is now used in a wide variety of ways, some of them pejorative. In using the word I am referring to the specific social/political philosophy that was shaped largely by John Locke and in this country by Thomas Jefferson and other founding fathers. The philosophy was the anvil on which a new political order was forged.

The liberal ideal grew out of the Enlightenment, that 17th- and 18th-century philosophical movement that was based on confidence in the power of reason to liberate people, order their world, and bring fulfillment to humankind. It was an axiom of faith that Reason, when unleashed in all its glory, could set us free from the narrow and provincial mentality that for so long enslaved our species. Democratic self-rule was thought to be possible only if enlightened individuals banded together in some sort of reason-based social contract to pursue the public good.

Notice the four key terms: reason, individual, contract, and public good.

1. Reason. "Reason" in the Enlightenment meant the analytic and synthetic exercise of the mind to think through the human condition and experience of the species in order to redesign the body politic. The faith was in individuals exercising the astonishing powers of the mind, freed from the shackles of ignorance and prejudice and the sheer brute power of the divine right kings. The watchwords: "Come, let us reason together." We can build a better world only if free citizens, who are adequately informed, engage in reasoned discourse about public matters.

2. Individual. Individuals, and not the collective mass, were the starting point. Individuals precede and form community, not the other way around. If we can but liberate the immense power and creativity of the individual through education and public discourse, we can establish a genuinely democratic world. If we can guarantee the rights of all individuals, we can secure "liberty and justice for all." Government can be "of the people, by the people, and for the people." Individuals, pursuing together their enlightened self-interest, are the best hope for human fulfillment and thriving.

As Michael Novak (1993) has written, democracy involves

> . . . citizens coming together to do what, traditionally, they had left to the aristocracy or state to dictate. According to socialist thought, the only way to overcome excessive individualism is to wait for directives from the party or state. Through their own initiative, however, free citizens are more than able to undertake and accomplish social tasks of considerable magnitude. (p.16)

3. Contract. Though human beings are individual, and though reason is a possession of individuals and not of groups, they must develop their individuality in concert with each other—hence the social contract. It is the only enlightened thing to do. To establish the contract, it is essential to determine the rights of each, as those rights derive from the general right to "life, liberty, and the pursuit of happiness." This is the basis of the individual's assertion of rights.

But we must note that classic liberalism asked not merely about what rights individuals may *claim* but about what rights all humans *have*. Unlike what happens in the modern world, in the classical liberal ideal, rights and duties are utterly inseparable. In the contract, each member pledges a duty to honor the rights of all others without regard to their station or wealth. Those who enter the contract promise to protect the rights of all individuals, a sacred duty. They are not merely empowered to assert their own individual rights against others, as in the right to choose abortion. This contract among individuals creates community. There is neither individualism nor collectivism here. There is instead a vision of genuine individuality in community.

4. Public good. Though the process begins with the individual, the ultimate goal is the common good. There is an interesting circularity here. The enlightened individual pursues self-interest by means of seeking the common interest, to build a body politic, in which individuals can flourish. That new generation of individuals is thereby equipped to pursue enlightened self-interest, so as to seek the common interest, to build a body politic, in which individuals can flourish. We can achieve the good life for all only by first guaranteeing the rights of each.

The liberal democratic ideal, therefore, thumbs its nose at the twin-isms: Take your individualism and your collectivism and stuff them! Individualism is inadequate because it fails to acknowledge a shared common heritage and destiny. Collectivism is wrong because it fails to note individuality.

Where do Cliff Christians and the communitarians fit into this scheme? Far from threatening liberal democracy, as some unreconstructed libertarians fear, the communitarians hold some promise of regaining the liberal ideal. In my judgment, liberal democracy is threatened by the general failure to acknowledge the duties and obligations that accompany individual rights. Thus I see Christians *et al.* as nudging the rudder to make an on-course correction, not as abandoning the libertarian individuality of Locke and Jefferson.

There also may be important parallels between the communitarians and a vastly older concept, the "Kingdom of God." Let us turn, then, first, to sketch an outline of one conception of the Kingdom of God and, second, to invite reflection on its possible utility as a conceptual basis for evaluating the communitarians and the ideals of liberal democracy.

The Anatomy of the Kingdom

The image of the Kingdom of God is central to the gospel account of Jesus' mission. Matthew's gospel, for instance, has John the Baptist announcing the messiah's arrival with the injunction to "repent, for the kingdom of heaven is at hand" (Matthew 3:1). Jesus then goes about Galilee "preaching the gospel of the kingdom" (Matthew 4:23).

The notion of the kingdom predates the New Testament, however. After the exodus from Egypt, the nation of Israel understood itself to be the people of God, members of God's sovereign kingdom. At Mount Sinai, about 1200 BC, Israel voluntarily covenanted with God to be His people. Thus was established what the Christians came to call the "Old Covenant." Jesus came announcing to Israel a New Covenant and further establishment of the kingdom. (It should be noted that the English word *testament*, as in "Old Testament" and "New Testament," is a translation of the Latin *testamentum*, which means covenant.)

> **These terms smack of involuntary servitude, of sovereignty imposed on a people by a state or other ruling elite—all of which is properly anathema to libertarians and communitarians alike.**

In this biblical notion, "Kingdom" must be understood in two ways, ways that are interrelated but separable. First, it refers to God's "kingship," to His status as king, as sovereign over the lives of His people. In this first sense of the term, individuals or whole communities commit themselves to being loyal subjects or servants, to following God's command.

Servitude of that sort is, of course, radically different from what terms such as "sovereign," "subject," "servant," and "slave" often convey to the modern ear. These terms smack of involuntary servitude, of sovereignty imposed on a people by a state or other ruling elite—all of which is properly anathema to libertarians and communitarians alike. Not so in the Kingdom of God. One enters the Kingdom only voluntarily, by invitation, never by coercion. One is called" (*vocatio* in Latin), not forced, and for a democratic people that makes all the difference.

The second sense of kingdom refers to a domain, to the collective body of people within a given Kingdom. Whereas the first sense of Kingdom is vertical—involving relationships between the terrestrial and the transcendental—the second sense is horizontal—involving relationships among people within the king's domain. Individuals in the Kingdom take on obligations to each other because each has a common bond to the "king." The voluntarily covenanted servants of the king also are voluntarily covenanted together as one people. (Does that sound like "social contract"?)

From this basic understanding of both the vertical and the horizontal dimensions of the concept of Kingdom, there flow some derivative points of ethics, points that provide the very foundation of Judeo-Christian morality. I mention three.

1. Equality. The first is the principle of equality. The vertical relationship of a people to God functions logically, psychologically, and spiritually to establish the absolute equality of everybody in the Kingdom. People are equally called and equally enrolled without any regard to accidents of birth (like race, sex, social status, height, or age). Galatians (3:28) affirms this view by noting that in Christ "there is neither Jew nor Greek, there is neither slave nor free, there is neither male nor female." Although people may not be equal in talent, achievement, or power, people are equally people, and that is all that counts.

This theme also appears in Isaiah. He was wandering around the temple one day and bumped into his god, Yahweh. It was an awesome vision.

> In the year that King Uzziah died I saw the Lord sitting upon a throne, high and lifted up. . . . Above him stood the seraphim . . . and one called to another and said: "Holy, holy, holy is the Lord of hosts; the whole earth is full of his glory." And the foundations of the thresholds shook at the voice of him who called, and the house was filled with smoke. And I said: "Woe is me! for I am undone." (6:1-5)

Isaiah saw Yahweh, creator and sovereign, to be so grand in power and splendor that any distinctions of status or worth between individuals paled into insignificance. Compared with Yahweh, none of us amounts to much. That is the theological base of the moral principle of equality.

The new communitarian philosophy, which at first glance appears to be designed for a secular age, thus far lacks this vertical element. What, then, is to provide the basis for equality in a secular world when the transcendent dimension is missing? Can it work in a secular age that seems to have abandoned not just notions of a personal deity but also any cosmic sense of a transcendent dimension to reality?

2. Freedom. The second point of ethics that derives logically from the notion of the Kingdom is the principle of freedom. Note that God *calls* people into his fold; he does not compel. Membership is voluntary, and we are free not to participate. (Is Locke's social contract theory significantly different from this Kingdom theory?) God calls his people into *service*, to be sure, but it is not a draft; there is no involuntary servitude here.

Freedom is limited, however, once inside the Kingdom, just as it is under the social contract. We must play by the rules of the Kingdom.

Those rules include, for example, the duty to love thy neighbor (Kant called it respect for persons as ends in themselves), to seek justice, and to walk humbly with God (Micah 6:8). Israel thought that the rules of the kingdom are expressed in the Torah, the law, especially in the Ten Commandments, which were, as the story goes, given by Yahweh to Moses on Mount Sinai. Functionally, it appears that the commandments were the constitution of Israel's social contract.

(If we combine these two points, the ethics of equality and the ethics of freedom, we have the intellectual base on which to address two of the absolute requirements of any modern democratic state: liberty and order.)

3. Independence. There is a third point of ethics of the Kingdom that addresses, and I think corrects, the concept of independence, a condition much vaunted and jealously protected by the modern press. (Black, Steele & Barney [1995] put it with seeking truth and minimizing harm.) In the concept of the Kingdom—and I think also in the sensible world around us—the notion of independence is a mere dream, an empty word "full of sound and fury signifying nothing." In the Kingdom, as well as in common sense, people are ultimately dependent on some antecedent reality, and they are radically interdependent on each other. We are neither fully independent of each other nor totally dependent on each other. Thus to proclaim independence without acknowledging dependence is sheer folly—spacey unrealism at its worst. It ignores the observable fact—no one chooses to be born—of our cosmic dependence.

But individuals are, of course, independent in some meaningful ways. For instance, they have the capacity to recognize their own individuality. The concept of the Kingdom also points to the fact that we are indeed freestanding individuals possessed of a serious measure of independence. But it points as well to the fact that we are communal beings possessed of a serious measure of dependence. Let me suggest that the more accurate word for the actual human condition is neither dependence nor independence, but interdependence.[1]

Conclusion

Where does all that leave us? I have not shown how to relate all of these philosophical notions to the practice of journalism. It is too soon for that because the journalistic community, its shapers at least, has not yet done its basic conceptual homework on the subject of humanity as simultaneously individual and social. Journalism, in the United States especially, has functioned largely from a sort of Adam Smith individualism, and it is that philosophical underpinning that is now being called into serious question.

With that I leave the matter hanging, save for a concluding observation: The current debate cannot move far forward unless we take into careful account the following four propositions.

1. We must re-enthrone thinking as a companion to feeling.
2. We should avoid the language of -isms altogether.
3. We must engage the spirit of mutual inquiry and eschew adversariness.
4. We can establish a realistic ethic for journalism only if we explore the professional implications of human interdependence.

Notes

[1] In this connection I find Erich H. Loewy's (1993) book helpful, especially chapter 4, "The homeostatic balance between freedom and community" (pp. 99 ff.).

References

Barney, R. (1997). A dangerous drift? The siren's call to collectivism. In J. Black (Ed.), *Mixed news: The public/civic/communitarian journalism debate* (ch. 5). Mahwah, NJ: Lawrence Erlbaum Associates.

Bellah, R. N., Madsen, R., Sullivan, W. M., Swidler, A. & Tipton, S. M. (1985). *Habits of the heart.* Berkeley: University of California Press.

Black, J., Steele, B., & Barney, R. (1995). *Doing ethics in journalism: A handbook with case studies* (2nd ed.). Boston: Allyn & Bacon.

Christians, C. G., Ferré, J. P. & Fackler, P. M. (1993). *Good news: Social ethics and the press.* New York: Oxford University Press.

Loewy, E. H. (1993). *Freedom and community: The ethics of interdependence.* Albany: State University of New York Press.

Novak, M. (1993, Autumn). Civility and democracy. *Creative Living,* p. 16.

— In other words... —

Ordinarily, what gets printed in a daily paper may be "newsworthy" for all sorts of reasons. Public journalism, however—despite the many forms it takes—inevitably comes to center on two tests of news values: Does this piece of writing or reporting help build civic capital? And does it help move the public toward meaningful judgment and action? Which means the final word on a public journalist's news choices can never come from the publisher, colleagues, or the Pulitzer Prize committee, but only from what happens or doesn't happen in the community as a whole.

Arthur Charity. (1995). *Doing public journalism.* New York: Guilford, p. 50.

How, citizens properly wonder, can people who profess to not care what happens be trusted to inform us? Why should the public value the perspectives on the importance of events offered by people who insist that they have no stake in those events? The journalistic determination to be properly detached also feeds into other cultural traits that have negative ramifications for journalism and public life:

• It not only supports but encourages transience. When caring about a place or circumstance is considered a negative, roots cannot be comfortably put down or useful relationships established; familiarity breeds professional discomfort.

• It insures that certain important things will not be seen as important, or perhaps not seen at all. Determined detachment leads to a kind of blindness about particular things, a trained incapacity to understand part of our environment and the people in it.

• It insures that more will be reported about what is going wrong than what is going right. Reporting on something wrong involves no risk, requires no extension of faith. But reporting on something right involves the risk that it can always go wrong. Detachment allows us to avoid that risk.

Davis "Buzz" Merritt. (1995). *Public journalism & public life: Why telling the news is not enough.* Hillsdale, NJ: Lawrence Erlbaum Associates, p. 19.

Public journalism calls on the press to help revive civic life and improve public dialogue—and to fashion a coherent response to the deepening troubles in our civic climate, most of which implicate journalists.

Jay Rosen. (1996). *Getting the connections right: Public journalism and the troubles in the press.* **New York: The Twentieth Century Fund Press, p. 1.**

Journalists are taught the pat theory that since "news" means events out of the ordinary, all the nondisastrous things that happen each day are not their business to report. Within limits this is true. . . . But if an awareness of the parts of life that go right is not built into an enumeration of what is going wrong, the news becomes fundamentally useless, in that it teaches us all to despair. . . . We have a system of news that tells people constantly that the world is out of control, that they will always be governed by crooks, that their fellow citizens are about to kill them.

James Fallows. (1996). *Breaking the news: How the media undermine American democracy.* **New York: Pantheon, p. 142.**

The big question journalists ought to ask is, "What do we love about journalism?" If we love the horserace, contention, conflict, our own careers—that's what we'll fight for. If we love our communities, that's what we'll fight for.

Marla Crockett. (1996, March 22). Remarks at Civic Journalism Teach-In, University of Missouri School of Journalism. (Crockett works at KERA-FM, Dallas, where she has a talk show called "The People's Agenda.")

Lynn Waddell
University of South Florida

San Diego Gets a Good News Solution

A mother murdered outside the drugstore. The last meal of death row inmates. Hundreds of civilians killed in Bosnia. These are the types of stories that dominate newspaper front pages on a daily basis.

Journalists' attention to the dreadful, horrid, and chilling has often prompted criticism from readers and those who shun the newspapers.

The *San Diego Union-Tribune* has attempted to combat that criticism with a continuing series about the good things going on within its community.

The occasional series "Solutions" runs several times a month and strives to recognize people who are improving the community but who normally don't get much attention. For example, one story focused on a woman who started a tree-planting campaign.

"That woman probably had never had her name in the paper before," said Gina Lubrano, *San Diego Union-Tribune* ombudsman.

Lubrano said the project has generally been welcomed by readers. She has received only one letter critical of it. That disgruntled reader voiced a complaint that several traditional journalists have shouted: The good news eats up space that could be used for more hard-hitting investigative stories

But the good news "Solutions" deserves a place in the newspaper too, Lubrano said. The bright stories aren't a gimmick to bond with readers, but an attempt to provide a more complete picture of the community, which is something newspapers have often failed to do.

"There is a responsibility to report what is going on in the community, not just the negative," Lubrano said. "If you pick up a newspaper and all it has are stories about robberies and murders that's really not giving you a true picture."

To some extent the public journalism projects aren't new to the *Union-Tribune*. The newspaper is just now giving those types of stories a logo and prominent play, she said.

The newspaper is also asking for more input from the community. Each "Solutions" story requests readers to write or call in about people who are improving the community.

Lubrano said she sees community journalism as just an evolutionary process for newspapers. Editorial pages have long taken positions. Now the news pages are trying to take a more proactive stance while maintaining objectivity.

Because of the delicate balance between traditional ideals and those of community involvement, the practice of public journalism is still evolving, Lubrano said.

"I think you have to be really careful about the topic you pick to become involved with. There was one reporter here who wrote a column about suicide and then was asked to be on a task force. He refused because he didn't feel comfortable with it. It's a different approach, and reporters are still feeling their way."

Communitarianism's Rhetorical War Against Enlightenment Liberalism

John C. Merrill
University of Missouri

The new communitarians are waging a vague rhetorical war against Enlightenment liberalism—against individualism and libertarianism. They talk of non-negotiable principles, universal and categorical claims in their emerging theory of journalistic ethics. They proclaim the necessity for the civic co-optation of the editorial prerogative. They mainly speak in vague and impenetrable terms: "universal solidarity," "a rich notion of accountability" that will "resonate in an organization's consciousness," the need for a journalism "that engenders a like-minded world view"— one calling for a "normative language for nurturing moral integrity in an age of fragmented lives" (Christians *et al.*, 1993, pp. 13-17). Such normative language, they say, is "apodictic to communitarian journalism," permitting "world-view pluralism" to "finally flourish within the public amphitheater" (p. 16).

Just what communitarians mean by all this is, in their language, "problematic," but the real meaning is not actually important. There is a vaguely spiritual, almost theological ring, to much of their rhetoric, which is alluring to many people. And it is often the tone and vagueness of their language that captivate the minds (or should I say *souls*, or *hearts*?) of many university professors and students. Also, it is rather chic to challenge the best minds of the Age of Reason and to trash their philosophies.

For instance, what we have thought of as press freedom is now passe, we have been told, and in its stead has arisen an enlightened, altruistic, cooperative, non-frictional concept of communitarianism. Liberalism has failed; society shows it, we have been told. The old ideas of Milton, Locke, Mill, Constant, Voltaire, and Madison may have been good for their day—but no longer. Instead, the communitarians are resurrecting the ideas of Rousseau, who tells us (Berlin, 1969, p. 148) that if we surrender our lives to society, we create an entity (society) that, being built on equal sacrifice of all its members, is in no one's special interest and thus cannot damage anyone else. But Rousseau's fellow countryman, Benjamin Constant (Berlin, p. 150), one of the fathers of liberalism, saw Rousseau as the most dangerous enemy of individual liberty. Why? Because, Constant declared, "by giving myself to all, I give myself to none" (Berlin, p. 164).

Today, the communitarians, sounding much like Rousseau, tell us that we need a more responsible media system, in which journalists, as members of the society, are willing to sacrifice their own freedom to the good of the whole. Reconstructing the basic tenets of the Hutchins commissioners of the late 1940s, the new civic journalism proponents stress media responsibility, not press freedom. They also stress the public (or social) leadership in press matters; they say they are democratizing American journalism—giving the people the say-so in editorial matters. No more mean, old selfish editors making journalistic decisions, many of which are detrimental to the moral health of the community. Listen to the people, they say. Find out what they want and give it to them. Increasingly, this rhetoric resembles what the old Soviet media managers meant when they talked of *freedom of the press.* They were talking about *freedom of the people*—or at least freedom *to* the press by the people. And we all know how much real freedom the media had in the Soviet Union—and even how much real impact the people had on press decisions.

> "Today, the communitarians, sounding much like Rousseau, tell us that we need a more responsible media system, in which journalists, as members of the society, are willing to sacrifice their own freedom to the good of the whole."

There has, indeed, been a tremendous shift of emphasis since the 1950s in press philosophy in the United States. Whereas previously the assumption was that journalists were rational and capable of making editorial decisions, the emphasis has now shifted (or is shifting) away from such freedom to become focused on the press's social obligations or responsibilities. These days the rationality and self-reliance of journalists have been called into question. The ability of journalists to make decisions is now doubted. What is needed, the communitarians are suggesting, is a more monolithic and positive media system that refrains from polluting the intellectual environment.

I reject the communitarians' suggestions that American journalism needs a more monolithic, responsible restructuring; that somehow the rational liberal theory of the Enlightenment has failed and must be trashed; that individualism is a flawed foundation for journalism and must be supplanted by a more collectivized, group-oriented and cooperationist theory, which will eliminate social friction and establish a kind of communitarian heaven on earth.

> I reject the communitarians' suggestions that American journalism needs a more monolithic, responsible restructuring; that somehow the rational liberal theory of the Enlightenment has failed and must be trashed; that individualism is a flawed foundation for journalism and must be supplanted by a more collectivized, group-oriented and cooperationist theory, which will eliminate social friction and establish a kind of communitarian heaven on earth.

I am a firm believer in individualism. The individual is prior to the community, not the other way around; individual perfection is the goal; as individuals get better, society will improve.

I believe in journalistic autonomy, in journalists having the maximum freedom in their decisionmaking. Such freedom should be permitted even if various individuals use this freedom in ways deemed harmful and irresponsible by others. I have dealt with this at great length in *Imperative of Freedom* (1970), *Existential Journalism* (1977), and more recently in *The Dialectic in Journalism* (1989).

I stand with the great Scottish thinker David Hume (1978), who touted development of a sense of personhood and pride that makes individuals cognizant of their own merit and gives them self-confidence. For me, personal ethics comes down to self-respect, to developing one's character in the Aristotelian sense—having a structure of life examined by ourselves as if we are our own spectators. Such an ethics, Hume said, is "the crowning attitude" for a person trying to live a moral life; such a person, for Hume, was a descendant of Aristotle's "great-souled man."

The Individualist Perspective

The individual ethicist insists that ethics is self-determined, voluntary conduct. It has to do with *self-legislation* and *self-enforcement*—no universal and non-negotiable principles here. The only universal value that I cherish is the value of the individual, a value that must be constantly protected against the inroads of various kinds of social engineers. I feel uneasy with the communitarians' advocacy of group harmony and solidarity. I prefer to retain a substantial degree of contentiousness, competition, and individuality, which makes life more interesting and is more likely to produce a greater degree of creativity in society—one of the foremost advantages of individualism expressed by Enlightenment thinkers.

Enlightenment liberalism must be defended in journalism. The belief that individual journalists can make rational decisions must be upheld, and even when such decisions are not made, they must be respected and considered. We libertarians of the press respect the free flow of information, the concept of pluralism of information and perspectives, and the belief that a diversity of ideas and opinions is good for society—even though it might contain disruptive and even false and wrongheaded messages. The liberal thinkers with whom I find congenial company repudiated the elitist and authoritarian ideas of previous times, had a healthy respect for all perspectives, and rebelled against communication control and paternalistic and monolithic notions of what the people ought to know. I, too, rebel against any communication philosophy advocating universal solidarity or pushing absolute normative ethical standards for everyone. I am suspicious of these elitists who claim to have some inside and correct notions of what is right in journalism—even the notion that the community, if consulted, will have the correct answers.

What Communitarians Want

A few other tenets of communitarians' new so-called "theory" follow. I rely mainly on the version articulated by Christians *et al.* (1993).

Communitarians see a need for the demise of pluralistic ethics—of libertarianism in ethical decisionmaking. They want a community-based ethic, a more monolithic or common set of ethical standards. They share a suspicion of libertarianism or classic liberalism and have all but discarded the Enlightenment concepts of individualism touted in the 17th and 18th centuries. They see these individual-based ethics as dysfunctional to the community and generally based on personal quirks rather than community-determined-and-agreed-on ethical standards. They see Enlightenment concepts as leading to a competitive and selfish morality that endangers any kind of community development.

Communitarians have not clearly explained how they would bring about their more absolutist normative ethics in a community. They haven't even clearly defined what they mean by "community." Would they bring their new theory to fruition by education, by persuasion, by intellectual dominance, by political means, or by religious sanction?

If they are willing to leave it to individuals to cooperate voluntarily, then they are really saying nothing more than the libertarian is saying. It is my belief, however, that they hope to go beyond this, and this is exactly what bothers me. For built into the communitarian world view is the same incipient authoritarianism and arrogance of the Hutchins Commission of the 1940s. What I wrote in *The Imperative of Freedom* in the 1970s by way of criticizing the *social responsibility theory*, I could say about the communitarian agenda, also.

The communitarians have a worthy goal. They want better journalism—journalism that fosters greater public concern and a higher moral level. That is also what I, as a libertarian, want. It's how we go about getting it that is the problem. The communitarians would somehow bring to bear public sanctions and some ill-defined sense of new direction on the media to reform them; however, I would hope that journalism would get better from within, from the journalists themselves. This does not mean that I would have journalists divorced from community thought and from community action. The press libertarian does not advocate making editorial decisions in a vacuum. Certainly, the rational libertarian editor, desiring to learn how best to serve specific segments of the public, will constantly assess public opinion. Libertarians are not nihilistic, unthinking "loose cannons." We must remember that the Enlightenment liberals or libertarians were much concerned with reason. They were not simply interested in freedom. Therefore they were *rational libertarians*, not hermit-like, selfish persons interested only in themselves. As rationalists, they knew the value of other people, the worthiness of community, and the need to extend themselves into the social fabric. The communitarians have misrepresented, certainly oversimplified, men such as Milton, Locke, and Mill. These liberals, too, believed in community, but they didn't consider the community prior to the individual, as do the communitarians. Neither did these men conceive of themselves as *atomistic* in the sense that communitarians describe them.

Christians *et al.* (1993) wrote: "In normative communities, citizens are empowered for social transformation, not merely freed from external constraints, as classical liberalism insisted" (p. 14). One must wonder just what is the deep meaning of *normative community*; just what is meant by citizens being *empowered for social transformation*. In addition, it should be stressed that classical liberalism did not mean simply being *freed from external constraints*. The Enlightenment liberals saw a utilitarian reason for freedom, a telos or an end. Libertarians (as made abundantly clear by such writers as Milton and Mill) were much concerned with the social reasons for freedom of expression.

It should be clear to you that I am opposed to communitarianism, but I am not opposed to *community* or to cooperating or interacting with others. I am not an isolationist. I like people (at least many of them); I enjoy talking with them, working with them, learning from them. I appreciate others—and I appreciate and value them as *individuals*. And I do so mainly because I appreciate and value myself. I believe in letting journalists formulate their own ethical codes and come to their own moral conclusions. If they are different from mine, so be it. In short, I am in favor of a pluralism—not only of ideas, perspectives, and bits of information—but also of *journalistic values*. This does not mean that I endorse every person's moral values; it does mean, however, that I respect his or her right to have them. This is, of course, a basic liberal position that is presently catching much flack from the anti-liberal communitarians.

> **I believe in letting journalists formulate their own ethical codes and come to their own moral conclusions. If they are different from mine, so be it.**

As hard as the communitarians try to divorce their philosophy from the ideas of socialism or of Karl Marx, it seems to me there is a disturbing similarity. Altschull (1995) notes the close resemblance between the communitarian press philosophy and that of Marx. In fact, chapter 11 is titled "The Communitarian Press: The Role of Karl Marx." Altschull wrote that it is "premature to consign the ideology of communism to the grave;" that "in its essence, communism is communitarian . . . with each person contributing to the community to the best of his or her ability" (p. 195). He further proposes that the communitarian ideal is alive and well today, although "the name of the movement has been changed from 'Marxist' to 'communitarian'" (p. 196).

Altschull and I are not imputing any fundamental disrespect with the basic humane concern that Marx had for society. We are saying that, under a different name, Marxist concepts are still being espoused. We are not saying this is bad. As a libertarian, I would not want to exclude any ideas or perspectives from the marketplace of ideas. I will admit, however, that a liberal position such as I prefer can lead to social stress. And it can disrupt, in varying degrees, the harmony of a community. It can lead to imperfections in a society or in a community—such as journalism. It can lead to cases of pompous and selfish individualism. It can also result in time-wasting arguments and debates. It is not as efficient as monolithic, authoritarian social action would be. Community-determined-and-directed journalism (if it could be realized) would obviously seem more valid than individual journalistic autonomy. But would it really be? Communitarian journalism suggests to me a kind of moral imperialism, a situation that the rational spirit of the Enlightenment was reluctant to tolerate.

I have tried to be long-suffering with the communitarians. Following the admonition of one of the greatest liberal spirits—John Stuart Mill—I have tried to enter fully into the mind of an intellectual opponent, who—though on the whole erroneous—may offer me some element of truth that can be useful. I have tried to understand what is bothering these modern antiliberals, and I must say that their concern over journalistic excesses, for example, is commendable. All of us can find some congenial ideas in the antiliberal (elitist) tradition. Just as generations of readers of Plato's *Republic* have nodded in agreement with many of his highly structured social tenets, people today are pulled toward any philosophy that offers social stability and freedom from the chaos that seems to be growing everywhere around the globe. The thought that all journalists, for example, would have the same ethical tenets and act in the same way is appealing. A kind of discipline and commonality of values would assure a far more efficient journalistic enterprise. This is what the new communitarians or antiliberals are advocating.

Public faith in the mass media is slipping fast, and we can see media filled with cheap, superficial, and vulgar material. We see shoddy journalism and deceptive media practices. Most of us—not only communitarians—want better, and we do have better, here and there. We have in our total media system a great deal of excellent, quality information and programming of a high moral tone. If we expect a consistently high quality in all of our media material, I'm afraid we will forever be negatively traumatized. But, fortunately, in our libertarian system we can choose; we can expose ourselves to our own particular kinds of information. It will not all be alike in kind, scope, or quality, and I'm sure that many segments of our public are happy that this is so. It is not only in theory that we as individuals like different kinds of journalism; it is empirically true as well. It is consistent with journalistic libertarian thinking, a liberal and flexible orientation that desires a broad pluralism of material that is available for the public—not just my kind of material. This was the spirit of the Enlightenment; this is the gist of classical liberal or libertarian thought.

But now, as Stephen Holmes (1993) has pointed out so well, the communitarians, or antiliberals, are currently laying siege to this legacy of

Enlightenment thinking. Under the banners of social ethics or group-determined morality, the communitarians, or New Elitists, are spreading their antiliberal rhetoric in classrooms, in books and periodicals, and in public speeches. Contrary to the liberals they criticize, the communitarians claim to know (or know how to find out) what is best for everyone in the society.

Challenging Communitarian Beliefs

It is not easy to extract from the communitarians' rhetoric exactly what their proposed journalistic theory is—what it is that journalism should be doing that it is not doing. But from the pages of *Good News* (Christians *et al.*, 1993), I have gathered a few prescriptions deemed important by the communitarian ethicists—some communitarian "oughts" or "shoulds" for the press, along with my short questions and comments, in parentheses:

1. Journalists should publish things that bring people together, not fractionalize them. (Just what would these stories be? How would the journalist know ahead of time what the outcome of the publication will be?)
2. Journalists should give the people of the community what they desire, not what the journalists want them to have. (What if the people, or large segments of them, want "tabloid"-type journalism and non-productive kinds of entertainment?)
3. Journalists should deal with positive news, not items that would tear down community spirit but those that would solidify and promote it. (What a monotonous, conformist media picture of the community that would be!)
4. Journalists themselves, within the community of journalism, should agree on a common ethics and should not fall into the trap of embracing situational or relativistic ethics. (Even a "community of moral philosophers" cannot achieve this.)
5. Journalists should discard the liberal politics of rights, which "rests on unsupportable foundations;" such rights should be "given up for a politics of the common good" (p. 45). (Maybe we should repudiate our country's *Bill of Rights*?)
6. Journalists ought not to ask, "What do I want," but "What do we want?" Not, "What should this newspaper do?" But rather, "What would the readers want this newspaper to do?" (Communitarians don't seem to realize that trying to give the public what it wants is basically what market-oriented libertarian journalism is all about.)
7. Journalists should throw out the old concepts of journalistic autonomy and editorial self-determination, along with individualism, and what communitarians call "negative freedom" (pp. 42-44). (If by "nega-

tive freedom" the communitarians mean "freedom from control" or "freedom to act freely", then if they throw out such freedom there will be no free space in which to pursue socially useful agendas.)

8. Journalists should make news reports accurate, balanced, relevant, and complete. (What if doing so fractionalizes the community—a practice anathema to communitarians?)

9. Journalists should hold fast to the underlying normative principles of truth-telling and the public's right to know—"non-negotiable principles" (p. 55). (Would negative and fractionalizing news be exempt from the truth and the public's right to know?)

10. Journalists should recognize that "morality always makes universal and categorical claims" (p. 61). (Whose morality and whose categorical claims?)

11. Journalists should realize that "universal solidarity is the normative core of the social and moral order" (p. 14). (Journalists might like to know what is meant by *universal solidarity*. Is such a sentence any more than saying that if all people join in accepting the very same ethics, there will be a consistent and monolithic morality?)

12. Journalists should recognize the falsity of the concept of the *Fourth Estate* or *watchdog* role of the press. (Why should they? Such concepts are theoretical, not empirical, and their falsity has not been proved. Therefore, why should journalist recognize such falsity?)

13. Journalists should not make ethical decisions on the basis of predicted consequences. (Why not make such decisions? Are the communitarians throwing out the theory of *teleology*—the moral value of concerned anticipation of consequences of their actions? Who are they to dispense so cavalierly such a legitimate and time-honored ethical theory?)

14. Journalists must realize that the Enlightenment philosophy of the press "currently generates confusion about the news media's rationale and mission and excludes the substantive issues from our media-ethics agenda" (p. 44). (Do communitarians have no such confusion? Are they certain of the news media's rationale and mission? If so, how?)

15. Journalists should reject "the Enlightenment's individualistic rationalism" (p. 185). (Are we to suppose that the communitarians had rather put their faith in the rationalism of the public or the masses? After all, the Germans in the 1930s and 1940s formed a kind of community whose rationality might be questioned. Maybe they needed more individual rationalists.)

Why Individualism Will Sustain Journalism

Proponents of individualism and free expression have always had their doubters and scoffers. These scoffers are with us today, and they will probably always be with us. They are welcomed by libertarians. When there are many—or a majority—who believe individualism has become so powerful that egoism eclipses social interest and the community is imminently endangered, then it is indeed time to become concerned about the limits of individualism. Runaway individualism and irrational use of freedom cannot be sustained by thoughtful, moral people. Therefore, such considerations need to be brought up, as the communitarians are doing. But individualism must not be abandoned. As American sociologist David Riesman (1961) has maintained, even though we are part of society, there is no reason to deny the importance of individualism. Although, as Riesman contends, social integration is a useful corrective to an earlier solipsism, it does not follow that social conformity is a necessity and a duty. If we go to that extreme, he said, we will destroy freedom, which gives life its savor and potential for advancement. Psychiatrist Carl Jung (1958), a passionate defender of freedom and basic individual rights, gave us a warning when he wrote that the individual matters more than the system. Here he was reversing the ideas of Plato, Hegel, Marx, Etzioni, and other communitarians. Jung believed, as I do, that the relatedness of the individual to his or her inner self is coincident with social relatedness. Nobody, Jung said, can relate to others if he or she has not first a relationship with the inner Self. I would add my belief that no one can respect others unless one respects oneself.

James Fitzjames Stephen, a 19th-century English jurist and philosopher, wrote:

> Each must act as he thinks best, and if he is wrong so much the worse for him. We stand on a mountain pass in the midst of whirling snow and blinding mist, through which we get glimpses now and then of paths which may be deceptive. If we stand still, we shall be frozen to death. If we take the wrong road, we shall be dashed to pieces. We do not certainly know whether there is any right one. What shall we do? "Be strong and of good courage." Act for the best, hope for the best, and take what comes. (Warner, 1993, pp. 212-213)

Stephens' kind of thinking is what is being challenged today. The individual will of a person is often suspect, especially by various kinds of modern Platonists, among them the communitarians. But, as Roderick Seidenberg (1974) stresses so well, "the spirituality of man is rooted in the freedom of the will" (p. 229) with the infinite worth of the person resting on this premise. Seidenberg warns that virtually every "free and noble-spirited writer"—from Kropotkin to Emerson, from Tolstoy to Thoreau—has defended the great Enlightenment tradition and the integrity of the individual against the steady encroachments of states and movements. Seidenberg says: "As the gravitational force of the mass increases, that of the individual decreases, relatively as well as actually, until a final condition of solidarity and conformity is attained" (p. 230). And, observes Seidenberg: "It is only when society tends toward a condition of stability, security, and eventual sterility, that exceptional men are doomed *a fortiori* to impotence and extinction; for in that phase of society either they will not arise or they will be suppressed" (p. 217). He warns that the individual is in the grip of forces that "draw him, irresistibly, into ever more rigorous orbits of collective procedure . . . that no longer sustains a sense of inward autonomy" (p. 113).

Seidenberg (1974) enthrones in modern terms the liberal, Enlightenment philosophy of freedom, rationalism, and individualism. Such thinking is still the foundation of a free and open society and of a vibrant press such as ours. It has not been swept away by the forces of history, as the communitarians contend. We must continue to espouse freedom and individualism if our journalism is to remain diverse and vibrant. We must, as one of my favorite philosophers, Soren Kierkegaard (1968), advised, put an end to collective identity and social roles and, instead, favor a deep respect for the individual.

Conclusion

Let us not give serious consideration to the communitarians' *non-negotiable principles* in journalism—those that supposedly define it as a profession and guide its practices. Let us seriously question the idea that morality makes universal and categorical claims on us.

Heaven forbid that we retreat into the elitism and arrogance of the Middle Ages when a monolithic moral universalism dominated the Western World. I refer to the communitarians' theory as vague rhetoric, and I think it is. But even worse, it is a rather ominous suggestion that a communitarian morality will rise like a gray and stupefying giant to erase cultural values and relegate ethical pluralism to nothingness. What we must do is to continue to espouse diversity that stems from freedom and individualism. We must, as Kierkegaard (1968) advised, put an end to collective identity and social roles and, instead, favor a deep respect for the individual. I am not saying Kierkegaard's thought is parallel to that of the Enlightenment rationalists, for it certainly is not. I am saying this early existentialist was a lover of freedom and an advocate of personal development and decision making.

Kierkegaard argued that a person who forsakes personal freedom, follows the crowd, and does not choose his or her own identity as an individual cannot even be said to exist. I heartily concur in this sentiment and highly recommend it.

References

Altschull, J. H. (1995). *Agents of power: The media and public policy* (2nd ed.). White Plains, NY: Longman.

Berlin, I. (1969). *Four essays on liberty.* London: Oxford University Press.

Christians, C. G., Ferre, J. P., & Fackler, P. M. (1993). *Good news: Social ethics and the press.* New York: Oxford University Press.

Holmes, S. (1993). *The anatomy of antiliberalism.* Cambridge, MA: Harvard University Press.

Hume, D. (1978). *Treatise on human nature.* In L. A. Selby-Bigge, Ed. Oxford: Clarendon Press.

Jung, C. (1958). *The undiscovered self.* New York: Mentor Books.

Kierkegaard, S. (1968). *Fear and trembling.* Princeton: Princeton University Press.

Merrill, J. C. (1970). *The imperative of freedom: A philosophy of journalistic autonomy.* New York: Hastings House.

Merrill, J. C. (1977). *Existential journalism.* New York: Hastings House.

Merrill, J. C. (1989). *The dialectic in journalism.* Baton Rouge: LSU Press.

Reisman, D. (1961). *The lonely crowd.* New Haven: Yale University Press.

Seidenberg, R. (1974). *Post-historic man: An inquiry.* New York: Viking Press.

Warner, S. D. (Ed.). (1993). *Liberty, equality, fraternity.* Indianapolis, IN: Liberty Fund.

In other words...

While to be truly free a press must be virtually unencumbered by public rules and regulations, that does not mean that only an unexamined press is worth having. Moreover, the very professionalism so treasured by members of the fourth estate must stand for more than simply what sells. At the very least, we can hope for an increase in peer pressure among journalists: more shame and guilt for the bad actors, and alternatively more approval and applause for those who cover the news responsibly.

Richard C. Leone, Foreword in Jay Rosen. (1996). *Getting the connections right: Public journalism and the troubles in the press.* **New York: The Twentieth Century Fund Press, p. vii.**

Most of the controversy surrounding civic journalism has centered not on its critique of the "disconnect," its different way of imagining public life, its embrace of deliberative dialogue, or its concern about the future of democracy, but on a single aspect of some newspaper experiments: their plunge into what is called "activism" or "advocacy."

To most of the American press, "advocacy journalism" is an anathema, and so the familiar charge is also a serious one. No movement could hope to succeed if it tried to persuade journalists to become advocates for a partisan "cause"—especially one they believed in. An acute wariness of being co-opted is one of the most prominent—and admirable—features of the professional culture of the press. More than most outsiders realize, journalists wage a daily struggle to separate their observations from their personal feelings, and they react with a certain intensity when they hear it suggested that this struggle is doomed or can be discarded.

Jay Rosen. (1996). *Getting the connections right: Public journalism and the troubles in the press.* **New York: The Twentieth Century Fund Press, p. 59.**

We dismiss many of our critics on the grounds that they are laypersons not washed in the waters of our culture, and therefore, knowingly or not, likely to put our independence at risk through the changes they propose. If they really understood our culture and the history and dynamics of journalism, we argue, they could never recommend such changes. Yet much of our own journalistic effort is based in our being "outside" critics of such institutions as government. In that case, we insist that our detachment, or noninvolvement, is precisely what legitimizes our criticism, yet we argue that a similar detachment from journalism on the part of our critics invalidates their criticism. That contradictory attitude comes very close to defining a priesthood, and it is one of the less endearing attributes that we show to citizens concerned about our influence.

Davis "Buzz" Merritt. (1995). *Public journalism & public life: Why telling the news is not enough.* **Hillsdale, NJ: Lawrence Erlbaum Associates, pp. 24-25.**

The rancor surrounding the public-journalism debate actually seems to arise from two misunderstandings. One concerns the nature of journalism's "involvement" in public life. When (editors) Leonard Downie (*Washington Post*) and Max Frankel (*New York Times*) hear that term, they seem to imagine drumbeating campaigns by a newspaper on behalf of a particular candidate or a specific action-plan for a community. What the editors who have put public journalism into effect mean is "just good journalism"—that is, making people care about the issues that affect their lives, and helping them see how they can play a part in resolving those issues.

And when big-paper editors hear that the public journalists want to "listen" to the public and be "guided" by its concerns, the editors imagine something that they dread. This sounds all to similar to pure "user-driven" journalism, in which the marketing department surveys readers to find out what they're interested in, and the editors give them only that. This version of public journalism sounds like an invitation to abandon all critical judgment and turn the paper into a pure "feel good" advertising sheet. It misrepresents the best conception of public journalism, which is that editors and reporters will continue to exercise their judgment about issues, as they claim to now, but will pay more attention than today's elite journalists do to the impact of their work on the health of democracy.

James Fallows. (1996). *Breaking the news: How the media undermine American democracy.* **New York: Pantheon, p. 266.**

Tremendous potential power comes with being a reporter. You have the negative power to say things about other people, in public, to which they can never really respond in kind. You have the positive power to expand other people's understanding of reality by bringing new parts of the world to their notice. Taking this power seriously means taking your calling seriously, which in turn means recognizing the impact of the tool or weapon in your hands.

James Fallows. (1996). *Breaking the news: How the media undermine American democracy.* **New York: Pantheon, p. 9.**

From (public journalism) assumptions flow that challenge the most deeply held principles of traditional journalism: detachment, objectivity, the belief that editors are the final judges over what is news. It also has led to some provocative redefinitions of journalism. . . .

I am concerned about the question of where news and editorial decisions are made. Are they made in the newsrooms or at the town hall meeting, within the deliberations of the editorial board or in the place where the editor sups with the civic coalition? (Or in the office of the consultant, where life goes on, no matter whether the circulation rises or falls, whether the community achieves capacity or not?) . . . We are . . . in a period of moral confusion. Public journalism has potential to help see us through into a better day. But it poses hard questions for traditions and values that we have held and respected for a long time. I fear that we are abandoning these too easily, letting them go without sufficient critical examination.

William F. Woo. (1995, Fall). Public journalism and the tradition of detachment. *The Masthead* **3(47), pp. 17, 20. (At the time of this writing, Woo was editor of the** *St. Louis Post-Dispatch.***)**

Since World War II, mainstream American newspapers have developed an ethical tradition that calls on reporters to forswear partisan advocacy, to be indifferent to the fortunes of individual candidates, to be agnostic as to public policy outcomes, to be dogged in the collection and delivery of information for its own sake.

(James) Fallows (author of *Breaking the News*) argues that such radical independence veers too easily into reflexive cynicism and that the reader will be better served by reporters who see themselves as civic stenographers dedicated to promoting worthy policies and well-motivated politicians. He condemns journalists who "lack a sense of responsibility for how public life turned out." . . . Fallows' philosophy flows from the . . . premise that journalism should be a service industry that tailors its work to help those involved in forming public policy. Such a view might be less erosive of the traditional values of the newsroom if it was not such a short leap from being a servant in the policy process to being a political advocate who uses journalism as a cover.

Howell Raines. (1996, Feb. 28). Bad advice for journalists everywhere. *St. Petersburg Times,* **15-A. (Raines is a Pulitzer prize-winning editor of** *The New York Times.***)**

Lynn Waddell
University of South Florida

The Sound of Discontent

It's tough practicing something you don't believe.

Just ask Bruce Gellerman, a reporter who leads some public journalism projects for WBUR-radio in Boston.

A long-time newsman, Gellerman loathes the current trend in journalism.

"I don't buy it. It's an intellectual circle jerk," Gellerman said. "People who don't do journalism or haven't done it in years are trying to tell us how to do it. I think it's garbage."

Gellerman was drafted to participate in public journalism projects in 1994 when his station in conjunction with the *Boston Globe* and WBZ-TV embarked on "The People's Voice" project. The public journalism campaign attempted to spark more community involvement in politics.

Therefore, his dislike for the practice goes far beyond where he thinks it is generated, academia. First, he is against the practice in theory because it advocates a proactive stance, which is contrary to the traditional role of the journalist.

"I'm sorry people don't vote. I'm sorry people don't listen, but my job isn't to make them listen. I'm not into advocacy journalism," Gellerman said. "I want everybody to hate me equally. That's what I was put on earth to do."

In practice, Gellerman said public journalism sometimes interferes with solid reporting. The trend toward community forums and polling often act as a disservice to readers, he said. There have been occasions when forums weren't worthy of stories, but stories were written because the news organization sponsored them, he said.

Polls have also missed issues of major concern to the public, because participants aren't always consciously aware of the basis for their fears and opinions, according to Gellerman. For instance, he said a poll done as part of "The People's Voice" showed voters' top two concerns as being crime and jobs.

"It didn't pick up even remotely about the distrust of government," Gellerman said. "We had it wrong."

There's similar danger in allowing readers to create the news agenda because they may not know as much about an issue as those specializing in it, he said.

"The idea that people have a better understanding of the issues than people who specialize in it is wrong. When we interview people we get opinions, not facts," Gellerman said. "For all those reasons it's a misguided experiment by people too sensitive to political correctness."

So why does Gellerman practice something that he preaches against?

"It comes down from the top," he said referring to upper station management. "It's a conspiracy of liberalism. The press has taken upon itself to become the whipping boy."

Gellerman, nevertheless, has kept his disdain for the practice no secret and credits his continuous employment to his years of experience.

"I'm not very popular around here, and I'm the one who has to run the programs. I've got to take out the garbage, but I'm a good soldier."

A Dangerous Drift? The Sirens' Call to Collectivism

Ralph D. Barney
Brigham Young University

The 1980s were widely viewed, with some justification, as the "selfish" eighties in America—a distressing period of apparent rampant individualism. The "chaotic excesses" of the period produced continuing demands for greater sense and cooperation in search of a calming social unity. Such cooperative efforts, the thinking goes, are our sole hope for breeding progress and producing solutions to mounting social problems. In short, the answer to the excesses of individualism is expanded communitarianism; cooperation.

Few, it seems, see danger—and certainly not social disaster—in a visceral drift toward communitarianism fueled by the mistaken belief that it conveniently holds solutions to the disorder and social confusion of individualistic behavior. Indeed, the idyllic vision of a cooperative society as the engine to drive social progress is the saving alternative to the individualism of a liberal democracy.

Societies through the millennia have inevitably grasped at communitarian discipline as an answer to the troublesome unpredictability of unruly individualists. To look today at 75% of the world's population (80% by the year 2000; Crossette, 1995), on all continents, is to glimpse peoples who centuries ago organized into freeze-frame, cooperative, change-resistant, consensus cultures which endure to this day much as they were those hundreds of years ago.

A fundamental weakness in these communitarian cultures is an obstinate resistance to change and, from a communication perspective, a compulsion to shape the system to facilitate community maintenance. In this context, the spread of communitarian philosophy has profound consequences for the communications professional and the communication industry.

Serious concern and reservations created by perceptions of individualistic abuse cannot, of course, be rejected. Yet, individualism—the inclination and ability of individuals to retain rights to self-determination in the face of community pressures—is not only the philosophy of choice at the moment for the American social system, but is the sole visible hope for maintaining a liberal, participatory democracy. As one begins believing a liberal democracy has outlived its usefulness, the attraction of a change-resistant traditional society rises.

Without doubt, collective, cooperative efforts are often desirable, and even critically necessary, for short term social good; enlistment and organization of individuals into unified groups is vitally necessary for the vast majority of project achievements.

But as cooperation rises as a highly seductive, and ultimately mandatory, alternative to hot-dogging individualists, it is imperative that the inevitable consequences of unconditional membership, based on observable historical examples, be explored. Therefore, this discussion concentrates on some structural tendencies of communitarian societies and the inevitable information philosophies they produce. The communitarian threat is the greater because changes toward communitarianism, unlike those toward individualism, tend to be irreversible, or reversible only at great social cost. Communitarianism at its most effective is intolerant of individualism and controlling of information. Individualism, on the other hand, must tolerate both communitarian and pluralistic information.

> "Individualism—the inclination and ability of individuals to retain rights to self-determination in the face of community pressures—is not only the philosophy of choice at the moment for the American social system, but is the sole visible hope for maintaining a liberal, participatory democracy."

The Appeal of Communitarianism

Communitarianism is defined as the relinquishing of one's individualism to the community for the greater good of the community. A community for Richard Rorty:

> is constituted by people who share enough of the same beliefs and values for each to be able to identify imaginatively with the other.

> Members of the same community can meaningfully attempt to re-
> solve their disagreements because fruitful conversation between
> them is made possible by the understandings they share; each has a
> heightened sensitivity towards the pain and humiliation of other
> members because each regards these others as 'one of them.'
> (Mason, 1993, p. 220)

Aristotle and St. Paul placed community in a thoroughly dominant position relative to individualism, arguing that :

> The community is in a certain sense prior to the individual; the in-
> dividual only exists through the community. For Aristotle, humans
> are political animals, and only gods and beasts would conceivably
> live outside society. For St. Paul, it is, of course, not a matter of an
> implanted social instinct; we are related to each other and to God by
> virtue of a covenant for which we were elected and which we did
> not elect. Autonomy is not a center concern. In fact, for Christianity,
> autonomy at its limit is best represented by Milton's Lucifer, who
> thought it better to rule in hell than serve in heaven. (Springsted,
> 1991, pp. 468-469)

Alasdair MacIntyre (1990) illustrated the dichotomy between the individualist and the communitarian by comparing values in Japan and
America. Two American characteristics formed his individualistic pattern:

1. The individual person possesses the resources for moral judgment
and right action within, so that each individual has the task of fashioning
his or her own morality, expressed in his or her choice, attitudes, and preferences and have correspondingly understood a shared morality as no
more than agreement in and harmonization of those individual choices,
attitudes, and preferences, perhaps an implicit social contract;
2. [Individuals] view social institutions merely as a means, as instruments through which individuals may give expression to and achieve the
various goals they have chosen.

The Japanese, by contrast, are clearly less individualist:

1. They find resources for moral judgment and action in the established
mores of the family, the workplace, and the like, rather than within themselves, and
2. They view the point and purpose of individual lives as being to serve
institutional needs and goals, rather than vice versa.

Briefly, in a communitarian setting, the individual is defined from the outside; in an individualistic setting, the individual is defined from inside.

It is not that communitarian effort is undesirable, or that individuals should not commit themselves to cooperative behavior. It is, however, the problems that emerge when the individual is submerged by communitarian structures to the point that the ability to make his or her own decisions, or to survive outside the collective community, is lost.

The community of shared values Rorty (Mason, 1993) described turns sinister in an entrenching process that immunizes those values to change, reducing the probabilities that the community will remain dynamic and progressive.

It must also be recognized that the communitarian will inevitably submerge the individual; there is no logical alternative to achievement of the cooperative ideal.

David Riesman (1961) suggested that sense of community is socialized into individuals; his outer-directed person needs to look to others for decisions. Similarly, current market research techniques identify probably two-thirds of a given population in this country as outer-directed and needing confirmation of correctness from others (Atlas, 1984). Such is the nature of a community with shared values and goals.

Cooperation or Corruption?

Despite the attraction of such cooperation, and the undoubted short term benefits of cooperative behavior in which resources are pooled for the common benefit and achievement of consensus goals, practical and crippling problems begin relatively soon, leading to the broad generalization that consensus groups (communities), by the nature of their evolutionary structure, corrupt and morally bankrupt themselves. Evolution from dynamic to static society (as occurred with today's traditional societies) is a particularly virulent corruption, despite the attraction and apparent comfort in such societies.

There appear to be two clear points at which the community becomes morally corrupt. The first of those thresholds is a necessary evil for all because of an inherent individual dependency in an increasingly complex society, but nevertheless deplorable on principle.

The first point of corruption lies in the loss of individuality and autonomy required by membership in the community. Whatever group we join requires some sacrifice of an individual's autonomy as a membership fee. This may range from innocuous adapting to a small group of friends (learning their minimum standards for continued association) to virtually total abandonment of individual rights entailed in entering the military in wartime. The dedicated individualist is likely to join groups from a self-interest, yielding a minimum of individualism and departing once his or her goals are achieved. The communitarians tend to find a home in the group and yields virtually all identity as they constantly seek clues about how they should behave.

The act of submitting to the collective immediately distances the communitarian from the individual, shaping the treatment of information and its distribution, and leading to power concentration for the collective good.

> **The act of submitting to the collective immediately distances the communitarian from the individual, shaping the treatment of information and its distribution, and leading to power concentration for the collective good.**

The second point of corruption, which I see as inevitable and merely a matter of time, is crossed when, as I will discuss below, the group itself becomes more important than the reason it was established. It is this second threshold that is more important from a moral perspective, although concerns should be expressed for individuals in a liberal democracy who turn themselves over to a collective without reservation.

This discussion will deal with polar views when the vast majority would actually place some distance from either pole. Dedicated individualists, for example, are soon in prison or in mental institutions. Unfortunately, however, social acceptability leaves many polar communitarians running loose and even achieving high and respectable position.

I would like to discuss two sets of conflicting principles affected by sense of community. First, Loyalty to a community is the inevitable price of acceptance, creating sharp conflicts with fidelity to Truth. Second, attitudes toward information shift from the need for a broad range of information (pluralism) to a reliance on information necessary to maintain community values and reinforce the status quo. Other conflicts are inevitable between the two philosophical positions, but these two have a particular relevance for communication professionals.

Loyalty Versus Truth

Sooner or later in formation and maintenance of a community, a threshold is crossed in which the importance of the group transcends the value of distributing accurate information both internally, to members of the group, and externally, about the community or group.

That is, it is not difficult to visualize a group established for strongly altruistic purposes with socially beneficial goals in mind (the trade union movement comes to mind) in which individuals must sacrifice for the benefit of the whole, and even for a broader social good. In the early history of the group, distribution of extensive and accurate information is important as the group strives to attract members, consolidate power, and carve a place for itself in the larger society.

The group often begins from a relatively powerless position, both in the society at large and in the enlistment of adherents. It is a sense of powerlessness in individuals that leads to the pooling of power into a cooperative. Recruitment of adherents is facilitated, by the way, in an individualistic society which values and encourages distribution of pluralistic information. It is that very pluralism that allows the group to proselytize and persuade in the face of superior public power.

Once the successful group has established itself, has expanded its membership to an optimum level, and has won its niche as a recognized social institution with power to pursue its original goals, emphases change. It appears an obvious evolutionary process. The drive changes from trying to achieve socially beneficial ends to maintaining hard-earned position in the social structure. Priorities subtly reverse.

> **Once success is achieved through the pooling of the power of shared values, the community inevitably turns to valuing itself and its perpetuation above individuals and surrounding communities.**

Once success is achieved through the pooling of the power of shared values, the community inevitably turns to valuing itself and its perpetuation above individuals and surrounding communities. This, of course, is at odds with the needs of a dynamic society in a liberal democracy committed to truth and accuracy. Such a society relies on the individualistic moral sense of journalists to place each of these communities in a perspective that reduces their probabilities of accumulating disproportionate power.

Group loyalty increases the power of the group, as well as contributing to the centralizing of power in the leadership. Groups intent on self-perpetuation find no shortage of adherents. As Hoffer (1951) said, "the chief passion of the frustrated is 'to belong,' and there cannot be too much cementing and binding to satisfy this passion" (p. 45). And, as Riesman (1961) suggested, the need to belong soon overrides the need to achieve and the organization soon exists for its own sense of community, though it may profess to seek goal achievement. Presentation of a united front, combined with confidence that mere belonging is a primary goal of many members, invests great power in a professional leadership, even in voluntary organizations, that has a vested interest in perpetuating itself.

It is not in the nature of a professional leadership to voluntarily work itself out of a job by achieving all goals, rendering the organization superfluous. Therefore, emergence of a permanent, professional leadership (a natural development in the evolution of a successful group) creates a class of individuals with a self interest largely independent of the group's interest. The group is most interested in achieving its goals. At an extreme, the professional leader has a greater interest in maintaining position, or in identifying new goals which may or may not be consistent with original group intent.

The communitarian wave, in this way, takes on a life of its own and tends to ultimately overwhelm individualists and to digest those members who commit themselves to collective behaviors.

Eric Hoffer (1951), in theorizing about mass social movements, described the composition and evolution of the groups which form to achieve the movement's objectives. Men of Words, rejected as timeservers and courtiers, discredit the prevailing order, after which the ruthless Fanatics, knowing the masses crave communion, the mustering of the host, and the dissolution of cursed individuality in the majesty and the grandeur of a mighty whole, become the architects of the new order. Soon, however, the restless Fanatic is necessarily pushed aside. Practical Men of Action, with the battle largely won, the niche assured, accept responsibility for "administering and perpetuating the power won" (p. 135). Such a characterization may appear applicable only in extreme cases of mass movement, but the elements tend to be common to virtually all enduring formations of community.

In this context, of course, an ideal community would be one that forms on an ad hoc basis, fills its function, and disperses without need for perpetuation; or whose leadership is, perhaps, voluntary and "amateur" without vested interest in maintaining power. Alternative newspapers of the 1960s and 1970s, for example, formed in protest of government policies at virtually all levels. Once the demand for such protest died (the end of the Viet Nam war, primarily), many alternative publications faded away (the *Los Angeles Free Press*, comes to mind). Others moved closer to establishment values in seeking stable readership in order to establish advertising rates (*Rolling Stone* magazine and the *Bay Guardian* of San Francisco, while still somewhat radical, are far milder of tone than they were 25 years ago) and perpetuate themselves through a form of corruption.

Students of these movements might find that anti-war, gender equality, and racial integration groups of the 1960s and early 1970s largely disappeared after relatively short shelf lives. Some did stabilize and struggle to find roles that would legitimize their organizations once the high profile of the cause had run its course. Anti-war groups, of course, disappeared almost entirely, suggesting highly individualistic involvement and the failure of professional managers to emerge and find diversionary "causes" that would perpetuate the order. As the urgency of both gender equality and racial integration subsided in the late 1970s, organizations for those two causes found themselves struggling to find new directions to justify perpetuating organizational infrastructures.

The manager who replaces the idealogue in the successful movement sets about demanding loyalty and establishing structures to maintain the group. Hence, members of the group who relinquish substantial individual autonomy for an altruistic purpose may ultimately find themselves lending little but their numbers to the perpetuation of the group, having been locked out of the administration by an efficient bureaucratic structure dedicated to, first, strengthening the organization and, second, advancing the cause, a reversal in priorities. Hoffer (1951) warned that "when hopes and dreams are loose in the streets, it is well for the timid to lock doors, shutter windows, and lie low until the wrath has passed. For there is often a monstrous incongruity between the hopes, however noble and tender, and the action which follows them" (p. 20).

> The need to perpetuate the organization reorders priorities to require that Loyalty to the organization transcends commitment to Truth.

This administrative development (the forming of a complex infrastructure) is critical for its effect on commitment to basic principles, such as Truth.

The need to perpetuate the organization reorders priorities to require that Loyalty to the organization transcends commitment to Truth. While the individualist has the possibility of exhibiting a commitment to Truth—no guarantees, of course—the goals of a community inevitably blind it to the value of truth if the community is endangered by truth. Protesters are banished from the community or otherwise punished.

Getting and Keeping Power

Communities established for noteworthy purposes—families; religions; corporations; professional, service, and fraternal organizations; and myriads of other groupings ranging from extensive to limited—soon move past their original purpose of goal achievement (concerted actions of trade union groups in improving the lot of workers, professionalizing of law enforcement officers, etc.) and into the preserving of the group as a primary goal. The reason such a transition occurs lies largely in the concept of power. Professional administrators exercise great powers over the group: They wield the group's power externally, and have a vested interest in perpetuating such a power position.

The ideal community, of course, sees little need for power struggle as leadership roles are defined, for it is established to achieve certain goals and disbands when those goals are achieved. Such a community is more likely to be composed of individuals who have a larger vision of life than the immediate achievement of short ranged goals. These individuals may see such achievement as a stepping stone toward the rest of the life's endeavors. The communitarian, on the other hand, is most likely to see participation in the group as the overriding activity that gives life meaning.

When group maintenance (Loyalty) overpowers commitment to Truth, a substantial subversion occurs. Such an end is inevitable when the communitarian dominates generations of members. Communitarian selfishness is now rampant: Public reaction of the law enforcement community, certainly of the Los Angeles police chief in the Rodney King case, was not based on truth and justice, but on the effect public debate and disclosure would have on the professional group's ability to make its own rules in filling what it saw as its public role.

Look at the lock step tradition of the Republicans when they were a minority in Congress, but with their own President during the 1980s. No one doubted that Republican Senator Orrin Hatch would, no matter what his personal feelings were, obediently accept the book (*The Exorcist*) handed him by the President's office and savage Anita Hill in the Supreme Court nominations hearing for Clarence Thomas. Similarly, Arlen Specter of Pennsylvania served the group loyally in much the same predictable way (He Said, She Said, 1991, pp. 37-40).

Dan Candee (1975) examined motives of Watergate defendants, categorizing them as Stage 3 or 4 on Kohlberg's scale of moral development (both centered broadly on external loyalties) to find that "it is understandable, at these stages, that in competition with other good motives such as 'loyalty to a man,' 'not being a team player,' or 'service to one's country,' the concept of [individual] rights may not fare well" (p. 191), adding that:

> One explanation of Watergate, thus, is that the participants were enthusiastic but essentially ordinary people who responded to the pressures . . . with decisions that from a stage 3 or 4 point of view seemed right or at least permissible. This view also explains how men who in other areas of their lives acted with probity could perform actions which, from the perspective of stage 5 (features which every human being desires to maximize: physical life and liberty), were unethical. In short, the Watergate actors can be seen as morally confused rather than morally malicious. (p. 191)

The area of concern, of course, is that the state of being a communitarian, seeking external guidance, is susceptible to "moral confusion" and cooptable into unthinking or confused support of group goals.

An extreme example of communitarian power (perhaps exemplary to some, but deplorable to the individualist) was the recently-disclosed plan by the Japanese government facing American occupation at the end of World War II. Recall MacIntyre's (1990) use of the Japanese as a typical communitarian culture.

Fearing soldiers of the occupying army would sexually ravage Japanese womanhood, a government plan to draft women to serve as prostitutes for the soldiery in government-established brothels was partially instituted. When the soldiers were neither as lusty nor as lawless as was feared, the plan was dropped as the normal sex industry was able to handle the load (Kristoff, 1995).

On the one hand, moral justification for the plan recalls the Kamikaze suicide pilot program near the end of the war in which young pilots accepted the duty to sacrifice themselves for their country. This displayed a deontological characteristic of blind obedience in which the young men— and later, the women—would recognize their debt to their culture and obediently submit to the plan. On the other hand a consequences-based judgment can use a utilitarian "greatest good" argument with equal validity: Sacrifice a few for the benefit of the many. Inevitably, however, cultural discipline finds its easiest moral path through the park of rules.

Communitarianism's Flawed Ideals

Lest it appear I am emphasizing the dark side of the communitarian personality, let me note that idealistic communitarianism of widespread cooperative effort, while desirable and laudable, is an illusion. Altruistic communitarianism is certainly laudatory, and would probably be very effective. However, Roberto Alejandro (1993) provided a Rawlsian view of community "anchored in the goals of cooperation, stability, harmony, and transparency, . . . entailing mutuality and reciprocity, . . . sharing in the distribution of benefits" (p. 76). Moreover, the individual in Rawls's community cooperates with others over a complete life, and "is transparent to himself to the extent that his ends cohere with each other, and he is transparent to others to the extent that his plan of life is part of a social plan just as individuals, through their institutions, are part of a 'social union of social unions'" (Alejandro, 1993, pp. 76-77).

> ## Idealistic communitarianism of widespread cooperative effort, while desirable and laudable, is an illusion.

Clearly, such a description lends itself to unquestioned acquiescence by the Japanese women when their community calls, a cooperation typical of traditional, communitarian cultures, but extremely difficult at the moment for most Western cultures to understand.

The weakness in the idyllic projection lies in the vision Rawls had of community as

> . . . institutional settings that comply with the precepts of justice and provide a space for mutual recognition and appreciation of the person's abilities. Associations socialize individuals into the principles of trust and friendship, strengthen the individual's self-esteem, and provide a 'secure basis' for the worth of their members. (Alejandro, 1993, p. 77)

Benefits yielded by heightened self-esteem are, again, undeniable. However, the price to be paid for self-esteem is one of dependency and loss of individual identity and autonomy to even the most unreasonable of demands. Alejandro (1993) saw associations as central for Rawls, since "self-esteem in Rawls's theory is 'the most important primary good'" (p. 77). Such a construct, while noteworthy, carries the seeds of its own destruction. Stress reduction and self-esteem bestowed by others in cooperative ventures reduce stress in return for stage 3 loyalty; attractive in an increasingly stressful society.

The ideal of a strong, society-wide cooperative community is flawed. Communities tend not to organize, according to Hoffer (1951), unless there is a sense of adversary against which the community contends—us against them. In the United States, for example, the 33 million member American Association of Retired Persons (AARP) thrives on an "us" of the elderly banding together for common cause against the "them" of the other 220+ million Americans. Communitarianism often is destined to be a battering at the walls of the establishment by a cooperative minority.

Whether power concentrations coopt a community or whether a communitarian organization, by the passive nature of its members, pushes power toward the center, a power bloc ultimately directs the efforts of members of the community. The troubles soon after reelection of Sen. Bob Packwood of Oregon in 1992 are an example of shifting power resulting from a community of effort—women had been largely powerless in the face of the mostly male-dominated community. The narrower community of women has formed in a combination of ad hoc expressions and formal organizations to consolidate power to breach male establishment walls. The communitarian test is whether the feminist community disbands once the perceived need is satisfied, or whether it perpetuates itself through organizations operated by professional administrators who, if my thesis is correct, will exercise their vested interest in keeping the movement alive as a matter of self-interest. The hallmark of such a community at that stage is exaggeration and deception to magnify the threat and continue to court support. In times of stress, such as in the Watergate affair, Truth and other virtues will give way to such a relative issue as Loyalty (Candee, 1975). That, in turn pollutes the entire information system. Deception for loyalty's sake denies the rights of individuals to liberty, according to Candee (1975):

> Liberty, the ability to make one's own decisions and to pursue one's own inclinations . . . necessarily includes the freedoms of speech, assembly, and action. From the moral viewpoint, such rights are basic to human beings and exist prior to societies. However, any action which purports to support a law or maintain a system at the expense of individual rights would be logically and thus morally incorrect, since the very legitimacy of the system is the maximization of such rights. (p. 187)

Loyalty, while a relative virtue, becomes destructive when it conflicts with the absolute virtues of Liberty. Such a statement, however, would be met with serious objections in Japan, MacIntyre's communitarian society.

Pluralism vs. Reinforcement

Communities and individualists require differing information systems. The difference, of course, revolves around the types of information required by an individualist to function in a competitive society, while the community information philosophy revolves around maintenance of the group and enhancement of group position in the larger community. There certainly is also the element of continuous group reinforcement as a central device for creating the individual self-esteem important to Rawls (Alejandro, 1993).

The individualist generally does not control the channels through which information flows, and thus has an interest in having those channels open to virtually every message as the only practical way of assuring at least the possibility of adequate information available to inform individual decisions.

In this circumstance, the individualist opts for an informationalist system with its general assumption that audience members, or consumers, have rational abilities to make decisions with some hope they will be informed decisions. Philosophically, the informationalist accepts the pluralist's responsibility to distribute broad information about causes he/she abhors. Implicit in this is acceptance of the likelihood that views, mine or others, can change as I add more information

> While communitarians envision societies in which participants with shared values discuss rationally and make decisions with community interests in mind, the basic information system installed by those with shared values will be inadequate to inform the discussions. Ultimately, decisions by these groups will be flawed by the ignorance resulting from restrictions on information.

to my knowledge base. Truth, of course, is of highest priority in this system, for it retains its validity only so long as there is a perception of routine breadth and fidelity. That is, a perception is necessary that the system is adequately constructed to warn me of agenda items that need my attention, and the warnings are substantially accurate. Such a system allows me a maximum of autonomy in my own decisionmaking processes.

The purposive community, on the other hand, requires a much different internal system and is probably ambivalent about the open nature of information systems surrounding—and penetrating—the community.

A communitarian, trading moral autonomy for group membership, necessarily becomes a cheerleader, or reinforcer. Such a stance assumes (for either selfish or altruistic reasons) the communitarian's view of the world is correct and should neither be challenged nor subject to change. A reinforcer makes group loyalty a primary virtue (making it almost an absolute, with other virtues relative) and is typically concerned about maintaining the status quo, suspicious of information that might threaten that state. Further, there is approval of utterances that will reinforce and strengthen the status quo. Truth is not a high priority with the cheerleader.

Thus, while communitarians envision societies in which participants with shared values discuss rationally and make decisions with community interests in mind, the basic information system installed by those with shared values will be inadequate to inform the discussions. Ultimately, decisions by these groups will be flawed by the ignorance resulting from restrictions on information.

Another scenario describes a community of passive individuals seeking self-esteem through the reinforcement system led by a "shared values elite" who have access to the broader world of information, but whose decisions, therefore, will not be decisions of community, but decisions of a questionably informed elite, with questionable goals, imposed on the community.

Under these conditions, there is an inherent conflict in communitarian arguments that cooperative behavior entails open discussion in a community of members with shared values. This must certainly be a fallacy, for the very nature of a group structure, with shared values and membership incentives, will inevitably—as restrictions on information that argues with the shared values increase—trend toward the views of strong leaders, or of the professional manager. A pluralistic, problem-solving dialogue in a communitarian setting is difficult to picture. More likely, a discussion based on shared values will work its way toward a foregone conclusion.

Group norm behavior, "seeing the system itself as more basic than the rights of individual members" (Candee, 1975, p. 185), almost naturally controls those who do not see legal and moral transgressions as of "different kinds" (Candee, 1975, p. 186), but, when they think of comparative virtues at all, lump loyalty with truth, a choice from among equals. Loyalty is a strong favorite, traditionally, to win such a battle in the community.

In the 1990 congressional elections in Utah, for example, serious last minute disclosures about the moral character of a candidate for the U.S.

House of Representatives placed an "assured" election in jeopardy. A major city mayor, the governor of the state, and two United States senators appeared in a political television commercial the Sunday before the Tuesday election with effusive praise for the character of the questionable candidate. They, as is typical, gave no indication of ambivalence about the candidate and offered whole-hearted support and fulsome praise. The state and national figures were elected representatives of the candidate's party. The non-partisan mayor later received an appointment to the State Tax Commission.

This is not to suggest that what these men did was wrong. Indeed, it was typical of communitarian behavior and a demonstration of communitarian value ordering. Under the circumstances, could there have been an open discussion among the four men before they made their political commercial? Even a pretense of a discussion would have predictably revolved around the party's (a group) best interest and not those of either the candidate or the public. In short, the group was willing to fellowship a morally questionable candidate rather than endanger party unity.

Cheerleading is a socially pervasive self-preservative state of mind for audiences, sources, supervisors, practitioners, all of us, that springs from the control effort previously explored. This tends, however, to be a thoughtless, short sighted state that results in stagnation emerging from absence of new information that would require changes in habits or behavior.

Professional Implications

Based on the aforementioned characterizations, it seems obvious to me that my degree of individualism or communitarianism will determine how well I do my job as a professional communicator. A journalist who is overly concerned about the impact of the information (how it will affect social action/attitudes in my areas of bias—feminism, abortion, religion, creationism, etc.) will be less inclined to write stories that will upset the status quo. Similarly, a journalist who seeks approval of sources (a communitarian characteristic) may also be reluctant to press sources for information, and will accept admonitions that a story should not be printed "because it will cause trouble," or "people don't need to know this."

A public relations person who is an individualist may feel moral stress when suppressing tendencies toward full disclosure in a situation in which persuasion occurs through selective distribution of generally reinforcing information. Rules of selection are very different between a journalist and a persuader.

What About the Individualist?

The individualist is often not a comfortable person with whom to associate. Individualists march to their own drummers, and their behavior is not predictable. However, we do need to make distinctions, based on moral development, with some comparisons of best and worst to the communitarian perspective.

Only through individualism is moral autonomy, and therefore moral development, possible and encouraged. A communitarian necessarily adapts to the moral stance of the community, Kohlberg's (1969) stage 3 or stage 4 behavior. As leaders become captives of the group, and the group, in turn, is captivated by its leaders, the group's values dominate, reinforcing the previous assertion in this chapter that moral corruption of those values is inevitable. Therefore, conformity is valued, not moral autonomy. If the group is "moral" the loyal individual will be moral. When the group corrupts the member goes with the group.

When moral development of the individual is short circuited, the individual becomes dangerous, for the group values that restrain the members are not present for the individualist. As a litmus test, the degree to which selfishness rampages through a culture may well be an indication of the moral development of its individuals, and the state of its communities in fostering and encouraging individual moral development. A communitarian community by its very nature shuns individual moral development, for moral development leads to moral reasoning, anathema in a cooperative community.

> **Only through individualism is moral autonomy, and therefore moral development, possible and encouraged.**

That is, nothing restraints the selfishness of the individual, nor does a corrupt, self-serving group contribute to a healthy moral climate.

So, by Barney's calculations, there is a two-out-of-three chance that a liberal democratic society will decline and disappear into the maw of communitarian shared value interaction. The subsequent lapse into the static, of course, appears to be as inevitable as the actions of today's traditional society hundreds of years ago, whatever the original intentions of the cooperative communitarian.

Consider briefly the example of this 75% of the world's people currently living—happily until options are presented—in the traditionalistic, conservative societies that formed themselves hundreds of years ago with "shared values conferences." Those conferences, we conjecture, sought

the idyllic, low stress, cooperative society of minimal conflict and high behavior predictability, a society in which members naturally cooperate for
the common good. The results are easily observable today, in vast cultures
that froze themselves in time by rejecting controversy and change and de-
ifying consensus and agreement. Information systems in those societies
reinforce the correctness of the conventions. Pluralistic systems become
alien intrusions to be rejected or converted.

The selfish individual who is the product of the stunted moral development environment is not likely to contribute to the social good, because
"there is very little to be said in favor of an individualism which takes its
orientation from a conception of the individual as essentially 'the propri-
etor of his own person, for which he owes nothing to society'" (Tucker,
1980, p. 3).

Ideally, the individual accepts a broad communitarian responsibility
and looks at effects on society at large of his or her behavior. With all due
respect, such behavior is, at root, individualistic/moral in nature because
groups inevitably lure the individual from the absolute moral virtues toward the self-perpetuating, or group maintenance behavior that favors
the smaller, immediate group at the expense of society at large:

> In Rawls's view, the morality of principles is the final and highest
> stage in the individual's moral development. For the morality of
> principles does not depend upon our relationship with our parents.
> Nor does it depend upon ties of friendship and mutual trust. It de-
> pends upon allegiance to the principles of right. (Alejandro, 1993,
> p. 82)

A prime example of a communitarian, collective society in embryo is a
new marriage, the beginning of a new family unit. With 47% of these units
currently disintegrating within a few years (Gallaher, 1996), the suggestion must be that selfish individualism is alive and strong. Among solutions to this problem are options for a communitarian-oriented uncritical
acceptance by marital partners of values that reject divorce as a option,
thus forcing some incompatible people to cohabit for life (one of them,
perhaps, to be brutally abused), or for principled individualism to recognize the need for early self-sacrifice by both partners for the later benefits
offered by a strongly supportive, cohesive family unit. Society is far better served by avoiding the short term attractions of collectivism and of
self-serving individualism, as painful and as taxing-of-patience as that
may be. Such a society should place a high priority on the development
of moral reasoning and the application of principles in the lives of its citizens—an education, rather than a conditioning, process.

As for the necessity for group unity as prerequisite to achievement of worthy goals, the group's ultimate purposes are best served when a substantial segment of the group consists of ideal, principled individualists with a willingness to cooperate but who reserve the right to, with principled judgment and knowledge, withdraw when the group loses sight of "end rather than means" attitudes toward its compliant members. Such a possibility constantly confronting leaders of the group, and continually threatening group existence, would have a sobering effect on the power centers, reducing their willingness to exploit members for sake of group continuance.

It is important to recognize that moral sensitivity is necessary for the individualist. A communitarian is largely regulated by the discipline of the group/organization while an individualist is largely a free agent; therefore, moral sensitivity is imperative in an individualistic society. On a pessimistic note, it is well to consider than when a society loses faith in the moral judgment of its individuals and opts for the communitarian protections, it is a sign that individualism is too dangerous to the overall well being of society to be allowed to survive. It is then that society will evolve to fit conditions described earlier in this chapter: rule-bound, predictable, and convenient; all questions answered, no new questions needed; all behavior prescribed; few examination of existing rules required or allowed.

Summary and Conclusions

This chapter presents stark contrasts between communitarian and individualistic philosophies, with their implications for the systems and content of information distribution. It predicts outcomes, suggesting that communitarianism ultimately corrupts itself and denies its members their rights to develop their own moral reasoning. In addition, the communitarian society will become highly rule oriented and static. The well being of an individualistic society, meanwhile, requires development of moral reasoning mechanisms in individuals to avoid the socially destructive behaviors of individuals unrestricted by group discipline.

Communities are corrupted when the emphasis shifts from advancing the cause for which the community was founded to maintaining and perpetuating the community, a shift that occurs when professional managers with a vested interest in group perpetuation replace the group's idealists, an inevitable evolution.

Communal groups thus develop self-perpetuating information systems, restricting information their members receive to that which reinforces the group's norms. In this context, fidelity to truth gives way to a lesser virtue of loyalty and truth declines in value.

The individualist, it is argued, has a strong interest in truth and in maintaining moral principles that maintain the individual as the key element of any society, the reason for a society's existence in the first place. This contrasts with the communitarian view that society is prior to the individual.

Groups with substantial numbers of individualists who are prepared, on principle, to leave the group and allow its collapse when it becomes corrupt and overly self-serving, are seen as the solution to maintaining community integrity and the validity of groups and the communitarian philosophy.

References

Alejandro, R. (1993). Rawls's communitarianism. *Canadian Journal of Philosophy*, 23(1), 75-100.

Atlas, J. (1984, October). Beyond demographics. *The Atlantic Monthly*, pp. 49-58.

Candee, D. (1975). The moral psychology of Watergate. *Journal of Social Issues*, 31(2), 183-192.

Crossette, B. (1995, September 10). The second sex in the Third World. *The New York Times*, p. 4-1.

Gallagher, M. (1996, February 20). Why make divorce easy? *The New York Times*, p. A19.

He Said, She Said. (1991, October 21) *Time*, pp. 36-40.

Hoffer, E. (1951). *The true believer*. New York: Harper & Row.

Kohlberg, L. (1969). Stage and sequence: The cognitive-developmental approach to socialization. In D. Goslin (Ed.) *Handbook of socialization theory and research*, (pp. 347-480). Chicago: Rand-McNally.

Kristoff, N. (1995, October 27). Fearing GI occupiers, Japan urged women into brothels. *The New York Times*, p. A1.

MacIntyre, A. (1990). Individual and social morality in Japan and the United States: Rival conceptions of the self. *Philosophy East & West*, 40(4), pp. 489-497.

Mason, A. (1993). Liberalism and the value of community. *Canadian Journal of Philosophy*, 23(2), 215-240.

Riesman, D. (1961). *The lonely crowd: A study of the changing American culture*. New Haven, CT: Yale University Press.

Springsted, E. (1991). Liberal individuals and liberal education. *Religious Education*, 86(3), pp. 467-478.

Tucker, D. (1980). *Marxism and individualism*. Oxford: Blackwell.

─── In other words... ───

Moral philosophy arises when, like Socrates, we pass beyond the stage in which we are directed by traditional rules and even beyond the stage in which these rules are so internalized that we can be said to be inner-directed, to the stage in which we think for ourselves in critical and general term (as the Greeks were beginning to do in Socrates' day) and achieve a kind of autonomy as moral agents.

William K. Frankena. (1973). *Ethics*. (2nd ed.). Englewood Cliffs, NJ: Prentice-Hall.

One of the striking things about the culture of the American press, which exerts such a strong influence on its members, is how conservative it is—conservative about journalism. There are a variety of reasons for this. Consider first the pressures that bear on the people who produce the news: the conflicting demands of audiences, media owners, political figures, sources, and especially the daily pressure of deadlines, a "monster" that has to be fed, whether the food is ready or not. Add to these the comparatively thin credentials of the journalist as a maker of professional judgments: no advanced training or licensing, no white lab coat, no obscure vocabulary to intimidate the layperson, no particular expertise in most of the subjects explored in the news, no scientific method or formal peer review. As press scholar Michael Schudson puts it, "Journalism is an uninsulated profession."

Jay Rosen. (1996). *Getting the connections right: Public journalism and the troubles in the press*. New York: The Twentieth Century Fund Press, p. 8.

My incestuous profession has become increasingly self-absorbed, even as its practitioners wring their hands about why fewer people seem to be listening. I hear this depressing talk every day, in newsroom meetings, in casual conversations, in my colleagues' bitter jokes about toiling for a dying business. For too long we have published newspapers aimed at other journalists—talking to ourselves, really, and the insiders we gossip with—and paying scant attention to our readers. . . . Where once newspapers were at the very heart of the national conversation, they now seem remote, arrogant, part of the governing elite. Where once newspapers embodied cultural values, they now seem mired in a tabloid culture that gorges itself on sex and sleaze.

Howard Kurtz. (1993). *Media circus: The trouble with America's newspapers.* **New York: Times Books, pp. 6-7. (Kurtz is media writer for the** *Washington Post.***)**

Before there were deadlines, or city editors, or county commissioners to catch in some moldy taxpayer ripoff, there was the First Amendment. The chronology is crucial. It helps account for journalism's fundamental toughness; a congenital, sleeves-rolled-up aggressiveness; a snarly conviction that nice guys don't get newspapers out.

The culture of toughness has more beneath it than the inevitability that many stories, by their nature, are going to make one person or another unhappy, and there is more beneath it than the pervasive maleness of the profession that persists even into the equal-opportunity 1990s. Such realities have helped form the cultural trait of toughness, but they alone cannot explain it. History can. The reality is that the free press was born in a defensive crouch. Its birth certificate was a declaration—significantly, an affirmative negative—that "Congress shall make no law. . . ."

Of course, the amendment does not guarantee that "the press" be fair, accurate, honest, profitable, or, of course, paid attention to—only that it be free to be none or all of those things, just as can any citizen who picks up pen and paper. Although it was originally written to empower people rather than any institution, it has become, for the organized "press," a license to self-define that is unique among U.S. institutions. Neither clergy nor bar nor medicine nor academe can claim, and have validated by the courts, more latitude in action and deed. That enormous latitude is a mixed blessing.

Davis "Buzz" Merritt. (1995). *Public journalism & public life: Why telling the news is not enough.* **Hillsdale, NJ: Lawrence Erlbaum Associates, pp. 13-14.**

The goal is to change the newsroom culture from one that values detachment to one that values proper attachment, but any step, small or large, beyond calculated detachment is encouraging if only in that it begins to dismantle the idea of One Journalism. The concept that there is and must be one homologous way of thinking and acting guided by immutable and arcane rules smacks of a priesthood, a status comforting to its introverted initiates but forbidding and unpersuasive to citizen outsiders.

Davis "Buzz" Merritt. (1995). *Public journalism & public life: Why telling the news is not enough.* **Hillsdale, NJ: Lawrence Erlbaum Associates, pp. 118-119.**

Civic journalists have encountered two valid lines of criticism. Some critics argue that if newspapers aim only to put more reporters "in touch" with ordinary people—without using their influence to sponsor social or political causes—then they're only doing what they should have been doing all along.

But other critics contend that the emphasis on "solutions" and "connections" will inevitably distort the news agenda, devalue problems for which no easy remedy is apparent, and end up compromising the paper's independence. . . .

The elemental tasks of describing events and discerning their causes are already beyond the skills and budgets of many American newsrooms. Running forums, finding speakers, and raising money are diversions for most television and newspaper staffs even if such activity had no compromising side effects.

Recipes for action that could safely "connect" a newspaper with its readers sound like recipes for making omelets without breaking eggs. Such action will be either superficial or extremely messy and embarrassing. . . .

American journalism sorely needs improvement. But redefining journalism as a quest for a better tomorrow will never compensate for its poor performance at explaining yesterday.

Reporters, editors, and publishers have their hands full learning to tell it right.

Max Frankel. (1995, Fall). Journalists should leave reform to reformers. *The Masthead,* **3 (47), p. 22. (Frankel is the former editorial page editor and executive editor of** *The New York Times.* **He won a Pulitzer Prize in 1973.)**

Voices

Lynn Waddell
University of South Florida

In the Beginning There Was Columbus

It began a trend that would incite rage and hope, inspire disciples and disappoint traditionalists, turn on some readers while turning off others.

The Columbus Ledger-Enquirer became a part of journalism history in 1988 when it took its coverage beyond the traditional newspaper fare into what has since been slugged public journalism. But although it led the way for award-winning public journalism projects at other newspapers and television stations, public journalism left some scars in Columbus, GA.

It began simply enough. *Ledger-Enquirer* Executive Editor Jack Swift initiated a series, "Columbus Beyond 2000: Agenda for Progress," to uncover the fears and concerns of Columbus residents. The newspaper conducted a survey of about 400 households, asking questions about issues such as race relations and jobs. *Ledger-Enquirer* reporter Billy Winn conducted a more informal survey and added a more subjective view to the series.

After 13 months of work, the newspaper ran the series, which included a list of recommendations for improvement, but to no avail. The newspaper saw little community response.

Frustrated after the series failed to generate reaction, Swift decided to take it further. He created and headed a community-based task force that sponsored town meetings and hosted backyard barbecues.

While some community leaders and outside journalism scholars praised the project, it was not a hit with the *Ledger-Enquirer* staff, said Winn, who was the lead reporter on the project and served on the community task force with Swift.

"There were the general complaints, complaints about why some people were on the A team and others on the B team, complaints from people involved because they were overworked, complaints that it was taking too long, complaints from reporters wanting to get back to their beats, complaints from people who thought it went too far that we were creating our own news and covering it," Winn said.

The project extended for two years and the news staff of about 45 and many readers grew tired of it. Reporters on average were working between 12 and 14 hours a day.

"It was absorbing all resources of the newsroom, and there wasn't enough left over to do regular reporting," Winn said.

The tension within the newsroom became clear when the newspaper's parent, Knight-Ridder, conducted an attitude survey in the summer of 1990 of the *Ledger-Enquirer* staff. Swift received harsh criticism.

On November 19, 1990, Swift put a gun to his head and pulled the trigger.

Winn, who worked closely with Swift, said he believes the criticism of the public journalism project wasn't completely responsible for Swift's suicide, but was one of several things that caused the editor's despair.

"I think it was related; how much is the question. It was a very tense time. A great many things were involved in Jack's death," Winn said. "There's no question he did take a lot of heat from Beyond 2000 from inside and outside the newsroom."

Before Swift's suicide, the newspaper had discontinued the Beyond 2000 series, leaving many supporters to feel abandoned, Winn said.

In hindsight, Winn said the project would have probably been more successful if the newspaper's goals had been made clear.

"A lot of the problems came from his inability to communicate the definition of public journalism and the goals of it," Winn said.

That's not to say the experiment was a complete failure. Winn said it jump-started the city's growth and gave the middle class and women a voice in the newspaper.

Winn considers himself a supporter of the public journalism in one sense, but does not salute the scholarly interest it has generated.

"We've had every guru through here, and they have all analyzed it to death," Winn said. "I happen to believe in public journalism. I just don't like all this talk about it being something new. We did a lot more when I first came into journalism in the '60s. Public journalism is a bad substitute for true journalism. This so-called public journalism offers them an opportunity to cover their own ignorance."

Winn said at times public journalism leads newsrooms to do projects on issues in which the community isn't interested. For instance, the *Ledger-Enquirer* did a project in 1993 on education. Winn, a Columbus native, said no one in the community was interested in that project.

"Public journalism projects have become a crutch for people who don't know their community. It's an excuse to do structured projects that are heavy on planning and teamwork, but short on knowledge, talent and genuine concern for the community. They are corporate buzz words," Winn said. "Sometimes I think public journalism is just an attempt to replace talent."

The American Newspaper As the Public Conversational Commons

Rob Anderson
Saint Louis University

Robert Dardenne
University of South Florida

George M. Killenberg
University of South Florida

The American newspaper suffers from a persistent, severe identity crisis, and no wonder. Critics complain that papers from the *New York Times* and *USA Today* to local dailies are aloof and elitist—or mundane and irrelevant; that they are biased by a liberal agenda—or by conservative monied interests; that they are too sensational—or too boring, or both. But the main criticism, the one that cuts deeply into journalism's pride and collective psyche, is that newspapers are no longer central to public life.

If this is true, it is not for lack of effort. Journalism finds itself awash in strategies for reasserting itself, many in the name or spirit of the "public journalism" movement (see Rosen, 1994). In cities throughout the country—Dayton (Ohio), Minneapolis, Columbus (Georgia), Charlotte (North Carolina), Huntington (West Virginia), Wichita, Bradenton (Florida), to name a few—newspapers have sponsored town forums, diagnosed community needs, established toll-free phone lines and computer bulletin boards, brought laypeople into news meetings and hired neighborhood writers, all of which at least demonstrate that publishers and editors are willing to experiment with ways of connecting to community.

Few within the journalism profession and the academy would disagree that something is seriously wrong and that something must be done before newspapers become superfluous in public life. The disagreement is about which course to follow. The public journalism movement, loosely defined as it is, would lead newspapers toward greater involvement in the community. Jay Rosen (1993; 1994), who directs the Project on Public Life and the Press at New York University, wants public journalism to invigorate the democratic process by encouraging people to think, speak, and act as citizens.

Newspapers, in Rosen's view, would become activists in community affairs. On the other hand, some editors, notably Leonard Downie of the *Washington Post* (see Case, 1994), find much of what is called public journalism gimmicky and packaged. "Whether you call it public or otherwise, [newspapers should] provide citizens with as much as possible of the information they need to conduct their lives, private and public, and to hold accountable the increasing number of powerful people and institutions that hold sway in our lives" (p. 14).

Perhaps they are both right. Perhaps newspapers need a public journalism that is, even by traditional standards, a good journalism. Despite Rosen's admirable vision, many public journalism experiments appear fixed on piecemeal marketing strategies. During the summer of 1994, for example, *Hartford Courant* staffers rented a van and conducted a "Greet the Press" tour of communities served by the newspaper. Passing out promotional trinkets, they sought feedback about the paper. At one stop, a reporter tried to engage supermarket shoppers. "We didn't have any in-depth conversations about coverage," he said. "They were kind of running in and out getting their groceries" (Glaberson, 1994, p. 23A).

The *Courant's* experience, while illustrating a commendable desire to know its readers, symbolizes the American newspaper's uncertain, drifting place in a rapid, confusing society of shoppers. Journalists try to connect with a public that has shown little interest in getting better acquainted. Despite much that newspapers do to become a vital force in public life, their audience and influence continue to wane. Even the piecemeal strategies can be valuable, but they are less important than the development of a larger, self-reflective discourse in which journalism explains itself not only to its public, but also to itself. The problem is that the practice of public or civic journalism is not driven by a common philosophy.

Recently the iconoclastic cyberspace magazine *Wired* published Jon Katz's "Online or Not, Newspapers Suck" (1994). The tone of the article was as blunt as its title. Katz wrote:

> For a long time, papers have demonstrated an unerring instinct for making the wrong move at the wrong time. At heart, newspapers are reluctant to change because of their ingrained belief that they are a superior, serious, worthwhile medium. . . . Over the past decade, newspapers have made almost every kind of radical move except transforming themselves. (p. 50)

Newspapers, indeed, need to be transformed. However, the transformation cannot simply be a more "public" journalism, although that is useful. The transformation of the American newspaper must be grounded on a fundamental redefinition that permeates the institution—

its ideas of news, its relationship with the community, its attitude toward citizens, its ways of communicating.

We advocate a particular kind of public journalism that is faithful to one of our oldest social structures, the commons (see Anderson, Dardenne, & Killenberg, 1994). Instead of a bundle of news reports, the newspaper becomes—like a town commons—a site for public dialogue shared by all citizens and accessible to all citizens. Constituted as our commons, the newspaper gives us both the means and the encouragement to encounter together the same ideas and issues and to test through civic discourse where we stand.

> **The transformation of the American newspaper must be grounded on a fundamental redefinition that permeates the institution—its ideas of news, its relationship with the community, its attitude toward citizens, its ways of communicating.**

Beyond the claim that journalism should assume greater public responsibilities, journalists must ask, *What kind of public institution are newspapers?* Does "public journalism" mean only doing journalism with more advice from the public? Doing it more in the open? Disclosing its inner sanctum more publicly? Adopting more stringently defined responsibilities to the public? Getting closer to communities and letting communities get closer to journalists? Yes, but a far more basic and important narrative is needed. Newspapers are unlikely to realize the ambitions expressed by advocates of change unless they become a *site* for public dialogue, an institutional *place for talk*, a *forum* in which citizens hear each other's voices—where positions that could not or would not be explored elsewhere are advanced, argued, assessed, and acted on. Newspapers can find a satisfying sense of purpose and a clarified course of action by becoming a conversational commons. In an age when identities are often presumed to be mutually exclusive, society needs the kind of forum in which citizens could be vulnerable to each other's cultural voices and political arguments.

A democratic polity demands more of journalism than it used to. Among all the institutions of democratic life, journalism, particularly in newspapers, is best positioned and qualified to become the conversational commons. Quite apart from playing its role as an informational conduit, newspaper journalism could provide a forum coordinated by professional communicators sensitive to the fullest possible range of community content and public argument. On-line news, electronic publications and other forms of Internet- and Web-assisted communication offer prodigious amounts of information and even inspire conversation in certain ways, but these technologies often keep people isolated, involved in their own independent information-seeking pursuits, or locked into specialized and often exclusive talk enclaves where newcomers are sometimes made to feel unwelcome.

Newspaper journalists now must decide what to say to others and to themselves about journalism. To do this, they must listen carefully to a wider public discussion about communication and democratic life—a discussion reflected in two basic questions. First, other than journalists, who cares about journalism's role as a public institution? Second, how can newspapers, and the journalists responsible for them, begin to enable a conversational commons at a practical level? The answer to the first question is a wake-up call for journalism. The answer to the second is a path to the transformation journalism needs to remain a viable force in society.

Who Cares About Journalism in the Public Sphere — Other Than Journalists?

Many journalists care deeply about contributing to a more effective, extensive, and inclusive democratic dialogue. How that is to be done is another matter. Pleas for a publicly grounded journalism seem directed more toward converting other journalists to the cause than toward leading the profession to the forefront of the debate now raging in other disciplines and fields about the condition of the public sphere.

Journalism is rarely an explicit part of that larger debate unless in the role of scapegoat for many of society's ills—a role journalists seem willing to accept without much complaint. The scenario is familiar: Politicians, celebrities, advocacy groups, corporate mouthpieces, and even media figures themselves use the popular rhetorical ploy of deflecting criticism by turning it against *the media,* as though *the media* is a singular rather than plural construction. Attacks on the media undoubtedly place journalism in the public arena, but those who lead such attacks consciously cast and recast journalism in a predominantly negative role, reinforcing a public image of a reckless, arrogant, and insensitive institution.

Therefore, much of journalism's presence in the debate is formed by people blaming the media for various problems. The scapegoat role is bad enough. Even more alarming is the virtual neglect of journalism by proponents of political community-building, who rarely mention institutional journalism, much less assign newspapers a vital role in stimulating democracy and citizenship. Moreover, journalism's wisest commentators are seldom cited or quoted in this dialogue of democracy. The neglect suggests journalism's thin credibility in the larger social discussion of democracy itself.

Without launching an exhaustive inventory, we cite several illustrations that document the extent to which scholars and commentators have dismissed or overlooked journalism as an institutional force in the public sphere. In an influential book of political theory, Sara M. Evans and Harry C. Boyte (1992), for example, referred to *free spaces* as

> environments in which people are able to learn a new self-respect, a deeper and more assertive group identity, public skills, and values of cooperation and civic virtue. Put simply, free spaces are settings between private lives and large-scale institutions where ordinary citizens can act with dignity, independence, and vision. (p. 17)

The authors emphasize the voluntary character of political conversation and wonder where citizens can associate viably in testing their ideas and civic skills. Evans and Boyte suggested that free spaces can be "evaluated in terms of their effectiveness as schools for democracy" (p. xix). Free spaces, they say, might include social clubs, neighborhood associations, ethnic organizations, self-help groups, and mutual aid societies. Evans and Boyte, however, do not include newspapers or other journalistic ventures on their list of potential free spaces.

Another public forum project, Manfred Stanley's (1990) 3-year study of civic conversation in an American city, likewise fails to accord journalism a central role. In fact, Stanley does not mention journalism in his insightful summary of concerns, "The Rhetoric of the Commons: Forum Discourse in Politics and Society." His models for public forums are politically based, dialogically motivated, and dependent on the kind of democratic alertness most needed in a complex and multivocal culture. At one point he asks how the debate among policy experts can be translated for the public: "Now the interesting question is: How do you take that debate, which is very important to the general public, and move it on to the public's agenda?" (p. 243). Stanley answered his question this way:

> Political conversation in contemporary democracy needs to be thought about in light of modern developments in rhetoric, philosophy of language, and social science. The forum adequate to capture the educational demands of democracy in a sophisticated secular age remains to be invented. Such a forum must find its way not only into the community lives of ordinary citizens, but also into the great cities of science and the professions. (p. 239)

Stanley's ideal forum may not exist at present, but its logical foundation—the community newspaper—is part of our daily lives. Stanley, however, seems to overlook the newspaper's potential as a place for dialogue.

Few recent critiques of our political system have been as pointedly concerned with public communication as James Fishkin's (1991; 1992) *deliberative democracy* project. Much of Fishkin's hope for democracy revolves around the concepts of public dialogue and social self-reflection, but his theoretical work relegates journalism to the political margins. Fishkin's notions ought to be fascinating to journalists, because he is less interested in what people think at any particular instant, as shown by collections of transitory whims and impressions turned up by local news polls and current 1-900 polling scams. Even more sophisticated polling methods simply present snapshot preferences of aggregated ignorance or opposed prejudice, inviting politicians to act selfishly to reinforce already popular policies. Fishkin is more interested in what people would believe about our collective fate after their personal beliefs have been tested in a crucible of dialogue that makes it difficult or impossible to avoid contradictory information and alternate opinions. Democracy does not need individual desires as its fuel; it needs tested beliefs in what Fishkin calls a *deliberative opinion poll.* There are positive signs that as Fishkin's ideas become more accepted they will necessarily involve journalists; he has implemented a version of his model in Britain and another version, with PBS journalists, in the United States.

Journalism now, however, also remains on the fringe for many scholars working in cultural theory and criticism. Perhaps most prominent among them are Robert Bellah and his colleagues (1986; 1992), who have explored how institutional life can invigorate community action and the common good. Newspapers and journalism are barely mentioned in Bellah's (1992) writing, except when described as providers of vast amounts of underassimilated and "uninterpreted" information that "bombards" or "floods" the public, leaving people dazed and unresponsive to real issues of concern (pp. 148-149).

Finally, journalism is either ignored or not prominently analyzed in many other significant treatments of political community (see Asante, 1987; Ackerman, 1980; Barber, 1988; Benhabib, 1992; Berube, 1994; Corlett, 1989; Etzioni, 1993; Gale, 1994; Glendon, 1991; MacIntyre, 1984; Mansbridge, 1980; Phillips, 1993; Sandel, 1982; Selznick, 1992; Taylor, 1989; West, 1993; Young, 1990). Even philosopher Jurgen Habermas and his commentators (Calhoun, 1992; Habermas, 1992), despite the centrality of media in many discussions of public sphere dialogue, put professional journalism backstage at best, away from the main actors and action. Ignoring journalism as a basic ingredient for political community seems to transcend the liberal-conservative and individualism-communitarianism skirmishes. Among most political theorists—liberals or libertarians, conservatives or communitarians—journalism seems peripheral.

Here is cruel irony. Journalism may be neglected because people bought the image journalists have been selling—that journalism is a neutral conduit to transfer bits of information, an image that reduces journalism to either a veneer or a vendor profession. In this view, when journalists do their job well, journalism becomes politically invisible; when they make mistakes, journalism becomes politically subversive. As an invisible conduit, journalists exert little influence, except as they disseminate influence for their sources and subjects. In its self-image, journalism is a common carrier, like the telephone company, transmitting information. When journalism becomes visible, it is frequently the subject of attack by those who see themselves or others as victimized. Journalism's visibility is most often as an object of fear, distrust, and sometimes vilification.

> **Among most political theorists—liberals or libertarians, conservatives or communitarians—journalism seems peripheral.**

Those who exclude journalism from the broader scholarly and political discussion about the restoration of community and citizenship are sending the profession a message: You may be part of the problem, but you are not considered part of the solution. If that assessment is correct, then what can journalists do to get involved, to establish journalism's identity, to fulfill a useful purpose, to find its relevance?

How Can Journalism Begin to Enable a Conversational Commons?

Journalists want to be full partners in the cultural conversation, but their own largely self-defined and curiously marginalized role holds them back. We admire the skill of reporters and editors in getting the news out and making tough, sensitive decisions about what the public may want and need to know. Journalists' function in providing accurate information that people can use to make rational decisions remains crucial. But journalism, as it is typically practiced, cannot afford to operate as a mere transmission apparatus for traditional news. Too much competition already exists for that job, with more competition emerging. Journalists must recognize that the basis for information and communication is rapidly changing from the *transmission* choices of a relative handful of media *senders* to the *access* choices of independent, active citizens or publics. That development blurs the old distinctions between sender and receiver, between media and content, between media communicators and the citizens they serve. People assisted by the latest technology and electronic links can gather and assess information from a virtually unlimited array of sources without the intervention or involvement of journalists. The tools of information in the hands of a communication-savvy public have altered our dated concept of communication. It has changed from sender-focused selection and transmission of messages, controlled by traditional mass media, including newspapers, to a liberating, spontaneous, interactive, public-oriented, and public-coauthored network of nearly limitless news and information venues.

This could be the end of newspaper journalism, or its salvation. Critics riding the crest of the cyberspace wave see the new electronic technologies, including capabilities of the World Wide Web to deliver millions of people to millions of sources of information, as rendering "old technology," or newspapers, irrelevant. Many of the critics describe a battleground in which new technologies are quickly eradicating the old, but the "battle," if it can be called that, encompasses more than technology. The Internet and World Wide Web are superior to newspapers and other more traditional technological forms in providing information or data to large numbers of people. But information and data are not news, serve different functions from news, and cannot replace news. The arguments are numerous and by now widely known, but information and data are worthwhile to the extent that they are accurate, contextualized, and otherwise interpreted to make sense. Certainly multiple sources of instantaneous information are helpful, even wonderful, but isolated individuals selecting data relevant only to them, without a broader base of information shared in common with other individuals, leads to a world of monologues.

That is antithetical to the kind of media world we see as necessary for citizens to deliberate about their common good. In the world we envision, people talk and even argue with each other; they bring in their own information and add it to the common store of news and information to which all can be exposed; and they come to encounter major issues affecting their lives. The newspaper remains uniquely placed to be the conversational commons where all this occurs. It cannot, however, be made to compete with information delivery systems. Such attempts will fail, or at best, with electronic delivery, newspapers will be merely another transmission channel. Neither can the newspaper (or all of journalism) become another chat room, where anybody's opinion on anything is dutifully recorded. Again, other technologies do that better, often leading to painfully dull and trivial reading.

Newspapers inform, but they also survey, analyze, interpret, and in many ways synthesize. They must also invite and engage. What is happening now in information delivery and interactive media is dramatic and profound, and journalists must react quickly before journalism's (particularly newspapers') reputation for irrelevance becomes terminal.

> **Newspapers inform, but they also survey, analyze, interpret, and in many ways synthesize. They must also invite and engage.**

If journalism is to make a difference, it will not happen as a result of embellishing outmoded roles. Journalism requires new versions of its own story and its contribution to the public dialogue. We argue that reporters and editors must embrace new responsibilities, taking on larger roles shaped by what we call the *conversation of journalism* (Anderson, Dardenne, & Killenberg, 1994). Those roles, in turn, will be determined as journalism imagines its potential as a conversational commons. Next, though, come the pragmatic, practical questions: What, concretely, will the commons enable? What might be its characteristics? Answers will emerge, we believe, once journalists accept two propositions: that journalism can serve as an inclusive civic university and that it can expand its listening-based inquiry without sacrificing its present strengths. We believe these propositions build on each other and can energize the larger social debate about democracy. Moreover, they point the way toward journalism's transformation as our conversational commons.

A New Civic University

As a rule, mature students at contemporary universities resent a transmission model of teaching in which professors talk at them, reiterate the textbook, prescribe platitudes, act haughty, or pile facts upon facts without analysis or interpretation. Discerning students expect professors to be knowledgeable without arrogance and to create spaces in classes where learners are encouraged to compare their judicious interpretations among themselves and with those of teachers. Telling students what to know and think may appear efficient and can even be done charismatically to garner praise for the instructor. But such an approach ultimately is sterile if not supplemented with extensive opportunities for teachers and students alike to test alternatives. A teacher who merely dispenses facts without opportunity for dialogue removes from consideration ideas, perspectives, and wisdom from those forced into silence, rendering education nonpublic, whatever its sources of funding.

One of our most able political critics, Benjamin Barber (1992), argued that education not only "has a civic mission" but "is a civic mission" (p. 222), echoing our argument about journalism. Education and journalism are institutions that can choose their own directions. They are also pervasive social activities in which we all participate in a public way. They share a mission: broadly stated, to facilitate the learning of an informed community of decision-makers. Education is journalistic, and journalism is educational. Knowledge, to Barber, "is an evolving communal construction whose legitimacy rests directly on the character of the social process. On this model, education is everywhere and always an ineluctably communal enterprise" (p. 222). Agreeing with Dewey (1927), Barber noted that "the point where democracy and education intersect is the point we call community" (p. 225).

Applying Barber's observation to journalism implies that a newspaper that tells only what it knows will create little more than a fractured public classroom in which citizens will not find their own voices or hear the voices of others. A more conversational and even pedagogical journalism will apply what it knows broadly to encourage greater opportunity for people to exchange ideas and opinions about what they are learning.

In the past, journalists have not been particularly good professors of public life. In fact, journalists share in the blame for a diminished civic discourse by too often telling people what to think and what to believe, or by offering journalism as the channel for such prescription. Journalists helped create the consumer creature by promoting the sale of commodities and by making journalism a commodity itself—a pretty package marketed to a target audience of consumers, not citizens. Commercial language and attitudes permeate journalism. As a result, communication corporations employ news largely to entice consumers rather than educate citizens; journalism, in general, encourages public passivity, not activity. Like students in a tightly managed classroom, presided over by a teacher who prefers monologue, people have been asked, even conditioned, to absorb what journalists tell them. Some feel comfortable in that classroom, but others, losing interest, move to the back row, closer to the exit, or withdraw altogether.

What kind of educational role should journalism play? What could happen in our university-like commons? Obviously, the conversation there will necessarily be about democratic decision-making. The commons will allow people to practice the endangered skills of talking, listening, questioning, debating, pondering, negotiating, and deciding public issues—all in public. Consensus and settled issues may be outcomes in commons journalism, but they are not crucial criteria. This type of journalism follows Dewey (1927) in the belief that community exists through discussion and debate among citizens, not just among their representatives. Journalists, of all public professionals, should be prepared to understand and investigate a wide diversity of attitudes necessary for the commons to work well. They should realize that it is unproductive and impedes public dialogue to divide complex issues into two sides thereby achieving pseudo-balance; to encourage a horse-race mentality in response to public controversy; to report personal attacks and accusations as automatically newsworthy without checking their veracity; or constantly to re-interview stereotypic spokespersons—authorities, leaders, officials, celebrities, and others in or with power—instead of nominating fresh voices.

> **Journalism can no larger rely on competent generalists who, in the past, have been able to shape issues and events into 12-inch articles on deadline.**

Journalism can no larger rely on competent generalists who, in the past, have been able to shape issues and events into 12-inch articles on deadline. To become an effective caretaker for the commons, journalism must supplement this approach by recognizing broader frames for community life. Evolutionary and ecological changes, for example, can be far more important than fast-breaking news of terrorist attacks or hurricanes, but journalism now typically underplays issues that unfold over months or years because they fit awkwardly with the standard forms and definitions of news. These complex issues also require journalists who are intellectually alert and capable of interpreting and integrating the social and behavioral sciences, the arts, and the natural sciences.

In sum, journalism—especially in its prototypical form of the daily newspaper—is the only public institution that can serve as our lifelong classroom and textbook as well as our free spaces of club, barber shop, general store, or post office in an otherwise mall-based society. Many papers now experiment with more dialogic methods, mostly out of economic fear, sponsoring forums and organizing focus groups. They use appropriate methods, but they cannot for long fake conversational journalism by glossy marketing of these features. A distinct difference exists between trying out new things to see if they will be popular (as, perhaps, with the roving news van idea) and making a profound change in underlying philosophy. Journalism should not create public measures to sell its current product more efficiently. Those public measures just become more commodities under the current philosophy in which everything done in the name of journalism is market-driven.

A Broader Public Inquiry: Assisted Listening

Daily journalism has been based on persistent inquiry, primarily because many stories are either hidden behind layers of bureaucracy and government secrecy or come from the statements of public figures. Observing, digging, and asking are valuable features of journalistic inquiry. Journalists point out that they have to watch carefully what is going on around them, read many varied and complex documents, and listen to sources and the public. They rightly define themselves as society's surrogate listeners; they have access to an array of information sources essentially unknown by and even inaccessible to the public. (Here we use *listening* as a metaphor for the receptive/interpretive functions of communication, that include reading, observing, and other sensory capacities.)

The demands of a conversational society require an enhanced listening responsibility for journalists. Beyond being effective listeners themselves, journalists must do more to sponsor a commons atmosphere to assist citizens in listening to each other. Sponsorship of occasions for citizen feedback, when it happens at all, now tends to come from organized civic groups (the League of Women Voters, school boards, etc.) or from government (public hearings, congressional testimony, etc.). While these occasions are often valuable, they are usually seen by journalists as events to be covered and analyzed. We argue that the character of public dialogue is strengthened if journalists see such occasions less as reportable events and more as opportunities to help people listen to each other. News organizations (as many are now beginning to do) could sponsor these *free spaces* regularly, advertise them proactively, facilitate them vigorously, and provide on-site explanatory context whenever possible for arguments that arise spontaneously. And, of course, these events could be reported in customary ways.

News organizations sponsoring issues forums routinely could provide electronic access to information sources, such as Nexis, Dialog, and others, to resolve petty disputes, to correct obvious misstatements of fact, to encourage citizens to listen beyond their existing prejudices, and to provide fuller histories of social problems. For example, imagine a community that is plagued by what residents perceive as increasingly violent teenage crime. Public meetings about such issues are usually held under the auspices of school districts, churches, or social service centers. They may or may not be successful in helping people share their fears or air their grievances. They may or may not be dominated by one or two charismatic people, or taken over by a series of careless but strongly worded assertions. In other words, they could be, for some, effective *expressive* events. They are rarely, however, the kinds of events in which a variety of citizens realistically check their own interpretations against the facts, feel free to compromise with others' solutions, or have access to enough accurate historical and social context to challenge demagogy.

Instead of this kind of meeting, imagine how local journalists could mediate the discussion within a conversational commons framework. By arranging for the forum in which the conversation would occur, by introducing a fuller cultural context for the dilemmas, and by providing the information services necessary to correct misapprehensions, a community's newspaper could serve both the traditional functions of journalism (informing a public) and the dialogic responsibilities of a genuinely public journalism (enabling that information to be transformed into helpful communication about mutual problems).

A man emotionally complains that his neighborhood is twice as dangerous as it was when he moved in two decades ago, "because of those damn kids;" yet the journalist, when requested, immediately can retrieve police reports from 20 years before to show that teenage crime was comparable then. When a group of the mayor's enemies attempt to blame her social-assistance policies for the rise of gangs, the journalist can access information immediately about quite similar problems in neighboring cities with very different social policies. It is even feasible that by evening's end, journalists could provide informational packets for all attendees that include representative quotations and summaries of arguments expressed in the dialogue. Thus subtle misunderstandings could be averted and the community itself would have constructed a more solid foundation for further discussion that would have been impossible without this active journalistic stewardship. Everyday citizens can more easily take responsibility for the *content* of public argument when journalists are willing to assist skillfully with its *process*. Arguments would not necessarily be settled, but they

> **Everyday citizens can more easily take responsibility for the content of public argument when journalists are willing to assist skillfully with its process.**

could certainly be clarified in ways no other civic institution could match. Such meetings, of course, raise questions about journalistic ethics—questions of slant, omission, semantics, differential treatment, and so forth. However, we must point out, these are the same ethical questions that have always confronted serious journalists, but they would now become more immediate and noticeable public issues. An interactive and conversational role could actually make journalism more accountable, as well as more communicative, in the long run.

Current public debate about political and cultural issues is severely truncated. Citizens become spectators as celebrity representatives wrangle over issues (and personalities), often from two extreme points of view, as in for abortion or against it, for gun control or against it. These debates rarely result in anything beyond the same tired refrains and highly polarized arguments. These extreme positions, in fact, may not be representative of the majority of citizens, whose views of highly complex issues often fall somewhere between. Citizens in a commons-based journalism can be expected to contribute a wider range of views because they will be listened to as commentators and critics, not just appealed to as an audience receiving the packaged rhetoric of special interests.

Contemporary journalism, to the extent that it participates in public forums, encourages special interest experts to adopt a monologic version of public talk that Stephen Claflin (1979) has called "The Rules"—the expectations that in front of significant audiences, experts should not be pressed to explain their reasons in light of opposing viewpoints. Claflin says that influential people have an "aversion to discussing in public, among themselves, certain issues they are perfectly willing to write about" (p. 4). They will write about them because journalism largely presents opinions in discrete packages, noninteractively. Journalists frequently publish—as in *USA Today*—opposing monologues on the same page. Broadcasters do the same thing on programs such as *Nightline*, where the interviewer asks often difficult questions of disagreeing spokespersons separately, but almost never asks them to relate to each other in any significant way. Arguments by people well-versed in fact are rare; instead, we get petty sniping and dueling monologues often without context. "There is no obvious reason," Claflin asserts, "why publishers and broadcasters can't call for dialogue on opposing views and give us the result in print and on the air. It should cease to be unthinkable" (p. 100). One model for effective dialogue discussed elsewhere (Anderson, Dardenne, & Killenberg, 1994) in terms of its symbolic meaning is the 1992 *Donahue* television show that gave an hour for presidential candidates Bill Clinton and Jerry Brown to talk with each other without a moderator.

A journalism that encourages dialogue also must be ecumenical and unapologetically multicultural. Some commentators have attacked multiculturalism as an excessively relativist postmodern philosophy, more worried about political correctness than with tradition, stability, or moral values. It is trendy for some to assume that a multicultural social order sanctions separatist identities and nitpicking language. A multicultural sensibility, as we mean it, does nothing of the sort. We mean that journalists must not only recognize the inevitability of cultural differences but also weave those differences into their daily professional practices. Minorities and majorities, males and females, young and old are no longer quotas, if they ever were, but necessities to provide insight and perspective to the community and the newsroom. Journalists who appreciate diversity know that a community cannot be captured through stereotypes, that turning something upside down sometimes reveals a telling perspective, that people learn and need to know in many different ways, and that the world reveals itself through multiplicity.

> A journalism that encourages dialogue also must be ecumenical and unapologetically multicultural.

Journalists sometimes talk piously about the public's right to know. Certainly, that is an important argument for access to public meetings and records. However, journalists would be wise to promote a listening-based kind of access—a public right to be heard. We do not want to create yet another "right" inherent in individual self-interest, but society is a multitude of formal and informal groups with distinctive cultural agendas and valuable perspectives on issues. Often journalism finds it more convenient to listen to and report a very narrow range of people, the so-called "usual suspects." Without a multicultural sensibility, don't we invite groups to splinter into alternative journalisms, or to forsake journalism entirely? Instead, shouldn't we sustain a journalism that can accommodate differences successfully and dialogically?

Newspapers appear stingy with space these days, except for advertising and large color displays. Little room exists for an essay from a secretary in Tampa because the paper is publishing an account of the mayor's press conference, or a shocking domestic brawl, or a drug bust, or the latest posturing from the legislature. There is no room for a welfare parent's story about being trapped by a city's disabled economy, or for stories about people who fought to escape the welfare system altogether, because the paper is running the text of a politician's speech about "welfare queens" and related columns by both Mona Charen and Anthony Lewis. While it may be commendable that newspapers provide an array of columnists with a range of opinions, columnists can become too smug or too predictable (or too cute), even becoming caricatures of themselves. National columnists are everywhere already, appearing on television regularly, assuming celebrity status, comparing safe, predictable, and often stale arguments with their just-as-predictable TV adversaries. New ideas, insights, and perspectives appear to be unwanted.

A similar range of community columnists—even rank amateurs—could not help but bring fresh perspectives and energy to what has become highly stylized, predictable journalism. What citizens have to say may seem relatively insignificant compared with what officials have to say. But what citizens have to say, and must be able to say, is significant to a conversational journalism. Several moves a paper could make would emphasize this importance without structural changes or terribly expensive investments. Add pages, start a weekly supplement dedicated to contextual follow-up articles, include more sidebar stories keyed to longer-term community change, create more neighborhood bureaus that require participation by neighbors. Give people video cameras and ask them to document the dilemmas and triumphs of their lives, then engage citizens from other groups to write about the relevance of the videos. In addition to traditional columns, create *dialogue columns,* in which politicians, journalists, and other citizens encounter objections to their views on controversial topics—knowing that not only their slogans but also their reasoning and responsiveness will become a part of public record. We do not by any means offer these as an exhaustive list of possibilities, but we argue that newspapers should be creative in enlisting participation of citizens in dialogue, debate, and conversation.

As Fishkin (1991) contended, public opinion should be more than the aggregate of a public's whims at the moment. If journalism, as an institution, wants to help democracy survive, even thrive, it has to help determine what people—and ultimately the community—would or could think after their ideas are tested by a fuller encounter with opposing ideas. People will always need to know what is happening around them, but as more and more electronic information outlets offer instant access to information and news, the public's need to assimilate, interpret, and synthesize—to make sense of the world and their place in it—becomes crucial. Assisted dialogue in public helps people define issues and define their places within the larger narrative that is community life. Such community activity in no way diminishes or devalues the importance of the individual or individualistic expression; in fact, such discussion and debate could not exist without many individuals expressing themselves openly.

The goal is not that everyone thinks and acts the same, but that reason-seeking, reasonably informed people can reach consensus on how they can talk with each other. The goal of public dialogue, we believe, is not to effect a consensus on the issues but to build a consensus on how we can communicate together about them. Journalism, particularly newspapers, can build such consensus.

Making the Commons Work

For the commons to work—for journalism to be a place where people learn about public life and work to build public life through fruitful conversation—those who edit our newspapers and report the news will have to share the commons, generously and sincerely, with the rest of our communities. Today's narrative journalists, like Tom French (1991) of the *St. Petersburg Times*, seek first to engage people—to enlighten, sensitize, and provoke. French uses narrative because it is conversationally effective; it gets people thinking, talking, and acting. After his weeklong series "South of Heaven," an absorbing account about a year in the life of an American high school, the *Times* held several public forums, attended by hundreds of citizens, to expand and continue the conversation launched by French. At the *Chicago Tribune*, sociologist Mitchell Duneier's (1994) six-part series about a working mother, "Andrea's Dream," appeared on page 1 each day from Christmas through December 30. His participant-observation story showed how well a journalist can listen to everyday life, integrating conversations of many engaging people into the larger cultural discourse about class, race, welfare, gender, parenthood, and career expectation.

Daring, provocative journalism is popping up throughout the country, suggesting that we are making progress toward a conversational journalism. For eight days in late 1994, *Washington Post* readers entered the life of 58-year-old Rosa Lee Cunningham in such intimate, disturbing detail that 5,000 people called the newspaper, most to complain. Writer Leon Dash (1994) powerfully told "Rosa Lee's Story," describing how she sold crack cocaine, prostituted her 11-year-old daughter, taught her grandson, 10, how to steal without guilt, and introduced heroin to a son's girlfriend, the mother of Rosa's grandson. The *Post* played the story on page 1 each day, setting aside other news to make room; in all, "Rosa Lee's Story" amounted to a 175-page book. Dash touched a sensitive nerve; that was clear immediately. "Why tell such a depressing story?" people asked the editors. "Why focus on poor blacks?" others objected. And they were good questions. The *Post*, with each day's installment, attempted to explain its motives—to show "the interconnections of racism, poverty, illiteracy, drug abuse and crime, and why those conditions persist" (p. 1).

The flood of complaints could be interpreted as a commendable experiment gone awry. But the *Post* dared to explore community life and values, and Leon Dash opened the conversation, that much is certain. He amplified, as well, an often-neglected voice that many Washingtonians paused to hear in a way they never would have otherwise. Thousands took the story into cafes, offices, and corridors, and talked about it, argued about it, analyzed its truth, and thought about its implications. In a sense, each day's installment became a meeting place for people whose voices sometimes clashed, maybe coalesced, but, at least, were heard. It was not precisely the commons we picture, but it was close. The series also won the Pulitzer Prize.

Conversational journalism requires that journalists become comprehensive communicators, recognizing that the news does not belong to them exclusively. They share the creation of stories with many sources and the community at large. A willingness to share—to allow sources some access to an article before it is published, for example—does not come easily to many journalists, who often claim "ownership" of their stories and therefore of the news. This notion of ownership, of personal creation or territory, may lead journalists paradoxically to discourage others who would talk about the news. For a conversational commons to succeed, the creation of news and opinion must include opportunities for potent community involvement, along with a willingness by journalists to accept and act on feedback before and after publication. News should not be treated as a commodity but as a co-creation of journalists and the people of the community; news is derived, in large measure, from their mutually defined relationship.

> **Conversational journalism requires that journalists become comprehensive communicators, recognizing that the news does not belong to them exclusively.**

Conversational journalism is more daring and risky than traditional journalism. It is more expensive because it requires a commitment to pay for the talent and resources to make it work. Yet it has the capacity to bring a diversity of voices into the public conversation and therefore to the news and the newspaper. We leave it to media economists to judge the long-term profitability of a commons approach, but we suspect its public appeal will be wide—at least as wide as public cynicism with present media practices is deep.

Conclusion

A final thought concerns all those with high hopes for the American newspaper. In what form will it survive, or will it survive at all? After all, circulation figures are static or dropping. Even advertising has not been as consistent as in the past. News holes shrink. Newsprint costs soar. Fewer students find journalism attractive as a career, in part because they perceive pay to be higher in other fields. Chains often move journalists around so much that many have little loyalty to or knowledge about the communities in which they work. Rivals in the news and information fields abound, with additional competition on the horizon from powerful telephone, cable, and computer conglomerates.

We remain guardedly optimistic about newspapers, and we know that without them we will lose the only institution capable of maintaining a protected place for public talk. People transfixed before idiosyncratically chosen screens of information will be less likely to find issues in common than a community that faces the same newspaper—its newspaper—every day. Even in the form of an electronic tablet, as some researchers predict, the newspaper can be our commons—once publishers and journalists accept that challenge.

Notes

The authors appreciate the helpful comments provided by Jay Black, Lee Peck, and John Pauly, who read previous drafts of this essay.

References

Ackerman, B. A. (1980). *Social justice in the liberal state.* New Haven, CT: Yale University Press.

Anderson, R., Dardenne, R., & Killenberg, G. M. (1994). *The conversation of journalism: Communication, community, and news.* Westport, CT: Praeger.

Asante, M. K. (1987). *The Afrocentric idea.* Philadelphia: Temple University Press.

Barber, B. (1988). *The conquest of politics: Liberal philosophy in democratic times.* Princeton, NJ: Princeton University Press.

Barber, B. (1992). *An aristocracy of everyone.* New York: Oxford University Press.

Bellah, R. N., Madsen, R., Sullivan, W. M., Swidler, A., & Tipton, S. M. (1986). *Habits of the heart: Individualism and commitment in American life.* New York: Harper & Row.

Bellah, R. N., Madsen, R., Sullivan, W. M., Swidler, A., & Tipton, S. M. (1992). *The good society.* New York: Random House.

Benhabib, S. (1992). *Situating the self: Gender, community and postmodernism in contemporary ethics.* New York: Routledge.

Berube, M. (1994). *Public access: Literary theory and American cultural politics.* London: Verso.

Calhoun, C. (Ed.). (1992). *Habermas and the public sphere.* Cambridge, MA: The MIT Press.

Case, T. (1994, November 12). Public journalism denounced. *Editor & Publisher,* pp. 14, 15.

Claflin, S. T. (1979). *A radical proposal for full use of free speech.* New York: Philosophical Library.

Corlett, W. (1989). *Community without unity: A politics of Derridian extravagance.* Durham, NC: Duke University Press.

Dash, L. (1994, September 18-25). Rosa Lee's story. *Washington Post,* A1.

Dewey, J. (1927). *The public and its problems.* Denver, CO: Alan Swallow.

Duneier, M. (1994, December 25-30). Andrea's dream. *Chicago Tribune,* A1.

Etzioni, A. (1993). *The spirit of community*. New York: Crown.

Evans, S. M., & Boyte, H. C. (1992). *Free spaces: The sources of democratic change in America*, (1992 ed.). Chicago: University of Chicago Press.

Fishkin, J. S. (1991). *Democracy and deliberation*. New Haven, CT: Yale University Press.

Fishkin, J. S. (1992). *The dialogue of justice: Toward a reflective society*. New Haven, CT: Yale University Press.

French, T. (1991, May 12-21). South of heaven. *St. Petersburg Times*, A1.

Gale, F. G. (1994). *Political literacy: Rhetoric, ideology, and the possibility of justice*. Albany: State University of New York Press.

Glaberson, W. (1994, July 4). Press note. *New York Times*, p. 23A.

Glendon, M. A. (1991). *Rights talk: The impoverishment of political discourse*. New York: The Free Press.

Habermas, J. (1992). *Autonomy & solidarity* (rev. ed.). In P. Dews, Ed. London: Verso.

Katz, J. (1994, September). Online or not, newspapers suck. *Wired*, 50-58.

MacIntyre, A. (1984). *After virtue: A study in moral theory* (2nd ed.). Notre Dame, IN: University of Notre Dame Press.

Mansbridge, J. J. (1980). *Beyond adversary democracy*. New York: Basic Books.

Phillips, D. L. (1993). *Looking backward: A critical appraisal of communitarian thought*. Princeton, NJ: Princeton University Press.

Rosen, J. (1993). *Community connectedness: Passwords for public journalism*. St. Petersburg, FL: Poynter Institute for Media Studies.

Rosen, J. (1994). Making things more public: On the political responsibility of the media intellectual. *Critical Studies in Mass Communication*, *11*, 363-388.

Sandel, M. (1982). *Liberalism and the limits of justice*. Cambridge: Cambridge University Press.

Selznick, P. (1992). *The moral commonwealth: Social theory and the promise of community*. Berkeley: University of California Press.

Stanley, M. (1990). The rhetoric of the commons: Forum discourse in politics and society. In H. W. Simons (Ed.), *The rhetorical turn: Invention and persuasion in the conduct of inquiry* (pp. 238-257). Chicago: University of Chicago Press.

Taylor, C. (1989). *Sources of the self: The making of the modern identity*. Cambridge: Cambridge University Press.

West, C. (1993). *Keeping faith*. New York: Routledge.

Young, I. M. (1990). *Justice and the politics of difference*. Princeton, NJ: Princeton University Press.

——— In other words... ———

People, not newspapers, convert ideas into reality.

Nelson Poynter. (Inscription appears on marker in Poynter Memorial Park in St. Petersburg, FL.)

It's worthwhile asking questions about what's the difference between this promised information highway, the promises of a warm, accepting virtual community, and what's being delivered. It just seems to me there's a wide gulf between the two.

Cyberspace expert and author Clifford Stoll. (June 6, 1995). Quoted in Nothing but 'Net, by Matthew L. Wald of the New York Times News Service in the St. Petersburg Times, p. 1D.

We need to re-evaluate the usefulness of conflict as the highest coin in the journalistic realm. We need to understand balance, not as contrasting polar extremes expressed by absolutists and experts, but as a continuum with myriad points between the extremes.

Davis "Buzz" Merritt. (1995, July 1). The misconception about public journalism. Editor & Publisher, 128 (26), 80.

If citizens continue to leave public life to the professionals and experts who are all too willing to have it to themselves, they have no need of journalism or journalists. In the long run, the democratic system will thus fail.

Davis "Buzz" Merritt. (1995). Public journalism & public life: Why telling the news is not enough. Hillsdale, NJ: Lawrence Erlbaum Associates, p. 114.

(J)ournalism ought to be conceived less on the model of information and more on the model of a conversation. Journalists are merely part of the conversation of our culture; one partner with the rest of us—no more and no less. This is a humble role for journalism—or it seems so at first blush—but in fact what we need is a humble journalism.

James W. Carey. (1992, Winter). The press and the public discourse. Kettering Review, pp. 20-21.

(T)he ways in which journalists habitually listen to people do very little to encourage them to sound like good citizens.

Arthur Charity. (1995). *Doing public journalism.* **New York: Guilford, p. 20.**

Journalism's central mission, as we see it, is to stimulate and guide the conversation that helps us recognize what we share, what we value, how we differ, how we are alike. In this sense, the search for "common ground," far from implying agreement or simple consensus, becomes a search for a metaphorical *place for social dialogue*—the ground the become "common" is the ground upon which the public's talk occurs.

Rob Anderson, Robert Dardenne, & G. M. Killenberg. (1994). *The conversation of journalism: Communication, community, and news.* **Westport, CT: Praeger, p. 74.**

Richard J. Kenney
University of Georgia

'South of Heaven':
A Community in Conversation With Itself

When *St. Petersburg Times* reporter Tom French embarked on the project that would become the series of articles—and later a highly acclaimed book—titled *South of Heaven*, he didn't envision a foray into community journalism.

He was just looking for a good story, one that went beyond common assumptions and political agendas.

Neither French nor then-managing editor Neville Green can recall having heard the terms *community/public/civic journalism* in 1990, when French began to spend a year inside Largo High School and its surrounding community to report on the state of education.

All French knew from years of reporting was that inside a Florida public school—and, more so, outside that school—was a story that needed telling, and which the public needed to hear.

His experience reporting and writing "A Cry in the Night," a 1988 series that examined how the judicial system operated in a single murder case, had shown him that. French wanted to provide the same kind of thick description of how the school system worked—or didn't work.

A *Times* editorial dismissing public schools as a poor educational alternative for parents seeking to place their children helped provide the impetus. French felt the editorial was uninformed and inaccurate.

"The assumptions people make really piss me off," French said. "I wanted to get past the rhetoric, past all these agendas. Politicians drive me crazy. Most politicians and editorial writers haven't spent time looking critically at the issues before spouting their rhetoric.

"It's not that simple. It's lazy, and it's very destructive."

Based on a year's worth of reporting inside and outside Largo High School, the series "South of Heaven" provoked an overwhelming public reaction. French said he felt the response at its ground swell.

As the seven-part series appeared daily in the newspaper, French would go to coffee shops and other places where people gathered. He heard them talking about not only the series, but also schools and their communities.

Green noted that the articles prompted an outpouring of letters to the editor—"unusual ones, intelligent ones, well-thought-out ones."

Roy Peter Clark, then dean of faculty of the Poynter Institute, which owns the *Times*, recognized in that response a community in conversation with itself. He and *Times* editors—and French—began discussing "whether, in fact, part of a newspaper's role is to carry the conversation beyond publication and into the community," Clark said.

The *Times* had already been sending editors into the community on other issues to improve public relations.

Clark suggested the newspaper sponsor a public forum, which the *Times* did, after advertising it as a sort of town meeting on education. French and several of the characters from the series were convened as panelists for a public discussion of schools. More than 750 people attended what was to be the first of two such forums.

One tangible, lingering effect of the series and the subsequent forums, Clark said, is the newspaper's improved schools coverage, including a regularly appearing page on which student achievement is highlighted. "That's not a bad outcome from a public meeting," Clark said. "It was a good response for the paper to make: 'Hey, we hear what you're saying.'"

And it all started, French said, because there was a story to tell to anyone who would listen.

"I have a very, very strong belief that story really promotes the idea of reading, and that reading is an essential act for people to engage in to really understand what's going on," French said.

"A narrative series can be an ethical responsibility. I'm not saying that all stories need to be as long as 'South of Heaven,' or even that all stories need to be told in narrative. Some can't be.

"But if you really try to get readers into issues like we did in 'South of Heaven,' you can't do it in 10 inches."

Adds Clark: "What interested me was the fact that this long story would become a conversation starter.

"What Tom did was deep immersion in what we might think of as a representative community and described it to a larger community, re-creating a world and allowing readers to enter it vicariously.

"By participating in that world, they began a conversation about young people in the 1990s."

And the powerful story suggested more be done.

"We said, 'Let's take this one step beyond. Let's see how people are talking. Since there was no set of solutions offered in the story, let's take the narrative and carry it over into public debate, which might lead to public work and take advantage of the power of the story to do good.'"

Public Journalism and the Prospects for Press Accountability

Theodore L. Glasser
Stanford University

Stephanie Craft
Stanford University

A line from the recent movie *Crimson Tide* nicely captures one of the sad ironies of public journalism. A gruff Gene Hackman, playing a submarine officer, reminds Denzel Washington, an idealistic and potentially insubordinate junior officer, of the important difference between what they do and how they do it: "We are here to preserve democracy, not to practice it."

It is remarkable, though not entirely surprising, how many journalists embrace the principles of public journalism but fail to see the importance of applying those principles to journalism itself. There are any number of examples—an autocratic and totalitarian newsroom is perhaps the most prominent contradiction[1]—but the principal paradox of public journalism is the failure of the press to recognize itself as a distinctively public institution bound by the same standards of accountability expected of other public institutions.

While the press seeks to sustain an open and unfettered dialogue with and within the community, the one topic of conversation least likely to come up is the press itself. While the press stands ready to expand the opportunities for public debate by inviting virtually everyone to participate, journalists typically exempt themselves by declining invitations others are expected to accept. While the press wants the public's business fully disclosed and thoroughly discussed, the decidedly public business of journalism, arguably the only business entitled to special Constitutional protection,[2] remains private, closed, and generally unexamined.

The argument we want to advance about the connection between public journalism and press accountability begins with the proposition that journalism cannot truly reform itself until it discovers new ways of talking about itself. We take this to be a particularly salient claim in the case of public journalism, for it implies not only a new vocabulary—new terms, new definitions, new conceptions—but a commitment to *publicizing* that vocabulary in ways that invite what public journalism regards as its *sine qua non:* public discussion.

120

Our argument unfolds with reference to what public journalism claims for itself, though we enlarge those claims somewhat by associating them with recent work, mostly unrelated to journalism, on the relationship between discourse and democracy. We then turn to a critique of what it means for a newspaper to express itself: What kind of discussion does an editorial page engender? Whose opinions, which opinions, belong there? We conclude with a proposal, grounded in the principles of public journalism, that equates news judgment with editorial opinion and that defines the role of the editorial page in terms of a newspaper's obligation to account for the quality of the agendas it sets.

> The principal paradox of public journalism is the failure of the press to recognize itself as a distinctively public institution bound by the same standards of accountability expected of other public institutions.

Public Journalism and Democratic Ideals

If there is no consensus on what to call it, most American journalists have no difficulty recognizing the term "public" or "civic" journalism.[3] It denotes a simple but controversial premise: The purpose of the press is to promote and indeed improve, and not merely report on or complain about, the quality of public or civic life.

Whether it is being celebrated or condemned, there is little disagreement about what, basically, public journalism expects from the press. It expects the press to recognize its role in fostering public participation and public debate. It expects the press to acknowledge that the decay of democracy, usually measured as a decline in voter turnout, requires a commitment from the press to improve the conditions for self-governance. It expects the press to abandon the traditional and still dominant view of journalism, which holds that the newsroom must stand detached from, and disinterested in, the affairs of the community. If public journalism stops short of equating "doing journalism" with "doing politics," it nonetheless "places the journalist within the political community as a responsible member with a full stake in public life." Public journalism, Rosen (1994) explained,

... does not deny the important differences between journalists and other actors, including political leaders, interest groups, and citizens themselves. What is denied is any essential difference between the standards and practices that make responsible journalism and the habits and expectations that make for a well-functioning public realm, a productive dialogue, a politics we can all respect. In a word, public journalists want public life to work. In order to make it work they are willing to declare an end to their neutrality on certain questions—for example: whether people participate, whether a genuine debate takes place when needed, whether a community comes to grips with its problems, whether politics earns the attention it claims. (p. 11)

In short, public journalism represents a departure, in principle if not always in practice, from certain time-honored norms concerning the "proper" separation between the press and its public(s). It thus represents an earnest effort to examine, though not necessarily reject, many of journalism's questionable premises and unquestioned assumptions. If it is not clear whether public journalism constitutes a fundamental "redefinition of journalism," as Merritt (1995b, p. 5) would have us believe, it is in part because so much of what passes for public journalism bears little resemblance to the original idea: "As new ideas diffuse throughout our business," Meyer (1995) pointed out, "they tend to get cheaper and cruder" (p. 3).

> The purpose of the press is to promote and indeed improve, and not merely report on or complain about, the quality of public or civic life.

The Principles of Public Journalism

Described by its proponents as a "grassroots reform movement" (Charity, 1995, p. 1) intended to "recall journalism to its deepest mission of public service" (Rosen, quoted in Merritt & Rosen, 1995, p. 16), public journalism emerged in the late 1980s and early 1990s in response to what was taken to be a widening gap between citizens and government and a "general disgust with and withdrawal from public life" (Merritt, 1995b, p. 6). It also emerged in response to journalism itself, namely the dismal performance of the press in its coverage of the 1988 presidential campaign, a performance Gitlin (1990, p. 19) characterized as "horse-race coverage . . . joined by handicapping coverage." Not only did journalists cover the 1988 election as a race, a contest, but more than ever before journalists insisted on giving readers, viewers and listeners an "insider's view" of politics, what Gitlin (1990) describes as a fascinating but mostly irrelevant tour "backstage, behind the horse race, into the paddock, the stables, the clubhouse, and the bookie joints" (p. 19). It was coverage of a kind that portrayed politics as an intricate and exclusive game, a public spectacle which attracted larger numbers of spectators. The press, serving as host, seldom questioned the assigned roles: politicians played, citizens watched.

Clearly, journalism was understood to be part of the problem—and part of the solution.

Public journalism's contribution to a solution, a contribution unabashedly in the "public interest" but also an appeal to journalism's self-interest, amounts to two basic sets of principles. One concerns changes in the role of the journalist. The other focuses on new ways of conceiving news.

First, public journalism rejects conceptions of "objectivity" that require journalists to disengage from all aspects of community life. To be sure, claims of objectivity run counter to the principles of public journalism insofar as the former encourage journalists to position themselves outside or beyond the communities they seek to serve. Public journalists, described by Charity (1995) as "civic capitalists" dedicated to improving "the productivity of the community," function as "fair-minded" participants in community life whose participation focuses on non-partisan processes and procedures (p. 11).

Merritt (1995b) prefered to distinguish between detachment and objectivity, which enables him to embrace the ideal of impartiality while rejecting the indifference often associated with it:

> One can be objective in looking at the facts and still care about the implications of those facts. For instance, a scientist seeking a cure for a disease must be objective in evaluating results, but he or she can still care very much about whether a cure is found. That's the difference between objectivity and detachment. (p. 80)

Merritt's distinction between objectivity and detachment hints at public journalism's reluctance to present itself as a form of advocacy journalism. If public journalism encourages a commitment to the quality of public life, it does so only if "quality" remains vague or defined by consensus. If public journalism seems aimed at making the community work, it is *not* aimed at making it work in any particular way. What public journalism wants, then, is something akin to what James Gordon Bennett wanted for his New York *Herald* in 1835, though nothing today compares with Bennett's boastful and flamboyant prose: "I mean to make the *Herald* the great organ of social life, the prime element of civilization, the channel through which natural talent, natural genius, and native power may bubble up daily, as the pure sparkling liquid of the Congress fountain at Saratoga bubbles up from the centre of the earth, till it meets the rosy lips of the fair" (quoted in Pickett, 1977).

Second, public journalism calls for a shift from a "journalism of information" to a "journalism of conversation," to use Carey's (1987) useful distinction. Readers need to be informed, of course, but they also need to be engaged by the day's news in ways that invite discussion and debate. The reader-as-participant, as opposed to the reader-as-spectator, needs to be addressed as a citizen rather than as a consumer. A journalism of conversation favors a publicly tested consensus over the spectacle of conflict; it takes seriously the "rational middle ground of issues," as Meyer (1995) put it, rather than "the tails of the normal distribution" (p. 3).

Accordingly, public journalism embraces a kind of "good" news, which is not to say a witless boosterism that uncritically accepts, or mindlessly supports, the status quo. Rather, it is good news in the sense that it conveys optimism about the future and confidence in "our" ability to get there. "No journalistic vision can be called complete," Rosen (1994) wrote, "unless it includes a vision of the community as a better place to live" (p. 15).

> Public journalism embraces a kind of "good" news, which is not to say a witless boosterism which uncritically accepts, or mindlessly supports, the status quo.

Put a little differently, public journalism strikes a hopeful tone. It stands as a corrective to a language of despair and discontent. It resists, specifically, the unmistakably *ironic* tone that enables journalists to report the news while conveying, quietly and discreetly, their disgust for it. "Like cops," to quote Rosen (1996) again, "journalists find bitter irony an attractive pose because, like cops, they are asked to live in the glare of society's contradictions, to witness at close range its stupidities and crimes, to absorb its hypocrisy—its claim to care, its utter carelessness" (p. 5).

Irony works only as it disguises journalism's contempt and cynicism.

But the disguise is wearing thin. What was once a clever invitation to "read between the lines" is now a pervasive and unrelenting reminder of the improbability, perhaps even the impossibility, of making things work. Irony unchecked summons derision, not indignation; it can easily undermine what public journalism wants to bring about: public discussion of what is true and good.[4]

Discourse and Democracy

Public journalism appears at a time when in virtually every corner of the academy, from law to the humanities and throughout the social sciences, one treatise after another seems focused on what Post (1993), among others, regards as "the disreputable state of contemporary democratic dialogue" (p. 654). These studies and discussions, some focused on the press (e.g., Carey, 1995; Christians, Ferre & Fackler, 1993; Glasser, 1991; Rosen, 1991; Peters & Cmiel, 1991), almost always pay an intellectual debt to Jurgen Habermas (1974; 1989) and his extended analysis of the "structural transformation of the public sphere."

Habermas (1989) lamented the demise of a press expected to play a political role through its "transmission and amplification of the rational-critical debate of private people assembled into a public" (p. 188). He (Habermas, 1974) lamented as well the corresponding demise of a robust and independent public sphere, a place where private individuals could come together for "[p]ublic discussions about the exercise of political power which are both critical in intent and institutionally guaranteed" (p. 50). Whether the public sphere—or at least the ideal of it Habermas attributes to the early stages of capitalism—disintegrated, degenerated, or simply relocated, the point is that the "communicative network of a public made up of rationally

> **The challenge for public journalism, then, is not simply to reconcile its rhetoric with its role but to transform its hopes into ideals and its assumptions into realities.**

debating private citizens has collapsed" (Habermas, 1989, p. 247; cf. Glasser, 1991, pp. 241-243).

But what has not collapsed, Carey (1987) reminded us, "is the ritual incantation of the public in the rhetoric of journalism" (p. 5). If the term itself has become a "symbol without a referent," a word that has "simply gone dead," its rhetorical force contributes enormously to journalism's sense of its own virtue. And that virtue, that self-image, constitutes the core of public journalism.

The challenge for public journalism, then, is not simply to reconcile its rhetoric with its role but to transform its hopes into ideals and its assumptions into realities, a challenge Dewey (1927) framed as the central problem of democracy: "Discovering the means by which a scattered, mobile and manifold public may so recognize itself as to define and express its interests" (p. 146). It is a challenge, as Peters and Cmiel (1991) recognized it, that at a minimum requires an appreciation for the public's scope and complexity: "An authentic public sphere is not a thin zone of politicians and journalists, but a gigantic realm between the state and the affairs of private life" (p. 212).

Nancy Fraser (1992) makes much a similar point, though for different reasons, when she insists on an historically realistic account of how democracy works and a normatively compelling critique of the kind of civic culture it requires. Fraser concentrates on "welfare state mass democracies" of the kind we have in the United States today; she thus focuses on "stratified societies," which is to say societies "whose basic institutional framework generates unequal social groups in structural relations of dominance and subordination" (p. 122). Under these conditions, Fraser argues, it makes no sense to operate under the assumption of "a single, over-arching public sphere" (p. 122).

While Fraser does not rule out the possibility of a unitary public arena—the "gigantic realm" Peters and Cmiel describe—the ideal of "participatory parity" is better achieved by recognizing and dealing with enduring inequalities rather than theorizing them away. Fraser's goal, then, is not to postulate the conditions for full participation in public debate and deliberation but to ask instead: "What form of public life comes closest to approaching the ideal? What institutional arrangements will best help narrow the gap . . . between dominant and subordinate groups?" (p. 122).

The model Fraser proposed, a model of considerable relevance to public journalism, is one of a multiplicity of publics. These various publics—"counterpublics," as Fraser described them—provide alternative venues for individuals whose identities, needs, and interests have been deliberately or unwittingly slighted in the "structured setting" in which day-to-day life unfolds. They are opportunities for what Fraser calls "discursive contestation," opportunities for other voices—other idioms and styles—to make themselves heard in a forum where they can be taken seriously.

What are the implications for public journalism? Should the press, especially the larger metropolitan and suburban dailies, which often serve increasingly diverse communities, begin to think in terms of a "plurality of competing publics" (p. 125), to use Fraser's phrase? How would these smaller publics feed into successively larger publics? What sense of community do—indeed, *should*—these various publics share?

These and other questions seldom get asked, let alone answered, in the debate over public journalism. And when they do get asked, they get asked by academics and others who talk to each other through journals and conferences and other obscure and inaccessible venues.

Is it reasonable to expect the press to express itself, openly and publicly, on these matters? Are the practices of journalism and the performance of the press issues of *public* concern? Does public journalism have a special commitment to this kind of discussion, an obligation to debate, specifically, the role and responsibility of the press in setting an agenda for public discourse?

The Independence of Editorial Opinion

Giving the public a space in which to form and debate opinions was, of course, a feature of the American press from its 17th century beginnings. Opinion writing dominated early newspapers well before the establishment of distinct editorial pages. In the colonial period, for example, formal editorials were a rarity and designated editorial pages unknown, but newspapers were filled with opinion in the form of essays, letters to the editor, extracts from books and pamphlets and even comments inserted in the news. Many opinion pieces were signed with pen names, but were often the work of the editor who preferred to write in relative anonymity (Mott, 1962).

Anonymity was important for maintaining the neutrality expected of an early colonial printer, who "was thought of, and thought of himself, as simply the operator of the machine rather than as an independent thinker whose function was to originate and present his own views" (Sloan & Williams, 1994, p. 65). Political and religious factions provided content—and their business—to the printer who shared their views. In towns with more factions than printers, the printer was expected to offer a roughly equal helping of all views. The newspaper was neutral.[5]

Preference for neutrality waned as political passions in the Revolutionary period rose and patriots and loyalists alike began to demand a partisan press. Until the advent of the penny press in the 1830s, these partisan papers, along with commercial and religious newspapers, typified American journalism. By the turn of the century the location of editorials became fixed, generally appearing on the second page under a local heading indicating the city in which the newspaper was published (Mott, 1962, p. 200). As Schudson (1978) noted, the pages were a great source of publisher pride, "strongly partisan, provocative and ill-tempered. Editors attacked one another ferociously in print" (p. 16).

Although the editorial "we" was in use as early as 1800 (Mott, 1962), and editing a newspaper was "an intensely personal matter" (Schudson, 1978, p. 16), editorials were not the voice of the editor so much as of his political or commercial sponsors. An editor's opportunity to speak his own mind emerged with the "independent" penny newspapers whose editors and owners were frequently the same person—and not merely the printer. Paradoxically, however, the dominance of "news" precipitated the decline of the editorial's popularity. In effect, the editor's moment to speak came just as the interest in hearing him diminished.

Early American readers may have worried more about equal representation of opinions than the separation of them from news, but the mass audience the penny press attracted seemed to care little for editorials. Their appetite for the new "news" found in penny papers made separating news from opinion a wise business practice as much as an ideal for fair political discussion. In the late 19th century, the *New York Times* and the *New York Herald* even considered dropping their editorial pages altogether (Schudson, 1978, p. 98).

The significance of the penny press for the development of editorial independence, however, is more than a matter of taste. That penny papers were free of partisan bonds and "claimed to represent, colorfully but without partisan coloring, events in the world" suggests that readers were encouraged not just to expand their notions of news, but to value the separation of political news—now "just a part of a larger universe of news" (Schudson, 1978, pp. 25, 22)—from opinion. Mott (1962) argued that the trend toward "neutral" journalism in the 19th century was "bound to happen as the papers came to recognize news rather than editorial opinion as their paramount function. News had been twisted and abused for partisan purposes; it was now more respected for itself" (p. 389). Neutrality, then, was defined in a new way; it was not, as the colonists conceived it, a matter of including all viewpoints, but of separating the viewpoints from the news.

The Newspaper and Its Opinion

Readers in the colonial period would have resented a printer's attempt to speak as the voice of the newspaper; the newspaper included everyone's voice, and the printer was merely the conduit. If the newspaper represented one opinion to the exclusion of others, colonists could identify the source of opinion by identifying which faction typically gave its business to the printer. Later readers also could link opinion in the newspaper with the party the paper represented. Likewise, identifying for whom "we" spoke was hardly difficult for readers of the penny press. Strong editors with strong personalities were closely identified with their newspapers and the opinions expressed in them. Perhaps what is most important for all these readers is not to whom the "we" referred, but that it referred to an identifiable someone.

Today, use of "we" or "this newspaper" to assert an editorial's authoritative voice has all but disappeared, at least in large newspapers (Hynds, 1990). In one case, the *Chicago Tribune*, "we" appeared in 42% of the editorials in 1955, but not at all in 1985. Perhaps the disappearance of the "we" is only a matter of changing style, but it is entirely appropriate; it speaks to the reality of how editorials are produced.

What could be more anachronistic than today's editorials, a holdover from a time when a newspaper's editor, often its owner, had a point of view and the means to express it? Editors seldom own newspapers these days. Chains and conglomerates own them. And chains and conglomerate are owned by shareholders, most of whom have no familiarity with, and certainly no interest in, a newspaper's editorials.

If editorials today do not—indeed, often cannot—represent the opinions of owners, they are just as unlikely to represent the opinions of editors and reporters. Editorial writers consider their editorial independence to rest, in part, on a "wall of separation" that isolates them from the newsroom (Wilhoit & Drew, 1991, p. 13). Many editorial writers do not object to occasional contact with the newsroom for the purpose of hearing reporters' observations about the news or clarifying, even sharing, information. But such contact can go only so far. Editorial writers want neither to compromise reporters in the eyes of readers or sources who expect reporters to deal only in "facts," nor to give the appearance that reporters can dictate the paper's views (Parrott & O'Neil, 1989, pp. 16-17).

> The two simultaneous claims of the editorial page—that it is independent from the rest of newspaper, and that it represents the newspaper's opinion—appear contradictory.

The limited contact between the newsroom staff and the editorial staff serves to reinforce the notion of separation rather than represent a departure from it. Each side recognizes itself as performing a distinct function in relation to the news: One reports it, one editorializes about it—and neither turns its gaze on the other.[6] Editorial comment is reserved for the issues raised in news stories or by the editorial page staff, not how the newspaper selects those stories and issues for attention.

The two simultaneous claims of the editorial page—that it is independent from the rest of newspaper, and that it represents the newspaper's opinion—appear contradictory. To represent the paper's opinion would seem to require connection with the paper, whether "the paper" is the owner, publisher, or editor. That most large newspapers are owned by shareholders with little interest in what the paper's opinion is, makes this claim of representation problematic. Even when a publisher asserts his or her traditional right to voice opinions on the editorial page, the contemporary editorial board is likely to be indignant, as was the *Miami Herald's* board when the publisher overruled a political endorsement. The appropriateness of the action aside, the incident illustrates how independent from the rest of the newspaper, including its ownership, the editorial page has become. A letter to *Editor & Publisher* about the incident asked, "Who works for whom at the *Miami Herald*?" (Gildea, 1985). Perhaps the relevant question here is, rather, who speaks for whom?

In sum, the independence of editorial opinion, now a hallmark at American newspapers, severs a newspaper's opinion from, ironically, the newspaper itself. Insulated from the presumably irrelevant judgments of editors and reporters, and at times even physically isolated from the rest of the newsroom, the editorial page staff operates in its own world, writing its own opinions. By design, the disembodied voice of the editorial represents nothing and no one, save an editorial page editor and a handful of editorial writers.

Judgments, Agendas, and Opinions

Of course, newspapers *do* have opinions, important ones, but they are usually disguised as "news judgment," which means, inexplicably, they don't belong out in the open and on the editorial page. Editorial writers express *their* opinions, nominally a "newspaper's" opinion, when in fact a newspaper's opinion can be best understood with reference to a newspaper's institutional perspective, its professional ethos, its occupational bias.

Newspapers play their most vital—and most effective—role not when they tell readers how to think, which is what most editorials presume to do, but when they tell readers what to think about. Implicitly, newspapers do that every day by virtue of the agendas they set on their news pages and elsewhere. Editorials, however, seldom acknowledge that role and are even less likely to try to explain it; to do so would be to violate the independence of editorial opinion.

Despite widespread use of "agenda" to describe what newspapers write about, outside academe the term is rarely acknowledged to refer to anything more than an assemblage of "newsworthy" events. Journalists prefer to characterize "news" as self-evident rather than selected, and to see news judgment, or "agenda-setting," as a technical routine rather than an an expression of values. It is something of a circular argument: The news agenda consists of important stories, important stories make it onto the news agenda. Underlying assumptions that play a role in determining how or why an event is deemed to be important are not addressed.

News judgment is denied a proper airing because it is seen as a kind of conventional wisdom; a newspaper's agenda is considered a natural result of applying rational journalistic principles, such as "whatever the president does is news" or "no one cares about Canadian politics." Because "everyone knows" these principles to be true, the logic goes, the feast of presidential coverage and famine of Canadian coverage appears unproblematic (Romano, 1986, p. 60).

Public Journalism and Press Accountability

Public journalism is at best ambivalent about its agenda-setting role. Merritt (1995a), for example, categorically denied it: Public journalism "isn't about newspapers setting a public agenda" (p. 80). Charity (1995), in turn, refered to the *public's* agenda and how the press might "hear" it (p. 24). No one seems eager to press the issue: Does public opinion exist prior to—and thus independent of—the press, presumably waiting to be discovered by politicians, journalists, or their respective pollsters? Or, to take the counterpoised view, does the press bring publics and their opinions into existance by stimulating discussion on issues of common concern?

The reluctance to acknowledge its agenda-setting role underscores public journalism's inherently conservative approach to public opinion and public discussion. When an agenda falls safely within a community consensus—when, that is, an agenda commands "the consent of almost everyone in the community," as Charity (1995, p. 146) prefered—there is no pressure to assume responsibility for it; "it" just exists "out there." But what happens to an agenda that fails to find a consensus? What *leadership* role should a newspaper assume? When Rosen (1994) called on newspapers to have a "vision of the community as a better place to live" (p. 15), was he merely asking for an answer to an empirical question?

Whether the press finds a consensus, brings one about, or operates without one, journalists invariably set an agenda by virtue of their everyday decisions concerning the newsroom's principal commodity, *news*: what gets covered, how much space or time it deserves, how it gets played, who counts as a legitimate source, and so on. More than that, journalists—and their managers—respond to a series of related questions about allocating resources (e.g., size of the news hole, number and type of special sections) and deploying personnal (e.g., hiring key editors, assigning "beats").

It is curious that public journalism favors "connections" over "separations" but hesitates to connect editorial opinion to the newspaper it supposedly "represents." It is also curious that public journalism promotes conversation and deliberation on virtually every topic but journalism itself. Bringing about a public sphere *for* journalism, Rosen (1991, pp. 278-280) cautions, will work in the long run only to the extent that the press can sustain a public sphere *about* journalism.

> **If the press is an important democratic institution, as newspapers and other news media remind us whenever their power or privilege is threatened, then the press needs to open itself up to the kind of scrutiny it demands of other democratic institutions.**

Our point, simply, is this: If the press is an important democratic institution, as newspapers and other news media remind us whenever their power or privilege is threatened, then the press needs to open itself up to the kind of scrutiny it demands of other democratic institutions. If indeed the press plays a vitally important role in creating and maintaining the conditions for self-governance, as journalists claim whenever they raise the banner of public journalism, then the press needs to assume responsibility for, and invite commentary on, the quality of its performance and integrity of its practices. The editorial page is a good place to begin.

Notes

[1] George Seldes (1938, p. 382) made just this point more than a half century ago, obviously long before public journalism came into vogue, when he pleaded for a demonstration of journalism's commitment to freedom and democracy; if self-governance means anything in and for the newsroom, Seldes argued, it means "letting the editorial staff run the newspaper." For a recent and worthwhile discussion of newsrooms and worker rights, see Hardt (1995).

[2] The most famous version of this position is Justice Potter Stewart's (1975), outlined in a speech at Yale in 1974, which holds that the First Amendment's press clause ought to be read as a structural provision designed to protect the "private business" of the press.

[3] We prefer *public* journalism because it reminds us that the "public" is a key concept in journalism and one that seldom gets the attention it deserves. Carey (1995) sums it up well when he describes "public" as the "God term" of liberal society—"the term without which neither the press nor democracy makes any sense" (p. 383).

[4] For a review of the elements of irony and their use in journalism, see Glasser and Ettema (1993). For a study of the language of irony and its implications for journalism and democracy, see Ettema and Glasser (1993).

[5] Sloan and Williams (1994) demonstrated that the expectation of neutrality did not protect printers from accusations of bias. Indeed, printers were often held to account for the views expressed in their publications, particularly the "propensity for publishing material on one side only" (p. 204).

[6] At some newspapers, the editorial page editor reports to a news editor; at others the chain of command links the editorial page editor with the publisher. In both cases, editorial page editors generally are committed to separation from the newsroom, valuing it as a basis of editorial independence. However, the chain of command under which an editorial page editor operates seems to influence his or her perception about the importance of separation, with those serving under publishers more likely than those reporting to a newsroom editor to give unqualified support to the principle, according to Parrott and O'Neil's (1989) survey. It is also interesting to note that editorial page editors under each command model find the other model to be troublesome in terms of maintaining separation. Those who report to publishers run the risk of being tainted by the paper's business interests, say editors who serve under a news editor. But those who report to publishers counter that having an editorial page editor report to the newsroom diminishes the value of opinion as a separate function of the newspaper and could damage the public's perception of the paper's objectivity in the news pages.

References

Carey, J. W. (1987, March-April). The press and public discourse. *The Center Magazine*, 4-16.

Carey, J. W. (1995). The press, public opinion, and public discourse. In T. L. Glasser & C. T. Salmon (Eds.), *Public opinion and the communication of consent* (pp. 373-402). New York: Guilford Press.

Charity, A. (1995). *Doing public journalism.* New York: Guilford Press.

Christians, C. G., Ferré, J. P., & Fackler, P. M. (1993). *Good news: Social ethics and the press.* New York: Oxford University Press.

Dewey, J. (1927). *The public and its problems.* New York: Henry Holt and Company.

Ettema, J. S., & Glasser, T. L. (1994, Spring). The irony in—and of—journalism: A case study in the moral language of liberal democracy. *Journal of Communication, 44,* 5-28.

Fraser, N. (1992). Rethinking the public sphere: A contribution to the critique of actually existing democracy. In C. Calhoun (Ed.), *Habermas and the public sphere* (pp. 109-142). Cambridge, MA: MIT Press.

Gildea, R. L. (1985, Jan. 12). You can't run a newspaper by consensus (letter to the editor). *Editor & Publisher,* 5.

Gitlin, T. (1990, Winter). Blips, bites & savvy talk. *Dissent,* 18-26.

Glasser, T. L. (1991). Communication and the cultivation of citizenship, *Communication, 12,* 235-248.

Glasser, T. L. & Ettema, J. S. (1994, December). When the facts don't speak for themselves: A study of the use of irony in daily journalism. *Critical Studies in Mass Communication, 10,* 322-338.

Habermas, J. (1974). The public sphere: An encyclopedia article (1964), *New German Critique,* 1, 49-55.

Habermas, J. (1989). *The structural transformation of the public sphere.* T. Burger (Trans.) Cambridge, MA: MIT Press.

Hardt, H. (1995). Without the rank and file: Journalism history, media workers, and problems of representation. In H. Hardt & B. Brennen (Eds.), *Newsworkers: Toward a history of the rank and file* (pp. 1-29). Minneapolis: University of Minnesota Press.

Hynds, E. C. (1990). Changes in editorials: A study of three newspapers, 1955-1985. *Journalism Quarterly, 67*(2), 302-312.

Merritt, D. (1995a, July 1). The misconception about public journalism. *Editor & Publisher, 80,* 68.

Merritt, D. (1995b). *Public journalism and public life.* Hillsdale, NJ: Lawrence Erlbaum Associates.

Merritt, D., & Rosen, J. (1995, April 13). *Imagining public journalism: An editor and scholar reflect on the birth of an idea.* Roy M. Howard Public Lecture in Journalism and Mass Communication Research (No. 5), Indiana University School of Journalism.

Meyer, P. (1995, Nov/Dec). Discourse leading to solutions. *The IRE Journal,* 3-5.

Mott, F. L. (1962). *American journalism: A history: 1690-1960,* (3rd. ed.). New York: The Macmillan Company.

Parrott, S., & O'Neil, S. (1989, Spring). Wall between editorial, news necessary, most editors agree. *The Masthead,* 16-18.

Peters, J. D., & Cmiel, K. (1991). Media ethics and the public sphere. *Communication, 12,* 197-215.

Pickett, C. M. (1977). *Voices of the past: Key documents in the history of American journalism.* Columbus, Ohio: Grid.

Post, R. (1993). Managing deliberation: The quandary of democratic dialogue. *Ethics, 103,* 654-678.

Romano, C. (1986). The grisly truth about bare facts. In R. K. Manoff & M. Schudson (Eds.), *Reading the news.* New York: Pantheon.

Rosen, J. (1991). Making journalism more public. *Communication, 12,* 267-284.

Rosen, J. (1994). Public journalism: First principles. In J. Rosen & D. Merritt, Jr., *Public journalism: Theory and practice,* 6-18. Dayton, Ohio: Kettering Foundation.

Rosen, J. (1996, Winter/Spring). Public journalism is a challenge to you (yes, you). *National Civic Review, 85*(1), 3-6.

Schudson, M. (1978). *Discovering the news: A social history of American newspapers.* New York: Basic Books.

Seldes, G. (1938). *Lords of the press.* New York: Julian Messner.

Sloan, W. D. & Williams, J. H. (1994). *The early American press, 1690-1783.* Westport, Conn.: Greenwood Press.

Stewart, P. (1975). Or of the press. *Hastings Law Journal, 26,* 632-637.

Wilhoit, G. C., & Drew, D. G. (1991). Editorial writers on American daily newspapers: A 20-year portrait. *Journalism Monographs,* No. 129.

———— In other words... ————

We have a journalism of fact without regard to understanding through which the public is immobilized and demobilized and merely ratifies the judgments of experts delivered from on high. It is above all a journalism that justifies itself in the public's name but in which the public plays no role except as an audience: a receptacle to be informed by experts and an excuse for the practice of publicity.

James W. Carey. (1987, March/April). The press and public discourse. *The Center Magazine*, **20, p. 14.**

Journalists should not huddle together in the press box, wondering how the story will come out. They need to rejoin the American experiment. But first they will have to drop the devastating illusion of themselves as bystanders, "watching the idiots screw it up." Public journalism begins there.

Jay Rosen. (1996). *Getting the connections right: Public journalism and the troubles in the press.* **New York: The Twentieth Century Fund Press, p. 6.**

In my experience, journalists talk easily about what they're "against." They're on guard against any threat to the First Amendment. As "watchdogs," they protect against misdeeds in government. They labor against the truth-shading tactics of politicians and spin doctors. They are naturally against anyone coming into the newsroom to tell them what to do. But occasionally it is necessary to ask: What are journalists for? To put a slightly stronger edge on it, what do they stand for?

Jay Rosen. (1996). *Getting the connections right: Public journalism and the troubles in the press.* **New York: The Twentieth Century Fund Press, p. 24.**

As surveys in the late 1970s and 1980s consistently showed a loss of credibility by journalists, we wrote it off as the burden of being the messenger. If we are mired far down in the trust ratings alongside politicians and aluminum siding salesmen, we told ourselves, it's simply because "they" don't understand. They really do want us to tell them the news; it's the news they don't like, not us.

But we were wrong. They really didn't like us, and the wound was self-inflicted. The increasingly high profile of political reporters, their constant appearances on television shows as pundits rather than reporters, the unceasing self-promotion of star anchors by television networks and local outlets, and the fawning celluloid celebration of the Watergate journalists began to meld politicians and political journalists into an amorphous and distant "they." Journalists and politicians looked and often acted like a cohesive establishment of elites: imbued with insider status; playing by arcane rules and keeping score with irrelevancies; seemingly indifferent, if not impervious, to outside challenge. Neither group seemed to relate to the lives of average citizens and neither was reflective of their desires, ambitions, or values.

Davis "Buzz" Merritt. (1995). *Public journalism & public life: Why telling the news is not enough.* **Hillsdale, NJ: Lawrence Erlbaum Associates, p. 47.**

It is interesting that journalism's binding axiom of objectivity allows, even requires, unlimited toughness as a tool as well as a credo, yet it rejects purposefulness—having a motivation beyond mere expose—as unprofessional. Without purposefulness, toughness is mere self-indulgence.

Davis "Buzz" Merritt. (1995). *Public journalism & public life: Why telling the news is not enough.* **Hillsdale, NJ: Lawrence Erlbaum Associates, p. 61.**

"It's absolutely correct to say that there are objectively occurring events . . . . Speeches are made, volcanoes erupt, trees fall. But news is not a scientifically observable event. News is a choice, an extraction process, saying that one event is more meaningful than another event. The very act of saying that means making judgments that are based on values and based on frames."

Cole Campbell, quoted in James Fallows. (1996). *Breaking the news: How the media undermine American democracy.* **New York: Pantheon, p. 262. (Campbell is editor of the St. Louis** *Post-Dispatch.*)

Public journalism has its risks. But they need to be measured against the risk of standing by as democracy becomes a spectator sport, as public cynicism deepens, as frustration breed failure and failure breeds contempt.

Jay Rosen. (1995, April 13). A scholar's perspective. In *Imagining public journalism: An editor and scholar reflect on the birth of an idea.* Roy W. Howard Public Lecture in Journalism and Mass Communication Research, No. 5, Indiana University School of Journalism, p. 24.

Lynn Waddell
University of South Florida

What's So New About Public Journalism?

For some journalists only the label "public journalism" is new.

Chris Waddle, editorial page editor of the *Anniston (AL) Star*, is among them.

For the past seven years, the 31,000-circulation Alabama daily has gone beyond its op-ed page to interact with readers. The newspaper not only invites letters, but rewards the authors of the better ones, based on individuality, with a printed star and an invitation to a banquet and lecture at nearby Jacksonville State University. At a recent banquet about 150 letter writers were invited.

"We're not isolated. I like to remind our staff that our biggest competitor is word of mouth," Waddle said. "It's hard to put something in the newspaper that gives people a connection. This letters policy allows the small-town wagging tongue a place in the newspaper."

The newspaper also occasionally does special requests for letters prompted by controversial local issues. For instance, about two years ago the city proposed cutting down old oak trees along the main city street in order to improve visibility. The newspaper asked people what they thought and dedicated more space to run the many letters it received. The trees remained.

"You wouldn't believe the response," Waddle said. "We had whole pages full of letters."

The onslaught of the public journalism movement has, however, influenced the *Anniston Star* to carry its proactive stance farther. The news section in 1995 ran the "Voices of Welfare" series, which was told by recipients and other citizens. The news staff is planning to continue that type of reporting, Waddle said.

Based in a town of 33,000 people and a county of 70,000, the *Anniston Star* has long encouraged reporters to be active in the community.

"We are citizens, too. I don't think we should give up our identity in the

138

community for fear we might appear something we are not. We are participants and taxpayers. Why should we ignore the reality that we have that interest?

"It is a genuine and real interest that we share with our readers. It's not advocacy in the sense of demanding special privilege. It's advocacy in protecting public interest," Waddle said.

Although the *Star* has long practiced what's now labeled public journalism, Waddle doesn't try to claim proprietary rights or get offended by the couching of it as something new.

"A lot of them are good ideas and good journalism. If having a new title to call it stimulates people to do it, then fine. I don't believe anybody in my generation has invented the ideas of getting people to write a letter to the editor or getting reader involvement. Those are both common approaches that go back a long ways. A lot of civic journalism is a rediscovery of that, but rediscoveries are okay, too."

A Crisis of Conscience: Is Community Journalism the Answer?

J. Herbert Altschull
Johns Hopkins University

Journalism is going through a crisis of conscience. In this, it is not alone. One after another, institutions grope their way through an impenetrable gloom, their anchors adrift in the murky seas that encompass them. Like the others, journalism seems ready to pitch overboard the illusions that have accompanied it on its way to This Place, wherever it is. It is turning to new (or freshly attired old) concepts. Public journalism. Civic journalism. Community journalism. Communitarian journalism. They are not all the same. It isn't easy to distinguish among them, but there is one constant: the belief—no, the conviction—that all is not well and that something new must be tried.

Jay Rosen (Merritt & Rosen, 1995), the chief spokesman for public journalism, said the world that journalism has inhabited for a long time has come to a dead end. Like many other commentators, he took notice of some very important developments: the takeover of news organizations by disinterested corporate America, the falling newspaper circulation, the melting together of television news and the big budget entertainment industry. He concluded that the only way for traditional journalism to survive is by abandoning its model of dispassionate, objective detachment and re-emerging as a proactive force for social change. A fair number of other political activists want journalism to retreat from worship at the shrine of the First Amendment and instead take the lead in an attempt to drive the corporate oligarchy out of the news business.

This is serious business. It is the kind of a crisis of conscience that other institutions have faced in the past. The therapy business comes to mind. Twenty-five years ago, the tradition of psychoanalysis began to crumble in an agony of charges and counter charges and a new brand of psychotherapy came to the fore. Whether the outcome was for good or ill is still to be determined. The point is, however, that the counseling business underwent a massive changeover.

Is this what we in journalism are facing? Well, listen to Davis "Buzz" Merritt, senior vice president of the *Wichita Eagle*, a newspaper that has been on the front lines pioneering the cause of public journalism. Merritt (Merritt & Rosen, 1995) thought it is likely that "the decline in public life" is correlated with "the decline of the efficacy of journalism" and that journalism has the duty "to do more than tell the news" (p. 6).

To stride firmly away from the old-fashioned press posture of objective detachment toward a stance of activism and committed participation is, Merritt (Merritt & Rosen, 1995) said, one way to shatter "an incestuous partnership of politics and the political press" (p. 4). His goal, he said without embarrassment, is to save democracy.

Merritt, Rosen, and their fellow visionaries launched their movement in an uncomfortable environment of public disgust with politics, a loss of a sense of purpose, a decay of public discourse, and steeply falling readership of the nation's newspapers. Moreover, Merritt (Merritt & Rosen, 1995) said, the trait of detachment has bred among journalists "a dangerous arrogance, a self-granted immunity [that] encourages us to ignore or demean outside criticism" (p. 9).

Well, that's where we are now. The topic of public—or civic or community or communitarian—journalism is one that has attracted my attention for a good many years, dating back to my days as a journalist for newspapers, magazines, news agencies, radio, and television. I have been a happy witness to the phenomenal gains in the stature and reputation of journalism that began with Cronkite and Brinkley and hit its height in the days of Woodward and Bernstein. I have been an anguished witness to the equally phenomenal collapse of the stature and reputation of journalism that reached epidemic proportions in the last decade or so. It is still with us.

I know that the appearance of public journalism (let's call it that at this point) marks a serious effort to return journalism to the reputation it once had and, even more important, to restore the role of the press to its original purpose—that is, to serve as a breeding place for ideas and opinions, a place worthy of elevation to the honored position it was given in the First Amendment.

So, I applaud the motives behind the campaign for public journalism. As a matter of fact, I have campaigned for it myself in my book, *Agents of Power* (Altschull, 1995), both in the original edition in the early 80s and the new edition published last year. Except, I did not speak of *public* journalism but of *participatory* journalism.

When I did this, however, I did not limit the idea to the print media. In fact, I saw then, as I do now, a critical activist role for the electronic media—meaning not only television but also radio. In fact, I see a very important, even critical, role for radio and especially its much-maligned stepchild, talk radio.

A Semantic Jungle

But before I get into that, let me address myself briefly to a semantic jungle, one that involves one of the three movements in the symphony of the press that I addressed in *Agents of Power* as a metaphor for the role of journalism in all corners of the world. It is a semantic jungle because every word you use to give them names comes with its own heavyweight baggage. I called these movements *market, communitarian,* and *advancing,* which stand for value systems that exalt the role of the individual, the role of the collective, and the role of the community. The movement to which I gave the name communitarian includes the values of Soviet Communism, the religious values of leaders like the Ayatollah Khomeini, and the messianic nationalist values of lands in Africa, Asia, and Latin America.

I understand and sympathize with some of the ideas in the communitarian doctrine spread today by thinkers such as the sociologist Amitai Etzioni (1993). Indeed, the doctrine can be found in all corners of the earth, in areas of the Third World and in our own market economic and social order. Much wrangling results from the slippery nature of words and definitions. As Clifford Christians, who like myself endorses a move away from the egocentric world of today's journalism, has observed elsewhere in this volume, "language is the marrow of community" (p. 26).

Yes, indeed, but taming our words is among the most intractable problems we human beings face.

In this country, commitment to shared communities has stirred political movements for two hundred years. Etzioni (1993) sought "a communitarian perspective" (p. 2) that avoids particular policies and instead aims at strengthening families (Abramson & Bussiere, 1995). Lamentably, for many but not all its supporters, communitarianism means the open use of the press as an avowed instrument of propaganda. It is an old idea, long part of the intellectual mainstream when Karl Marx was born in 1818.

> **Lamentably, for many but not all its supporters, communitarianism means the open use of the press as an avowed instrument of propaganda.**

I do not advocate this kind of communitarianism for the American press today. Christians (1993) and Christians, Ferré, and Fackler (1993) argued for journalism in the service of the public good, and I certainly agree with that end. But the means used to reach that end worry me. And, as he correctly points out in these pages, there is always the risk that a community will turn its back on the outside world and root for only its own gods. The definitional jumble is further confounded by the fact that sometimes communitarianism is portrayed as the direct opposite of libertarianism and thus a philosophical support for limited government controls to challenge the might of media empires (a worthy enough idea but outside the scope of this discussion).

Nor am I comfortable with all the ideas in the public journalism advocated by people like Merritt and Rosen (1995). Perhaps the designation that comes closest to my sense of values is of *community journalism*. So, let me settle on that, because I believe most strongly that something must be done if we are going to salvage the traditions of journalism from the cesspool into which it seems headed.

A Personal Journey

Before we return to matters of substance, I would like to burden you with some clearly personal feelings. I began my journalism career a long time ago fresh out of the University of North Carolina. I started out as a reporter for my home town paper in York, Pennsylvania. I was a news junkie from the beginning. I covered sports and wrote editorials for my high school newspaper and spent more than a few afternoons hanging around the home town paper city room. I was an idealist, like many of my colleagues. I believed whole-heartedly in government by the people and I was sure that democracy could be served only when journalists presented to the people the information—the news—that they needed if they were going to fulfill their duties as citizens of a democracy. In my book, I call this belief the democratic assumption, and I believe those words are accurate.

My career as a journalist led me all over the world. I covered the McCarthy hearings in Washington, the Berlin crisis, and summit meetings. I telephoned in reports from Capitol Hill and Checkpoint Charlie and I believed all the time that I was performing a crucial public service for the people of America. Sure, I came to see the underside, the lying news sources, the dissembling governments, the crooked politicians, but somehow I remained convinced that if I and my colleagues could only report the facts and give the public the truth, democracy could be saved, just as Buzz Merritt believes today.

In the end, I went back to graduate school, got a master's degree in Political Science and a PhD in History. I had always done a lot of research as a reporter and editor, but I learned more in graduate school about the rigorous application of the scientific method to my research. In any case,

I was no longer involved in daily journalism with all its constraints of time and space, I thought longer and harder about what I had always known but had somehow ignored. At the time I was a working journalist, I didn't know anything about cognitive dissonance.

> I came to see the underside, the lying news sources, the dissembling governments, the crooked politicians, but somehow I remained convinced that if I and my colleagues could only report the facts and give the public the truth, democracy could be saved.

So I came to realize what was wrong with my thinking. Like so many of my journalistic colleagues, I had ignored Money. Sure, I knew that the news media were profit-making institutions and I knew they were reluctant to share their financial bonanza with us working stiffs. I had even been active in the American Newspaper Guild in Washington and had seen the books. But cognitive dissonance was at work. I still worked long and hard for what I believed was the main mission of the press, that is, serving the public interest.

My writing as an academic and a free-lance journalist has concentrated on money and how the quest for higher and higher profits has done its insidious job. I have witnessed the fall of newspaper after newspaper, the rise of supermarket tabloids, the decline of competition, the switch of the public from veneration to disgust with their newspapers.

I have worked in radio and television, too. I guess I can say my happiest days as a journalist were in the glory days of television when I was a news analyst free to speak my mind no matter how my words might damage the station's profit potential. At the wonderful facility of KING-TV in Seattle, we were permitted to take on Boeing and Weyerhauser. But we fell victim to the invincible lure of ratings, and I moved off to academe to document what I had learned.

There was still no getting over my despair, born of recognition that I had spent my entire life for naught, pursuing the flawed dream of the democratic assumption. So I read the papers and the magazines every day, watched the news on TV and listened to it on radio, and mumbled and grumbled again and again as news began to vanish in the irresistible embrace of entertainment.

Still, somehow, I couldn't give up. So I believe that the appeal of Merritt and Rosen's public journalism is that it offers a thin ray of hope, a sort of quixotic belief that the mission of journalism may yet be restored in the forbidding world of Time Warner, Ted Turner, and Rupert Murdoch. Anyway, I never was able to withstand the appeal of Schadenfreude when some of the Lords of the Global Village went under, like Robert Maxwell.

In any case, still tilting at windmills, I embraced in *Agents of Power* the cause of participatory journalism in which Reporter and Reader could jointly agree on a definition of news and work together to provide the people the information they need to carry out their role in the democratic assumption. To some degree, this is also the goal of the public journalism movement.

Beyond Merritt and Rosen

But if we are going to go, I would like to go beyond what seems to me to be the modest goals set by Merritt, Rosen, and company, even though these goals are disturbing to some journalism philosophers like my good friend John Merrill (1997). He rejected what he called their "incipient authoritarianism and arrogance" (p. 58), and warned journalism not to stray into the dangerous arena of social engineering away from the libertarian ideals of Locke, Voltaire, and Hume.

I would like to agree with him, for I admire his cheerful optimism and his belief that somehow America's journalists will yet arrive at the sunny uplands that he sees as still within their reach. I used to believe that myself, before I had come to recognize that individual tilters at windmills are simply unable to challenge Money. We are, however we may complain, egoists, men and women who as individuals are so profoundly concerned with bettering our lot and that of our families that we easily fall prey to the goodies that corporate America dangles before us.

I am convinced that we cannot compete by ourselves but only in union with one another. We may not succeed. In my own despair, I don't really think we can. But the choice is there. Either we can give up and abandon the dream that undergirds the democratic assumption or we can join together as a *community* and take our place on the battlements.

The goals of public journalism as set forth by its backers seem, as I have said, to be too modest. But, Rosen (Merritt & Rosen, 1995) warned that if journalists don't take action, they may find themselves "standing by as democracy becomes a spectator sport, as public cynicism deepens" (p. 24). If that is the risk we take by doing nothing, it isn't enough for reporters to write in greater depth about election campaigns or to organize town meetings so that citizens might speak their mind. Rosen (Merritt &

Rosen, 1995) applauded my old colleague David Broder of the *Washington Post* as an inspiration to the public journalism movement by urging reporters to "become activists, not on behalf of a particular party or politician, but on behalf of the process of self-government" (p. 21).

> **Either we can give up and abandon the dream that undergirds the democratic assumption or we can join together as a community and take our place on the battlements.**

Fine, I say to Mr. Broder and Mr. Rosen, but all of us who proclaim ourselves adherents of the process of self-government still need a buck to buy a cup of coffee. That kind of talk exposes what we believe but it doesn't change a thing. Merritt is proud of his *Wichita Eagle* as are the editors of the *Charlotte Observer* and other newspapers that have worked hard to give their readers a portrait of the real meaning of election campaigns, rather than simply a horse race and a parade of public opinion polls. But that isn't enough, either.

Rosen and Merritt noted that their modest movement is only a beginning, one that is scoffed at by much of the news media, especially the elite newspapers, and not to mention the television news empires, which very likely haven't even heard of something called public journalism. Imagine Rupert Murdoch or Ted Turner pausing at the counting house to discuss public journalism.

I am not suggesting that it is wicked or immoral to work for profit. That isn't the point. The point is: That is the way the world works. Profit is neutral. It isn't good; it isn't bad. What counts is what profit is used for. It is socially immoral, we can all agree, if it is used merely to line one's own pockets and to pay no attention to the needs of the community we live in. Immoral it may be, but nothing is going to change it, not even public journalism.

Our choice—my choice I can say, since this is a personal document—is not a happy one. Either we give up or we make a stab at trying to carry out the democratic assumption. And here I can take a broadside at the American press, as I do in the pages of *Agents of Power*. Chapter 16 deals with a move by Third World nations inside UNESCO, a branch of the United Nations, to work for what they called a New Information and Communication Order. This is how Chapter 16 begins:

News and opinion reporting has rarely descended to a lower level than it did in dealing with the story of "a new international information order" during the last quarter of the 20th century. No story illustrates more clearly the linkage between news and politics. It is filled with overtones and undertones of racism, colonialism, ideology, and power politics. It is shot through with the perhaps insurmountable difficulty of squaring emotional realities and concrete reality. The setting for this lugubrious portrait of journalism was, ironically, an international organization that had been created with the hope of encouraging a global brotherhood and sisterhood for the peoples of the earth. The role of the news media in striving for the French Revolution's goal of Fraternity was considered central by the organization's founders. The moral doctrine advanced in every resolution and every policy developed by the organization was the doctrine of brotherhood through social responsibility. What happened? How did the world press fall so short of achieving its dreams of moral grandeur? How was its reporting so barren, so incorrect, so inclined to deepen rather than bridge the rift between races, between nations, between ideologies? How did the news media go so wrong? This book attempts to answer that question. (Altschull, 1995, p. 293)

You can see I was pretty much worked up over this issue, but this chapter is about community journalism and I had better get back to that. Let me just say that UNESCO has never adopted an information order; it has never approved the licensing of journalists; it has never campaigned against a free press. What it did was to propose a free and more balanced press around the world.

Incidentally, one idea popular with the great majority of the Unesco delegates was something called *community journalism*, a kind of participatory journalism promoted by UNESCO in remote rural areas; it is not generally considered feasible in industrialized society, not even in the large cities of Africa, but I think it has some possibilities, even here. The idea is to offer the citizen direct access to the pages of the news media (as is already possible in on-line services) but, more importantly, to enable him or her to participate in editorial decisionmaking. Like the rural press concept, this form of community journalism seeks to carve out a new role for the press, where it serves not as the agent of paymasters or of political power, but as the agent of the consumer, the interested and articulate citizen (Berrigan, 1981). Worth a try, anyway.

A New Direction for Journalism

It is foolish, I believe, to reject the idea of a new direction for journalism. Many of the ideas we have been discussing here agree on the need for a new direction. Some, like John Merrill (1996), fear that any new direction will eliminate what tradition sees as the proper role of journalism, that is, to be a fourth branch of government, a watchdog, to keep its eye on those who really wield the power: the government, those who make the law and those who enforce the law; the corporations, the churches—and without fear or favor to report what they see to the public.

> Objectivity simply does not exist. Even if it did exist, it would be wrong—because objectivity always works on behalf of the status quo.

Michael Gartner (1995), chairman and editor of *The Daily Tribune* in Ames, Iowa, is even more outraged. He called public journalism "a menace" (p. 86). Actually, I agree with some of the things Gartner said. He is for covering the news, for giving the readers facts, for analyzing the news, and reporting what it all means. But where I part company from him is his insistence on objectivity. Objectivity simply does not exist. Even if it did exist, it would be wrong—because objectivity always works on behalf of the status quo. It is true that the typical American journalist perceives this to be his highest calling: To get the facts and to lay out the facts for the reader, who may or may not act on those facts, as he or she sees fit. But objectivity is a mechanism for ensuring the status quo; it is an instrument to guarantee the preservation of institutions and the social order. It permits criticism of individuals but not of the fundamental system, political, economic, or social. The state of impartiality is, in fact, defensive of the system. That in this model the press retains the potential to challenge the social order is the element that poses a threat to those who exercise power. Inasmuch as the press fails to live up to its potential, it is carrying out the political role that is desired of it by those in power. To the extent that the press endorses the idea that it is above politics it is serving the needs of power.

Gartner (1995) is properly fed up with some of the high-flown definitions that have been given to public journalism, like "democracy-enhancing journalism" or "journalism that seeks to define and learn a different set of reflexes" (p. 89). To me, community journalism is journalism in a quest for *information* and not *misinformation* or *disinformation*. Community journalism works together with the citizens of its circulation area in a joint effort to dig behind the cliches and distortions in *search* of that most elusive of goals: truth.

I don't mean simply arranging for town meetings where citizens can air their needs and their desires, although there is nothing wrong with doing that. I don't mean simply sending out questionnaires to the citizens to find out what they care about, although there is nothing wrong with doing that, either. I mean drawing in the citizen at every step of the news process, from defining the news to determining the news sources to even helping to gather the news.

Why not?

Isn't it the business of journalism to help the public understand? High up there among the reasons why I have been so murderously disappointed in today's press is, if you'll pardon the expression, its know-it-all-ness. The First Amendment was not written for the benefit of the press. It was written for the benefit of the people. Under the First Amendment, everybody has the right to be heard. It isn't only for the people with the resources to own the newspapers and the broadcasting stations and the fiber-optic bitstreams.

Why are the media so unpopular? They always come in at the bottom in public opinion polls along with the politicians. I don't know all the reasons, but one of them, I'm sure, is their arrogance, their assumption outlined every day in the newspaper columns as well as on the Sunday TV shows where Sam Donaldson and George Will let us know every week how clever they are and how stupid we are.

> **High up there among the reasons why I have been so murderously disappointed in today's press is, if you'll pardon the expression, its know-it-all-ness.**

When I was a journalist in my own arrogant mode, I used to think down, too. If we filled our newsholes with stories of murders and rapes and high crimes and misdemeanors, why, we were just serving the needs of our readers, our audience; that's what they wanted, the dumbbells. We knew better, but we also knew those dumbbells wouldn't read the paper or tune in the evening news if we covered a complicated story about tax codes or foreign aid or library acquisitions. We didn't deal with those stories unless there was a scandal about money or sex or, best of all, both of them with a little blood and guts added for extra spice. So, we gave them what they wanted. And, privately, at our own watering holes we put them down.

When I was reporting in Washington, we always used to report movement: Who was up? Who was down? That's what the dumbbells wanted, we told each other. They didn't want to hear about issues, certainly not the complicated ones. . . . Well, don't let me go too far. We did do the complicated stories; we did try to report what the Hutchins Commission recommended, that is, the truth behind the facts. Some newspapers still do. Some TV reporters still do. But they are all losing ground—to tabloid papers and tabloid television. Or to *USA Today* and its many clones. Short and very spicy.

The Voice of Money

Let me play preacher now and remind you that one of the ideas behind what we cheerfully speak of as the freest press in the world is that it gives voice to those among us who are the hardest to hear. Of course, I am talking about the poor, the homeless, the Black, the gay, the native American. Mainstream journalists need to listen to them, too. I think the Finnish Television Network did the right thing when its reporters went out into the community and asked ordinary people what they wanted to know more about. When they learned what it was, they went out and produced documentaries giving everybody a chance to be heard. Unfortunately, it has dropped the program. Even in Finland, I guess, it's very difficult to challenge the bottom line.

But why not here? What have we got to lose, except—aha!—Money? It wins every time.

> Is it really in keeping with the idea of democracy for us to invoke the First Amendment just to avoid engaging a tough problem?

Still, giving up is not the answer. Money is for the most part indifferent to content. And audiences will very likely be stimulated to pay attention to substantive news when they have participated in defining what it is. Definition is the key. Reporters can and should be devoting their time to finding out what matters to their audiences and then laying out the story for them with suggested solutions. This is what participatory journalism is all about. News is no longer defined in terms of the journalist's amorphous news judgment.

Permit me to raise yet another counter-cultural idea (I am using that phrase here to refer to something that runs counter to the standard culture of journalism). Is it really in keeping with the idea of democracy for us to invoke the First Amendment just to avoid engaging the tough problem of excessive violence on television? All of us know there is too much violence on programs on the Tube and that children don't have the experience or the wisdom to place that violence in perspective. It is not hard to see the importance of Newton Minow's (1993) suggestion that we use the First Amendment to protect and nurture our children, rather than as an excuse to ignore them.

Journalists could, with profit, devote more time to helping make our world a better place to live in than to the rolling of eyeballs, the scrambling for high salaries, and the rigid insistence on our rights under the First Amendment (Bok, 1994; Glendon, 1991). Whatever we write or broadcast has consequences. Don't we have to pay attention to those consequences? We also have responsibilities, don't we?

I suppose some of this sounds as if I am fed up with journalism and into bashing the press. But this is far from the truth. I love journalism and *that* is why I am angry at the state of American journalism today. I want it to be better, much better. It could be so much better. I wish there were less time and energy devoted to standing up for our rights and more devoted to carrying out our role in the democratic assumption.

What Community Journalism Demands

Now, let me get into what I believe community journalism demands of the journalist, certainly of reporters and editors; I hope we can also include publishers and owners, but this means they will have to lower their financial expectations. Edward R. Murrow, I believe, said it for all time. Speaking to the Radio and Television News Directors Association in 1958, Murrow, who was then quarreling with CBS, argued (Friendly, 1967) that the public interest is more important than the demand for private profits. He was not, Murrow said, and I quote, suggesting "that networks or individual stations should operate as philanthropies. But I can find nothing in the Bill of Rights or the Communications Act which says they must increase their profits each year, lest the Republic collapse" (p. 252). His quarrel was not with making profit or with the free-enterprise system. His objection was to maximization of profit at the expense of the public interest.

So, community journalism demands putting the public interest ahead of the maximization of profit. Think about that. But the working stiff, no matter how high, can't force this formula on the people or the corporations that pay their salaries. That's a weakness in community journalism. Utopians hope that weakness will go away. In my new mood of guarded optimism (I love that phrase), I would like to try to persuade the bosses that by bringing the people *into* the process of journalism, they can continue to produce earnings while serving the needs the people.

The world we live in is an unstable place. We all know that. Crime is rampant. We don't feel safe on the streets, especially at night. Crime has also become the staple of news, every day, every night. It is clear that if the journalist is going to serve the public interest, he or she will have to deal with crime. The Old-Time Journalists of whom Michael Gartner is proud fulfill their job when they tell the story of the latest murder at Market and 5th and when they reports what the experts tell them about the causes.

It isn't enough. The community journalist goes beyond the facts. Beyond them. I have come to respect the research and analytical insights of the English sociologist, John Burton, who wrote (1979) that if we are to have a stable society—and that means for the journalist, his or her boss, and all the people who live in the community—then everybody, all the people, all the social units, must have equal access to the community's resources and the skills they need if they are going to act within the rules of society. Those denied this kind of access, Burton says, will turn to "alienation behavior." And that means going outside the norms of society to a life of what we, who have that access, call crime (pp. 188-189).

Obviously, the community journalist knows, these needs include adequate access to news and information and, indeed, to the way news and information are defined. What an opportunity for the community journalist! By drawing outsiders into the news process, he or she may even help to combat crime. Because all of us are interested in what is going on around us, the people who play no part in the way we define news and information are likely to be frustrated and bored. When they are frustrated and bored, outsiders are likely to withdraw and shrink into apathy or perhaps to find excitement on the fringes of the law or, worst of all, turn to activities outside the law.

I don't mean to say community journalists can conquer crime. Of course not. But they can help the entire community by expanding their reports to provide, with empathy and understanding, coverage of the needs and wants of all the people, not only those we sometimes absurdly refer to as "newsmakers." Community journalists know that there is no such thing as the Black community or the gay community. Of course, plenty of reporters already go after stories about "ordinary" people, but these are usually haphazard. The "man in the street" story tells the audiences mainly about who is available to be interviewed.

There is a special role for community journalists here, maybe the most important of all. They could become a third party to conflict. It's an idea that appeals to me, an idea that makes people in the media real mediators. Buzz Merritt (Merritt & Rosen, 1995) mentioned this role when he argued that the idea of detachment needs rethinking. "We needed," he said, "a viable philosophical foundation that could give both new hope and new purpose while protecting the truly essential third-party role of journalism" (p. 10).

Rosen (Merritt & Rosen, 1995) spoke of a weekend retreat organized by the *Virginian-Pilot* of Norfolk where fifty participants, mainly journalists, talked about what public journalism demands by way of changes in attitudes and techniques. There was talk about political reporting as a search for solutions to public problems (pp. 15-16). This was in keeping with a movement to return journalism to its deepest mission of public service. Mentioning public service somehow gets our foes' juices to bubbling. They say it isn't the business of journalists to hunt for solutions. The job of the journalist is to air the problems and turn them over to politicians.

> **I don't believe journalists are obligated to shy away from solutions. In fact, they offer solutions all the time.**

My concept of community journalism lies somewhere between these two positions. Some might say it's more far out than either of them. But I don't believe journalists are obligated to shy away from solutions. In fact, they offer solutions all the time. Read the articles labeled "analysis" in the papers. Tune in to David Brinkley's show on Sunday morning. We need to be careful, however. Community journalists have every right to suggest solutions; they have every right to agree with President Clinton or Newt Gingrich, with the mayor or her opponent, with Arthur Modell or the Cleveland football fans he left behind. The community journalist has every right to express an opinion. But—and I want to emphasize this—the community journalist must have the courage to inform his or her audience about his or her own political views. It isn't fair to the reader to keep that information secret. If you're a Democrat, say so. If you' re pro-life, say so.

Let the Media People Mediate

Best of all, however, the community journalist can and should bring the two sides together. Let the media people mediate. Most problems can be solved, or at least alleviated. Here is the classical third-party role. Study the background. Recognize that you can provide the data that shows the antagonists don't have to play the zero-sum game, where one wins and the other loses. The mediator finds the places where the antagonists are in agreement, no matter how small the area. After all, most of us believe in our personal survival. And most of us believe in the survival of the community. That's a start. It may not be the journalist's job to bring the two sides together, but ask yourself: Who else is going to do it? You can be the *link* that facilitates communication and decision-making by the actors (Burton, 1979, p. 219). The journalist is not the one who comes up with a solution, but certainly a solution is what is meant to be the end product of the process.

This role is a kind of extension of the First Amendment. It speaks not of our rights but of our responsibilities. It is the positive side of freedom. The negative, which is embodied in the First Amendment and the rest of the Bill of Rights, set forth what the government may *not* do. These are our civil liberties, the liberties that protect us from an abusive government. We are not told what we must do in return. Many have written of the social responsibility of the press, but that is a term that has no meaning in itself, because it doesn't tell us what we are responsible *for* or who we are responsible *to* (Altschull, 1990, pp. 85-92, 127-132).

Why not be responsible *to* the community and *for* helping the community solve its problems?

There are risks. Very serious risks. That arrogance I have been talking about is one of them. We don't need journalists in the pulpit, but they can help the people in the pulpit, and that's no mean role to play. To carry this fearsome burden, reporters will have to be what they should be under any circumstances, well educated and learned in analysis. Here journalism really plays a part in what matters most and becomes a true fourth branch of government.

Community journalists are always involved with their own community. They are out talking to people in the community all the time, finding out what is important to them and building stories that are both interesting and relevant. And encouraging the men and women in the community to participate, to write letters to the editor (pause) and to tune to the good radio talk shows.

The Virtues of Talk Shows

What? Aren't talk shows the worst thing we've run across since Frankenstein's monster? Sure, some of them are, but the worst talk shows are on television, not on radio. I'm not talking about TV shows about husbands with six wives or teenagers sleeping with their grandfathers. I'm speaking about shows like those on public radio, like Diane Rehm in Washington or Marc Steiner in Baltimore.

Having been on both those shows, I can assure you the people who call in are interested in public affairs and raise very good questions. There are programs like these all over, where the host is not a comedian like Rush Limbaugh and has no political axe to grind. If you haven't tried them, tune in. You may be surprised.

Marc Steiner, who has a show on WJHU, the Johns Hopkins FM station in Baltimore, said in a talk recently that his responsibility goes beyond radio—to dialogue. Taking that dialogue into the communities is something that interests editors of the suburban weekly press too; they would like to increase their columns of letters to the editor. In other words, community journalists don't have to work for metropolitan dailies; they can do the job of bringing the community together through weeklies.

Steiner said his goal was to help the people go a step beyond, to cross the boundaries we are afraid to cross—with the help of radio talk shows and community journalists. As part of the process, I would like to see newspapers large and small encourage readers both to write letters to the editor and articles for the Op-Ed pages. Newspapers can expand both and follow the pattern of the press in Europe. Letters columns are often the most interesting section to read. And they can serve as springboards for action.

Steiner said his show features "provocative discussion, intelligent talk." Not a bad motto for the community press. How, he was asked, might we get a consensus from differing voices that merely repeat the same things. The answer was one we can all agree with. It's not the media's job to bring consensus but to encourage dialogue. We are never going to have consensus in a democracy. We need to inch our way toward solutions.

Journalistic objectivity and detachment may have been fine once upon a time, but that doesn't bring communities together. They may even drive them further apart. The well-known apathy of the public is going to grow deeper and deeper if the public continues to see itself as separate and disconnected, uncared for and uncaring. People need to *care* if they are going to tune in to and read the news.

A "growing gap" has developed between journalists and readers, *Washington Post* media critic Howard Kurtz (1994) has pointed out (p. 6). And Hodding Carter III, onetime journalist and State Department spokesman, noted "the current lack of connection to the general public." What journalists need to do, Kurtz declared, is to "stop preaching at people, even if it means ceding some of our precious newsprint to those outside the priesthood." Participatory journalism has at least a shot at bridging that gap, at restoring that connection.

I have one last confession to make. I was really pleased to be invited to submit this chapter. And I had a secret motive for doing it. I thought that in preparing this chapter, I might rid myself of my own cynicism about the state of the American press, with which for a good many years I have had a sometimes rocky affair. I think I may have succeeded.

References

Abramson, J., & Bussiere, E. (1995). Free speech and free press: A communitarian perspective. In A. Etzioni (Ed.), *New communitarian thinking: Persons, virtues, institutions, and communities* (pp. 219-228). Charlottesville, VA: University Press of Virginia.

Altschull, H. (1990). *From Milton to McLuhan: The ideas behind American journalism.* White Plains NY: Longman.

Altschull, H. (1995). *Agents of power: The media and public policy* (2nd ed.). White Plains, NY: Longman.

Berrigan, F. (1981). *Community communications: The role of community media in development* (No. 90). Paris: UNESCO.

Bok, S. (1994). TV violence, children and the press: Eight different rationales inhibiting public policy debates. Discussion paper D-16. Cambridge, MA: The Joan Shorenstein Barone Center.

Burton, J. (1979). *Deviance, terrorism & war: The process of solving social and political problems.* New York: St. Martin's Press.

Carter, H. (1996, March 4). Comments, *Getting the Connections Right.* Symposium sponsored by the Twentieth Century Fund, National Press Club.

Christians, C. (1997). The common good and universal values. In J. Black (Ed.), *Mixed news: The public/civic/communitarian journalism debate* (ch. 2). Mahwah, NJ: Lawrence Erlbaum Associates.

Christians, C., Ferré, J., & Fackler, M. (1993). *Good news: Social ethics & the press.* New York: Oxford University Press.

Etzioni, A. (1993). *The spirit of community: Rights, responsibilities, and the communitarian agenda.* New York: Crown.

Friendly, F. W. (1967). *Due to circumstances beyond our control.* New York: Random House.

Gartner, M. (1995, Nov./Dec.). Give me old-time journalism: 'Democracy-enhancing' label runs counter to what media ought to be about. *Quill,* p. 86.

Glendon, M. A. (1991). *Rights talk: The impoverishment of political discourse.* New York: Macmillan.

Kurtz, H. (1994). *Media circus: The trouble with America's newspapers,* (rev. ed.). New York: Random House Times Books.

Merrill, J. (1997). Communitarianism's rhetorical war against enlightenment liberalism. In J. Black (Ed.), *Mixed news: The public/civic/communitarian journalism debate* (ch. 4). Mahwah, NJ: Lawrence Erlbaum Associates.

Merritt, D. & Rosen., J. (1995, April 13). *Imagining public journalism: An editor and scholar reflect on the birth of an idea.* Roy M. Howard Public Lecture in Journalism and Mass communication Research (No. 5), Indiana University School of Journalism.

Minow, N. (1993, August 3) How to Zap TV Violence. *The Wall Street Journal,* A14.

┌─────── In other words... ───────┐

Journalists as journalists need to define ourselves, not as being in the information business, or in the watchdog business necessarily or solely, but rather define ourselves as being in the business of public life, the business of democracy. Because if people aren't attentive to public life, they have no need for journalists or journalism of any sort.

Davis "Buzz" Merritt. (1994, Summer). Quoted in The emerging electronic democracy. *Nieman reports*. p. 54.

If politics has lost its hold on citizens, the solution is to start with what does have a hold on citizens. The political reporter needs to be redefined as someone who enters into the common life of the community in search of politics.

Jay Rosen. (1991, October). To be or not to be? *ASNE Bulletin*, 735, p. 18.

Realistically speaking, there's no point in publishing information people can't (or won't) use; consequently the newspapers in this book expend unprecedented effort on helping citizens buy in to the decision-making process. A community can't make progress on its problems if the public dialogue is polluted; so they refuse to let anyone's grandiose claims, wishful thinking, or sheer laziness pull their discourse off track—even if it's the public's own laziness or grandiosity. Far from pandering to readers, public journalists challenge them (and all other citizens) to do what really has to be done if public life is to succeed. They work from a conviction that citizens will come to see this kind of newspapering as a more essential part of their lives, will continue to read it (and pay for it) even if they balk now and then when their own complacency, bigotry, or wishful thinking is put on the spot. Public journalists, in short, are the clear-eyed pragmatists that conventional journalists only pretend to be.

Arthur Charity. (1995). *Doing public journalism*. New York: Guilford, p. 51.

(I)f journalists are to have any sort of critical voice or challenging role within a community, they must live in some fashion as members of that community. The force of their reporting will originate not in the distance they keep but the connection they make to the real aspirations and daily struggles of the people they report to. A certain distance is indeed required, but the distancing can only begin once the connection has been made. If the thread of trust and sympathy is broken, or never established, "tough" reporting falls on indifferent ears. It becomes impotent.

The whole notion of toughness as a property inherent in journalism and journalists is deeply misleading. What makes tough reporting effective as an act of communication is the same thing that makes a trusted friend the best person to give us the painful criticism we sometimes need. Truth-telling at its most difficult draws on the strength of a prior relationship, a bond deep enough to withstand the strain of asserting uncomfortable or depressing facts. So it is in daily journalism. The watchdog must know the house, be minimally welcome in the yard, understand the occupants well enough to sound the right alarm. These are genuine problems of connection. They cannot be waved away with pious rhetoric about "detachment" and scare stories about "getting into bed" with the authorities. Public journalism is not about the authorities. It is about regaining a relationship in which journalists and their publics understand and value each other.

Jay Rosen. (1996). *Getting the connections right: Public journalism and the troubles in the press.* New York: The Twentieth Century Fund Press, p. 63.

It seems almost perverse . . . that journalism, an important intellectual activity that should involve a careful balance of values, thoughtfulness, judgment, precise word selection, and attention to nuance, must often be performed under severe time and space restrictions. That practicality in itself requires that its practitioners be "powerfully conditioned to its rules and values" . . . that they be able to operate on reflex alone.

Davis "Buzz" Merritt. (1995). *Public journalism & public life: Why telling the news is not enough.* Hillsdale, NJ: Lawrence Erlbaum Associates, p. 16.

(Public journalism) moves beyond current practice because it requires a fundamental shift in thinking. It is not a formula or a set of rules. It is a conviction, and a resultant attitude, about the relationship between journalism and public life.

Public journalism is journalism that involves these mental shifts:
• It moves beyond the limited mission of "telling the news" to a broader mission of helping public life go well, and acts out of that imperative.
When public life goes well, true deliberation occurs and leads to potential solutions.
• It moves from detachment to being a fair-minded participant in public life.
Its practitioners remember that they are citizens as well as journalists.
• It moves from worrying about proper separations to concern with proper connections.
If we get the proper connections right, the separations will take care of themselves.
• It moves beyond only describing that is "going wrong" to also imagining what "going right" would be like.
By describing realistic possibilities that lie beyond immediate solutions, it informs people of their potential choices for the future.
• It moves from seeing people as consumers—as readers or non-readers, as bystanders to be informed—to seeing them as a public, as potential actors in arriving at democratic solutions to public problems.
It therefore relentlessly seeks ways to encourage public involvement and true deliberation; ways to build the public capacity to talk about and form solutions.

Davis "Buzz" Merritt. (1995). *Public journalism & public life: Why telling the news is not enough.* **Hillsdale, NJ: Lawrence Erlbaum Associates, pp. 113-114.**

The Norfolk *Virginian-Pilot's* conceptual journey to doing better journalism:

Starting With . . .	Leads to . . .
Readers	Public listening
Public listening	Deliberation
Deliberation	Framing issues/ positioning citizens
Framing issues/positioning citizens	Engagement
Engagement	Social capital
Social capital	Stronger public life

Cole Campbell. (1996, March 23). Remarks at Civic Journalism Teach-In, University of Missouri School of Journalism. (Campbell, former editor of the Norfolk *Virginian-Pilot,* **is now editor of the** *St. Louis Post-Dispatch.)*

Voices

Lynn Waddell
University of South Florida

Adding Color to Public Journalism

When the first two parts of a series on race relations in late 1992 failed to generate much reaction in Akron, OH, *Akron Beacon-Journal* editors decided to take the campaign for racial harmony beyond the news pages.

The newspaper began to hold community focus groups and contracted two facilitators to organize the meetings. Businesses and churches became interested and formed an organization to help combat racism. Before long so many people and businesses were involved in the organization that it had to publish a newsletter just to communicate with all its members.

The *Beacon-Journal* reported on the discussions it stimulated in a five-part series titled "A Question of Race." The five parts gave an overview of the racial problem and looked into the areas of crime, housing, economic opportunity, and education. It began on February 28, 1993, and ended late the same year with cut-out coupons pledging to fight racism. The coupons were returned to the newspaper signed by more than 22,000 readers, whose names were printed in a special section of the newspaper.

But the project not only generated a community reaction. It also drew accolades from some in the news industry and won the Pulitzer Prize for public service in April, 1994.

Nevertheless, the initial decision to do it wasn't an easy one for those at the newspaper trained in the tradition of objective reporting and detached observation.

"Sure, we were worried," said *Beacon-Journal* editor Dale Allen. "We asked ourselves, 'Is this something appropriate for us?' We were somewhat uncomfortable with it initially. It did take us out of our initial role as an observer."

Part of what led editors to go forward with the campaign was that there didn't seem to be anyone else in the community suited to do it, Allen said.

"Government is distrusted by minorities. Civil Rights organizations have lost their luster. Churches who rightfully take moral leadership are so splintered they are unable to do anything," Allen said. "When we looked around at the other public agencies we concluded we were probably more compatible than anyone in the community to do something about it."

Still, in order to protect the integrity and freedom of the newsroom, the *Beacon-Journal* decided to set up safeguards. One of those was the hiring of two outside facilitators to oversee the campaign. The part-time facilitators didn't report to anyone in the newsroom except Allen.

"We didn't want editors to feel they had to cover it. We also said from the beginning if anything happens in this program that backfires we will cover that, too. "

As it turned out, the project did backfire once, and the newspaper covered it. One man involved in the campaign promoted an event for residents to join hands across a long, local bridge as a message to combat racism. As it turned out, the man also was putting out brochures to try to make money from the event.

"We wrote all the organizations involved and told them he was trying to make money. The whole idea was we're going to cover it warts and all. Fortunately, there have been few," Allen said.

Since that event was quashed, a similar one has occurred without monetary profits. The hands-across-the-bridge project linked people for more than a mile.

The *Beacon-Journal* covered it, but because it was newsworthy, not because the newspaper was a sponsor of it, Allen said. That's another safeguard: Editors choose what stories to cover on the basis of news value. That way, newsroom editors and reporters maintain autonomy.

"We let the editors make the same decision as they would (regarding) any other community event," Allen said. "We covered the hands-across-the-bridge because it was a news event. With a meeting at the schools this week we didn't cover it because there wasn't any news value to it."

The project lives on in the community and the newsroom. The various groups formed as part of the movement continue to grow. Initially, 85 organizations and about 10,000 people were involved. Those numbers have grown to about 160 organizations and 15,000 people.

The group formed by the newspaper is now seeking nonprofit status. The *Beacon-Journal* has been spending roughly $150,000 a year to support it. With nonprofit status, the organization will be more capable of receiving grant money, he said.

The project's success, however, is still difficult to measure in terms of whether it has changed people's attitudes about race. The inability to determine this has not dissuaded the *Beacon-Journal's* resolve.

"If a few more people in the community begin having dialogue, start talking to each other for the first time in their lives, then there's been some success," Allen said. "Not that it is vastly going to change things overnight. That's going to take a couple of more generations."

The Ethics of Civic Journalism: Independence As the Guide

Robert M. Steele
Poynter Institute for Media Studies

"The job of the newspaper is to comfort the afflicted and afflict the comfortable," journalist and humorist Finley Peter Dunne said as he described the role of his press brethren at the beginning of the 20th century. While some of that comforting and afflicting still exists in journalism as this century ends, there is a range of additional roles played by a much more broadly defined "press" that includes electronic media as well as print. With those new roles comes considerable debate.

Should reporters be investigators of system failure or initiators of solutions? Should journalists be detached observers or activist participants? Should newspapers be independent watchdogs or conveners of public forums?

Significant ethical questions are embedded within this debate, a debate that swirls around and cuts beneath what we have come to know as civic, public, or community journalism. It is a debate that often gets bogged down in polarized positions as advocates and critics stake out their respective territory. That polarization may ignore the common ground. It may prevent us from capturing the best elements of civic journalism and moving beyond those approaches that serve poorly both the profession and society.

Before we can explore the ethical issues of civic journalism we should consider just what this approach to journalism means, accepting that it means different things to different people. Here's how it has been described by various proponents and opponents.

Doing Journalism Differently

Civic journalism is "helping the public find the solutions to problems," said Frank Denton, editor of the *Wisconsin State Journal*, a newspaper in Madison that has been deeply involved in the practice of public journalism. The *State Journal* has employed a number of approaches, including organizing town meetings on public policy and convening panels of community leaders to give feedback to stories before they are published (Glaberson, 1995).

Civic journalism is "a fundamental change in the way we do our business," said former broadcast network news executive Ed Fouhy (1994, p. 18), who heads the Pew Charitable Foundation's efforts in supporting civic journalism. Fouhy sees civic journalism as a change in "how we define what news is and how we serve our viewers." As TV stations jockey for success or survival in an era of converging technologies, Fouhy said he believes there is an incentive in civic journalism. The strategy, Fouhy said, is "reporting the issues on the peoples' agenda, even though they may not necessarily be on the journalists' agenda" (p. 19).

Cole Campbell, former editor of the *Virginian-Pilot* and now editor of the *St. Louis Post-Dispatch*, has put into practice various elements of civic journalism. He said news organizations must create a different sort of relationship with the public, one that re-examines the journalist's role to sources and to readers. Campbell said newspapers must reframe the questions and change conventions about what is news and how it is covered. He said journalism must "cover tension, not just conflict; ambivalence, not just certainty" (personal communication, February 26, 1995).

That connection between the journalist and the public was on David Broder's mind when he wrote a column on coverage of politics in 1990, a column that in many ways jump-started the public journalism movement. While he didn't use the term *public journalism,* Broder (1990) spoke eloquently about the need for journalism to move closer to those we serve, of better fulfilling "our obligations to the people who read, listen to and watch the news" (p. B1). It should be noted, however, that Broder talked about "shoe leather reporting, walking precincts, talking to people in their living rooms" as the modus operandi of journalism serving the democratic process.

> **Broder talked about 'shoe leather reporting, walking precincts, talking to people in their living rooms' as the modus operandi of journalism serving the democratic process.**

Broder's comments were focused primarily on how journalism covers the political process and his fear that journalists were leaving the public out of the press-politics equation. Public journalism has come to mean many other journalistic ventures and adventures in the 1990s, however.

Newspapers and TV stations have championed causes related to children, welfare reform, and community volunteerism.

The *Portland (ME) Press-Herald* news staff pioneered what it called "expert" reporting. Writers spend months studying and researching an issue of community concern and then write in-depth stories on it, going so far as to propose reforms. That last step—proposing reforms— is what takes expert reporting into the public journalism category and beyond traditional reporting. In one case, as part of a project on workers' compensation, the newspaper convened a meeting between the governor of Maine and other involved parties when the reporting and the call for reform did not produce solutions.

Poynter Institute senior scholar Roy Peter Clark (1994) tied the evolution of public journalism to the way journalists have perceived their function:

> Our role as detached observers has gotten us into a kind of problem, reflected in distrust by the public. The creation of a professional class of journalists may have produced an alienation between journalism and the public . . . the media need to be more like the public. Journalists need to be more like the people.

Some advocates of public journalism believe that news organizations move from the traditional standards of objectivity to play a more activist role in community activities, affairs, and issues. Clark said public journalism asks us, on occasion, to step across the traditional line of journalistic independence—to go across the line that separates observers/reporters from conveners/builders.

The Newspaper As Problem Solver

That notion is not foreign to the *Miami Herald*. Doug Clifton, (1994) the *Herald's* executive editor who said the newspaper that practices public journalism should be able to provide help, wrote:

> related to problems of public education, health care delivery, and criminal justice, not by dictating a solution, but by facilitating broad, purposeful discourse on the issue, by celebrating victories, by diagnostically noting failures, by encouraging citizens' involvement, by outlining and assessing available courses of action. (p. C4)

That emphasis on solutions was the inspiration for how *The Charlotte (NC) Observer* covered racial tension that grew out of a dispute in the use of a local park. Rick Thames, the *Observer's* assistant managing editor, said the paper's reporting "turned from just reporting conflict to interviewing a lot of people about what should happen, what is the solution here. The dialogue began to take place inside our newspaper that wasn't taking place in any other forum" (Glaberson, 1994, p. D6).

We see in that example and others the proactive role embedded within public journalism. In Akron, Ohio, the *Beacon Journal* went to great lengths in bringing elements of the community together to discuss and improve race relations. The paper hired outside consultants to serve as facilitators in that exploration and public dialogue. While playing the convener role, the paper also played the reporter and analyzer role in traditional newspaper fashion. In fact, the news staff played it so effectively that the *Akron Beacon Journal* won the Pulitzer Prize for public service in 1994.

It is that problem-solving focus that Jay Rosen often spoke of. "Public journalism," Rosen (1994) said, "is not a settled doctrine or a strict code of conduct but an unfolding philosophy about the place of the journalist in public life" (p. 6)

Rosen spoke of journalists "connecting with their communities in different ways" (p. 6). He said, "Journalists will have to redefine their own standards of proper conduct, draw new and imaginative lines that mark off their special functions but also connect them to the work of others" (p. 18).

Rosen's compatriot in the public journalism limelight is newspaper editor Davis "Buzz" Merritt, Jr. of the *Wichita Eagle*. Merritt (1994a) said public journalism is "about fundamental, cultural change in journalism; about attitudes and traditional concepts that no longer serve either us or our communities well" (p. 17A). He believed that journalism can improve the quality of public life in communities, can improve "the public capacity to solve problems."

Both Merritt and Rosen challenged the tradition of objectivity in journalism. Merritt said that in order for news organizations to "help revive public life" (p. 17A), journalists must move beyond telling the news to become what he calls "the fair-minded participant." He said one does not abandon "fairness, balance, and . . . truth" (1994b, p. 23).

> But it does mean employing those journalistic virtues on the field of play, not from the far-removed press box, not as a contestant, but as a fair-minded participant whose presence is necessary in order for outcomes to be determined fairly. (p. 23)

Merritt added:

> The public journalist's newspaper would view a problem such as public safety not merely as an opportunity to report what is hap-

pening but as an obligation to promote the discourse that leads to solutions; to act as a conscientious citizen would act. (p. 26)

Challenges to the Citizen-Journalist Role

Therein lies a major question about the role of public journalists. Are they merely conscientious citizens, or is there something in the role of journalists that distinguishes them from other citizens? Is the newspaper merely a recorder and reporter of events, or is it a catalyst to change?

Let me suggest that yes, there is something special about journalists and their role in society, something special about newspapers or television or radio stations and their journalistic role in a community—a role that is unique. In fact, it is that unique role that prompts some journalists to challenge and even condemn this public journalism concept.

> **Are they merely conscientious citizens, or is there something in the role of journalists that distinguishes them from other citizens? Is the newspaper merely a recorder and reporter of events, or is it a catalyst to change?**

A clear voice of opposition comes from Leonard Downie, executive editor of *The Washington Post*, who challenged both the methods and motives of its practitioners. "Too much of what's called public journalism," said Downie, "appears to be what our promotion department does, only with a different kind of name and a fancy evangelistic fervor" (Case, 1994, p. 14).

An equally critical voice came from Richard Aregood, editorial page editor of *The Philadelphia Daily News*. "What in God's name are we thinking about?" he asked (Case, p. 14). Aregood argued that the public journalism crusade is only what good newspapers have always been doing.

Joann Byrd (1995), former ombudsman at *The Washington Post*, expressed her concerns in a less demonstrative manner.

> The goals of civic journalism can be accomplished without compromising journalism's important principles. It does not help the community—or the paper—to have the paper acting as booster or as champion of its own agenda. Communities always need a newspa-

per that can stand back, take the long, broad view of the conflicts and the possibilities and avoid, in service to the whole community, taking sides. (p. C6)

Jane Eisner (1994), editorial page editor at *The Philadelphia Inquirer,* said it's true that public journalism may have a good ring for many journalists, touching their chord of idealism and their desire to "make the world a slightly better place" (p. E7).

But, Eisner said:

> owning part of the public stage comes with a price. Our central mission is to report the news, to set priorities, to analyze but not to shape or direct events or outcomes. Subsume or diminish the central mission, and we become like any other player in society, like any other politician, interest group, do-gooder, thief. (p. E7)

Eisner said she is not willing to relinquish this unique role that journalism plays in society. "I have trouble where we are seen as convener of the solutions and responsible for the solutions," Eisner said (personal communication, 1995). Eisner spoke passionately about the unique role of journalism in society: "There's no lack of lobbyists in this country." Still, she said she believes that the discussions about public journalism have heightened her sensitivity to how journalism functions. She now sees more clearly how newspapers overemphasize conflict elements of community activities and issues. She suggested that the public perception that journalists are arrogant may be connected to how we select stories with such a heavy emphasis on conflict.

The Trap Door of Involvement

Arrogance was a word used by William F. Woo (1995), former editor of the *St. Louis Post-Dispatch,* in a speech on "Public Journalism and the Tradition of Detachment":

> Yes, we have been isolated, detached, arrogant, disconnected, narrow in our definitions of what's news and what isn't. We have thrived anaerobically, in airless environments. Damn right that we should listen to the public. But should the consensus at the town meeting automatically become our agenda, not merely in editorial support but in the expenditure of resources that determine what other stories do not get covered?

Woo continued:

> Proponents of public journalism declare that at the end of the day
> every newspaper must make its own decisions in light of its own
> values and principles. Fair enough. But I have yet to hear of a paper
> that said "No" to what the citizens wanted when the paper itself
> mobilized the people, of a paper that said to its community, "Sorry,
> the agenda we helped create is not for us after all." (p. 21)

So, what does the public think about public journalism? It's interesting
that much if not most of the debate is among journalists, with only a smat-
tering of the voices of people. Ironic—isn't it?—because the voices of the
people are central to the notion of public journalism.

The *Inquirer's* Eisner asked her readers for their thoughts on public journalism. "Nobody says we should be more active in the community," she
reported, though some said the *Inquirer* was out of touch with the community and that newspapers are arrogant (personal communication,
1995).

Also from the public side, Paul Soglin, the mayor of Madison,
Wisconsin, said he worried that a newspaper can get too much power by
mixing the roles of reporting the news and creating it. Soglin said the
Wisconsin State Journal has been "wearing two hats" by reporting a story
it helped create, in this case on economic development issues (Glaberson,
1995, p. C6).

Searching for Common Ground

We can view the debate over civic journalism from a good-and-bad,
right-and-wrong perspective, but that would be both unfair and short-
sighted. The issues are too complex to be scored that way. It is not just
about winners and losers, and much of the debate can be examined by
going from the philosophy of public journalism—*what* it is—to how it is
practiced. That is the next step in exploring the ethics of civic journalism.

Make no mistake, just as public or civic journalism is defined in different ways by different journalists, it is practiced in different ways by different news organizations.

That was the point made recently by John Dinges, who directed
National Public Radio's *Election Project* in 1994. That project involved a
partnership between NPR and local newspapers and NPR affiliates, as
well as several television stations.

"Questions of objectivity and advocacy have not been a factor in any of
our projects," Dinges (personal communication, January 27, 1995) said,
pointing out that NPR stations and newspapers did not "organize" in the
community. Rather, Dinges, said, these news organizations shared resources in developing what Dinges called "tough reporting" on "the is-

sues, tradeoffs, and solutions associated with the 'citizens' agenda.'" That emphasis on citizens was key to NPR's election project, in terms of identifying the issues on the agenda to frame the coverage and then to keep *citizens* as a prominent part of the story.

The focus on citizens was at the heart of *The Charlotte Project*, a reshaping and renewing of political and election coverage at *The Charlotte Observer*. Poynter Institute associate Edward Miller (1994) who was very involved in that experiment, said that "journalism's allegiance to 'objectivity' need not come at a price of community understanding and engagement" (p. 87). Writing about lessons learned from Charlotte, Miller said that "Communities need journalism's insights, skills, experience, disciplines, ethics, perceptions, hard work, and above all, passion to be involved. All can be compatible with the traditional values of journalism" (p. 87).

Eisner (personal communication, February 28, 1995) of the *Inquirer* worried that the discussions on public journalism are falling into extremes, and feared that the more "bells and whistles we put on what we do, the more readers will turn off on journalism. A lot of the stuff we do is very simple." She cited the work of her *Inquirer* colleagues Donald Barlett and James Steele on their 1991 series, "America—What Went Wrong," as an example of good public journalism without calling it that. The paper committed great resources to that reporting project, then distributed free to the public some 400,000 copies of the report, which also became a best-selling book. That, she suggested, and I wholeheartedly agree, is a significant journalism project focusing on the public. Furthermore, Eisner said, it did not involve the type of community activism that worries many journalists.

Woo (1995) did not shine a totally negative red light on public journalism. He raised cautions in the spirit of a yellow light. Woo liked the connections to improving democracy, and he said he is "intrigued by what may lie down that road, beyond the bend" (p. 9). But he also urged journalists to listen to what he called the

> old bells ringing for objectivity, detachment, independence, for the courage to print stories that are unpopular and for which there is no consensus. . . . I hope we listen for them again, before we grow so old and so wise that they no longer matter. (p. 22)

Avoiding Polarization

Woo's wisdom and the ringing bells metaphor provides us with a starting point for examining this issue from a different perspective. Let us start by drawing a line to help us examine this issue—the ethics of civic journalism. Our tendency is to draw the line vertically, creating two sides, two positions. In fact that's the way we often speak of ethical dilemmas: We worry about "crossing the line," stepping across the traditional line of journalistic independence. On one side is independence and detached reporting, and on the other side is participation, advocacy, and activism. We see one side as right and good, the other side as wrong and bad.

That two-sided approach is not the most productive method of analysis, as it creates a polarizing effect and ignores the gray that most often exists between the black and white when we explore journalism ethics. It's a blueprint for both frustration and, I would suggest, failure as a way to explore the ethics of civic journalism. A crossing-the-line model simply does not work.

Instead of drawing a vertical line, let us draw the line horizontally. That horizontal line may be both substantive and symbolic—a level playing field on which to examine the ethics of civic journalism.[1]

See the line as a "continuum" along which we move back and forth depending on a variety of circumstances. Our movement is guided by principles.

Let's identify some terms to describe various roles journalists play:

Independent Reporter	Messenger
Detached Observer	Interpreter
Advocate	Watchdog
Supporter	Promoter
Opinion Leader	Intermediary
Agenda Setter	Convener
Builder	Participant
Activist	Thinker

In the vertical-line model, I argued against putting the terms on one side or the other of that line, which connotes their goodness or badness, and their rightness or wrongness with what we see as the journalist's role.

But with a horizontal line we see these positions of activity differently.

Independent reporter >——————< Messenger

Detached Observer >——————< Interpreter

Advocate >————————————< Watchdog

Supporter >————————————< Promoter

Opinion Leader >————————< Intermediary

Agenda Setter >————————< Convener

Builder >————————< Participant

Activist >————————< Thinker

They rest side by side on a continuum, separate from each other but also blending together. We recognize that an individual journalist or news organization might play the different roles to varying degrees depending on circumstances while still honoring journalistic principles. For instance, a newspaper might move from traditional reporting on the issue of medical care for the children of illegal immigrants to a position of advocacy when no other organizations or governmental units respond to a crisis that is endangering lives. Or a local television station may move from messenger and interpreter of information about an educational crisis in the community's schools to a convener of a town meeting on the issue when no other organization is willing to take the lead in seeking solutions.

In Service to the Public

We can see these blended journalistic roles in the work of Jeffrey Good of the *St. Petersburg Times*. He is a news reporter who brought his journalistic skills to the editorial page. His 1994 series, "Final Indignities," focused on the issues of estate planning and the significant problems associated with weak state regulations and the horrendous quality of some legal work for those seeking estate-planning assistance. Good researched, he reported, and he wrote, publishing the series in the Perspective section of the paper where editorials and other opinion pieces run. Good and the *St. Petersburg Times* also editorialized on the same issue, again within the commentary section of the paper. Then, the paper moved further on this issue, organizing a public forum on estate planning. The series had significant impact on the community and on state officials responsible for making laws and regulating their enforcement. The series also drew the attention of the journalism profession, earning Good and the *St. Petersburg Times* a Pulitzer Prize.

If we take this example of journalism and apply it to the horizontal line model, we can see how the project employed a number of those roles we identified earlier. It was an example of a journalist as reporter, watchdog, analyst, and interpreter. It was also an example of a newspaper as advocate, activist, agenda setter, and community convener.

If we see these roles as different positions on that continuum rather than as being identified as right or wrong, good or bad, it is possible to see more clearly the role of civic journalism in society. It may be a more productive way to consider the ethical issues embedded within such reporting projects.

We could do the same with other examples of what we might call civic or public journalism, giving some clarity to what decisions we should make on how far we should go in our actions and our involvement.

Principles as Guideposts

A horizontal line is not enough to guide us in making such decisions, however. This is where ethical principles come into play.

It is in the ethical principles that we find our clarity and our guidance for how we should move along this horizontal line, for when we might move, say, from detached observer to agenda setter—for when we might move from independent reporter to community convener.

Journalistic independence serves as a moral compass and a moral gyroscope

Journalistic independence is a guiding principle, at the heart of our role as truth seekers and truth tellers (Black, Steele, & Barney, 1995). This guiding principle serves as a moral compass to tell us where "true north" is, where to find the polar star. The guiding principle of journalistic independence also serves as a moral gyroscope to tell us where we find some balance, a level point in an environment where we are constantly buffeted by the winds of competition, the pressures of deadlines, the forces of business decisions, and the countervailing influences of our own self-interest and of peer pressure. The principle of independence guides us as to our role in society, clarifying our responsibilities to our customers, to the public, and to our communities.

Some may question why independence is a proper principle for ethical guidance. Don't the proponents of public journalism challenge journalism for being too detached from the people we serve? Isn't public journalism about *connectedness*, bringing journalism and the public together to better serve community, to provide for civic good, to accomplish democratic goals?

Well, yes and no. Goals related to community, civic-mindedness, and democracy are noble. But let me suggest that journalism's role in society is, as Eisner (1994) at *The Philadelphia Inquirer* said, "unique" (p. E7).

Journalism is a one-of-a-kind profession. There is nothing equivalent to it in a community. Doctors, ministers, architects, and teachers all have essential and unique roles to play in a community. As do attorneys, law enforcement officers, bankers, government workers, and entertainers.

So it is with journalists. Journalists are unparalleled in their responsibility to gather information and present it to the public, to seek out the truth and report it as fully as possible. Journalists must apply excellence of craft in fulfilling a societal mandate to tell the community about significant issues, so people can make important decisions in their lives—important decisions about their children's schooling, about their personal safety, about the people they choose to hold office, about the choices their government makes, and on and on.

That is the singular responsibility of the journalist. Carrying out that role with excellence is what real civic journalism is all about. It reflects the consummate public service.

To fulfill this unique role, we make choices. As Eisner (personal communication, 1995) at the *Inquirer* put it,

> Our function does require a certain amount of independence. We have to give up some things personally in terms of activities and collectively as a newspaper in order to maintain a certain amount of distance so that we maintain integrity.

It's clear that Jane Eisner sees her role as a journalist as unique. So does Woo as he hears the ringing of the bells.

This role for journalists might be termed a *special calling,* to use the words of Paula Ellis (personal communication, February 28, 1995), the managing editor at *The State* newspaper in Columbia, SC. Ellis is both very idealistic and very practical when she sees her role as a journalist as a "life of service. . . . Once you identify your special gifts, you need to use them to make your community better."

Ellis is no detractor of public journalism. In fact, she sees some strong connections between this "service of journalism" based on traditional values and connections to the public.

Journalists must apply excellence of craft in fulfilling a societal mandate to tell the community about significant issues, so people can make important decisions in their lives

"My journalism and my concern for community have always been tied together," she said (personal communication, February 28, 1995). And that connection is reflected in the impressive work she and *The State* newspaper have done on important community issues related to young people, to AIDS, and to education. Ellis believed in a solution-based model for journalism.

> The old-line investigative project laid out the problems, leaving people feeling desolate and helpless. So we'd come up with solutions from experts within our mix. That was equally disempowering for the public. People still don't know what they can do about the problems. Civic journalism is about building new models to help citizens find ways to have power.

Civic Journalism As Ethical Journalism

If we examine the work of journalists like Good and Ellis, if we consider the quality projects of the *Akron Beacon Journal*, National Public Radio, *The Philadelphia Inquirer*, and the *St. Petersburg Times*, we can find some strong connections between the old brand of journalism and the new brand of journalism. The differences are not as great as they are sometimes painted. There is considerable common ground.

We can use the principle of independence to guide us as we explore that common ground in our quest to best serve citizens and society. Civic journalism, if it is practiced with great skill and deep commitment, and if it is guided by leaders with high ethical standards, can produce reporting that honors that century-old responsibility to "comfort the afflicted and afflict the comfortable."

Notes

[1] I owe thanks to Joann Byrd, former ombudsman at *The Washington Post*, for giving me insight on such a model. She once used this horizontal line to examine issues of news reporting versus infotainment.

References

Black, J., Steele, B., & Barney, R. (1995). *Doing ethics in journalism: A handbook with case studies.* Boston: Allyn and Bacon.

Broder, D. (1990, Jan. 14). Five ways to put sanity back in elections. *The Washington Post,* p. B1.

Byrd, J. (1995, Feb. 5). Conversations with the community. *The Washington Post,* p. C6.

Case, T. (1994, Nov. 12). Public journalism denounced. *Editor & Publisher, p.* 14.

Clark, R. (1994, Nov. 6). Unpublished comments at *Seminar on ethics at Poynter Institute for Media Studies,* St. Petersburg, FL.

Clifton, D. (1994, March 6). Creating a forum to help solve community problems. *Miami Herald,* p. 4C

Dinges, J. (1995, Jan. 27). *Internet bulletin board* (ELECTION@NPR.EP) *communication to National Public Radio Election Project Participants.*

Eisner, J. (1994, Oct. 16). Should journalists abandon their detachment to solve problems? *Philadelphia Inquirer.* p. E7.

Fouhy, E. (1994, May). Is civic journalism the answer? *Communicator,* pp. 18-19.

Glaberson, W. (1994, Oct. 3). A new press role: Solving problems. *The New York Times,* p. 6D.

Glaberson, W. (1995, Feb. 27). Press: From a Wisconsin daily, a progress report on a new kind of problem-solving journalism. *The New York Times,* p. C6.

Merritt, D. (1994a, Oct. 30). Public journalism: a movement toward fundamental cultural change. *The Wichita Eagle,* p. A17.

Merritt, D.)(1994b). Public journalism: what it means, how it looks. In J. Rosen & D. Merritt Jr. (Eds.), *Public journalism: Theory and practice* (pp. 19-28). New York: Kettering Foundation.

Miller, E. (1994). *The Charlotte Project: Helping citizens take back democracy.* (Poynter Institute Paper). St. Petersburg, FL.: Poynter Institute for Media Studies.

Rosen J. (1994). Public journalism: first principles. In J. Rosen & D. Merritt (Eds.), *Public journalism: Theory and practice* (pp. 6-18). New York: Kettering Foundation.

Woo, W. F. (1995, Feb. 13). As old gods falter: public journalism and the tradition of detachment. *The Press-Enterprise Lecture Series.* (No. 30). University of California, Riverside.

———— In other words... ————

What exactly is public journalism? Well, it's at least three things: First, it's an argument about the proper task of the press. Second it's a set of practices that are spreading (slowly) through the American press. Third, it's a movement of people and institutions.

Jay Rosen. (1995, April 13). A scholar's perspective, in *Imagining public journalism: An editor and scholar reflect on the birth of an idea.* **Roy W. Howard Public Lecture in Journalism and Mass Communication Research, No. 5, Indiana University School of Journalism, p. 14.**

(S)ome people are natural common-grounders and some aren't. Some take quite naturally to public listening and deliberation; others take naturally to investigative reporting and "gotcha" Q&As. Each has a place even in a public journalism newsroom. Many editors begin by separating beats that require the skills of public journalism from those that require the skills of Woodward and Bernstein, then they assign staff to whichever beats make them most comfortable and productive.

Arthur Charity. (1995). *Doing public journalism.* **New York: Guilford, pp. 123-124.**

Traditional journalism's sense of objectivity has often led it to be passive; one might argue that public journalism is trying to discover how to be neutral instead.

Arthur Charity. (1995). *Doing public journalism.* **New York: Guilford, p. 149.**

I have sometimes used the phrase "proactive neutrality" to describe the public journalist's approach. It is neutral because it prescribes no chosen solution and favors no particular party of interest. It is proactive in its belief that journalism can in certain cases intervene in the service of broad public values without compromising its integrity.

Jay Rosen. (1996). *Getting the connections right: Public journalism and the troubles in the press.* **New York: The Twentieth Century Fund Press, p. 13.**

Objectivity can mean many things in journalism. The disinterested pursuit of truth, the care to ground reporting in verifiable facts, the principled attempt to restrain one's own biases and avoid prejudice are core values from which the press draws practical guidance and moral strength. No one should trifle with them. But objectivity also has its weaknesses. Under its influence "facts" tend to be placed in one category, "opinions" or personal views in another; with this division the journalist's mind appears to be successfully mapped. This works for some purposes . . . but there is a whole category of intellectual work that eludes the language of objectivity, with its attendant concerns about "bias."

Jay Rosen. (1996). *Getting the connections right: Public journalism and the troubles in the press.* New York: The Twentieth Century Fund Press, p. 29.

Journalists traditionally talk about "the line" and "crossing the line" as if there were one line, with everything on one side of it being good journalism and everything on the other side being something else. The formulation assumes that all important journalistic points—fairness, ethical behavior, proper detachment/attachment—fall neatly along that single line, "the line," and that everyone in the profession understands where it is and sees it the same way.

A more useful—and realistic—formulation considers two lines that define a continuum. At one edge, say the left side, is the traditional idea of total detachment. At the other, the right side, is total involvement and extreme political manipulation. Adopting the continuum model immediately changes the philosophical environment. Suddenly more possibilities exist for making journalistically proper connections, for the two lines define some middle ground.

Journalists who venture into that new ground will have to decide, over time, whether they and their communities are best served by that movement.

Davis "Buzz" Merritt. (1995). *Public journalism & public life: Why telling the news is not enough.* Hillsdale, NJ: Lawrence Erlbaum Associates, p. 118.

Richard J. Kenney
University of Georgia

'Final Indignities': Finally, a Voice for the Community

Jeffrey Good's editorial series, titled "Final Indignities," concluded with a rare feature: the voices of the public—citizens whose lives and livings were connected dramatically to a probate court system that "had failed people at perhaps the most vulnerable time," in Good's words.

"What I wanted to do was make reaction from readers and officials an integral part of the series," Good said. "We invited people to make themselves heard.

"In effect, we convened a town meeting on the editorial pages."

The series, published in 1994, earned Good and his newspaper, the *St. Petersburg Times*, the Pulitzer Prize for editorial writing.

The idea behind the series was to prod public officials—namely lawyers and legislators—into fixing the system, but also to involve the public—in a community with many elderly citizens—in the probate reform process.

As a reporter, Good had been "frustrated, despite disclosures that these problems [in the probate court system] existed, that nothing really changed." Then, promoted to the *Times'* editorial board in 1994, Good sought to use the high profile of the editorial pages to publicize the issue, using both that forum and his skill as an investigative reporter to have the paper "speak in a unified voice."

In fact, Good had his editors' full support in the unusual enterprise. Normally, editorials aren't allotted enough space for counter argument, Good says, regardless of its validity. "The more critical I was going to be, the more I wanted to incorporate a balance of views and voices," he says.

The unconventional approach to editorial journalism—integrating solid reporting with an editorial perspective and call to action and giving the public a chance to speak out, all resulting in a lengthy series—drew more notice from within the newsroom than from without.

"There was the predictable resistance from lawyers over the issue," Good says, "but not about the media forum.

"The only raised eyebrows were from reporters who thought there was too much news for it to be an editorial issue."

Publishing a part of the series on the front page of the Sunday Perspective section also "gave it extra weight," Good says.

The *Times* followed up the series by sponsoring a public forum on estate planning, attended by about 750 people. The meeting, Good says, was neither political not editorial; just informational. "That part of it was not activism," Good says. "I would distinguish between what we did and what others do and call public journalism."

Then, too, came the Pulitzer.

"Forget about the prize," Good says. "The thing here was, this issue touched the community.

"What I'll remember most are the handwritten notes that would come in the mail, thank-you's saying, 'Now we can control our destiny.' "

Public Journalism, Independence and Civic Capital . . . Three Ideas in Complete Harmony

Davis "Buzz" Merritt
The Wichita Eagle

During two years of sometimes fierce debate over public journalism, the question has often been posed: How can a newspaper that attempts to set the agenda for a community maintain its independence? Sometimes the question has arisen in another form: How can a newspaper that promotes its own solutions to public problems remain and be perceived as independent?

The answer is that it cannot.

The problem with those, and other, oft-heard challenges is that they broadly misconstrue what those of us writing about public journalism are recommending.

The questions assume, wrongly, that public journalism is about journalists doing things directly; that public journalism replaces traditional journalism (and its valuable separations, ideals, and virtues) with something else. It doesn't. The way journalism has come to be practiced in recent decades is not so much wrong for the 1990s, we argue, as it is insufficient; in need of an additional dimension.

Thus much of the debate about public journalism hasn't actually been about public journalism; it has been about what journalists—including some critics and some journalists who claim to be practicing it—think it is.

To understand this confusion, start with the fact that journalists, by nature and necessity, are pragmatic, results-driven people. For the most part we say, "Don't bother me with philosophy. Tell me how to do it; I've got a paper to get out." Or, as often, "Just give me a two-graf definition and I'll decide if I like it or not."

Public journalism isn't that easy; if it were, it wouldn't be potentially important or particularly interesting; it would be merely a different, if controversial, technique. But public journalism is much more than technique. It requires a philosophical journey because it is fundamental change in how we conceive of our role in public life.

The yearning for a facile definition and the fact that public journalism was first expressed in large projects invited journalists to regard it as a set of practices rather than a philosophy. Public journalism became "focus groups" and "polling" and "holding forums" and "setting agendas" and "getting involved in the news" and "asking readers." A parallel definitional trap would be to define investigative journalism as "going to the courthouse to look up records." The tools have become identified as the thing itself.

Therein lies an irritating irony for those of us who have taken the necessary philosophical journey. Most of the writing about public journalism has been done by journalists, who bring to that task much of the baggage of traditional journalism: devotion to stark contrasts as opposed to subtleties; astigmatic focus on "how" as opposed to "why;" determined adversarialism as opposed to healthy skepticism; a gadfly reluctance to spend much time on one subject before flitting off to another; gnarly defensiveness that grows out of the free press's sanctification in the First Amendment. The irony: Public journalism can be said to have had journalism done to it.

> **The irony: Public journalism can be said to have had journalism done to it.**

So What's It Really About?

A crucial fact is that public journalism is still experimental; it is a philosophy in search of printed expression. The lack of a simple, one-paragraph, practical definition seems to arouse great uneasiness in its detractors. "Tell me what it is and I'll tell you if I like it," they say, ignoring the fact that they could not easily respond to a similar demand about investigative journalism or computer-assisted journalism, or, indeed, simply journalism itself.

Journalists, being pragmatists, tend to be more interested in "how" than "why." Public journalism at this stage is mostly a "why." The search for "how" is still underway at newspapers and broadcast outlets from coast to coast. It is a search that has, in my view, taken strange and, in some cases, wrong turns.

But the "why" of public journalism seems clear to those of us who have thought about it for very long, and it is on the "why" that the profession's debate should be centered, not on the experimental and vestigial "how." If the "why" is sound, and we believe it is, the correct "how" will be developed over time.

The "why" answer lies in a two-step thinking process.

The first step involves accepting the fact that journalism, in the media age, has a direct and important impact on how well public life goes. Whether or not journalists like it, or are comfortable with it, that fact is inarguable. In a world glutted with information, how journalists organize and relay that information, how we frame issues, which facts we report and which we omit, has a great deal to do with how people respond and thus how things go.

The second step: The fact of our undeniable impact imposes an obligation on us. The obligation is to do our journalism in ways calculated to help public life go well *by engaging citizens in it*. This philosophical step is seen by many journalists as highly challengeable. They miss, or dismiss, the last five words and assume, in their pragmatism, that "helping public life go well" means journalists saying just how that ought to occur; or that it means doing journalism in ways to help public life go quietly and peacefully. What we mean when we talk about public life going well is that citizens are engaged in making the decisions of public life, a participatory democracy milieu in which "quietly and peacefully" are the last things one would either expect or want.

> **The obligation is to do our journalism in ways calculated to help public life go well by engaging citizens in it.**

Why Is Public Journalism Needed?

Public journalism is a response to two 1990s dilemmas: First, Americans are increasingly withdrawn from public life, cynical about their leaders' ability or interest in doing the right things and at the same time increasingly discouraged about their own ability to affect that woeful situation. And secondly, the fact that journalism is rapidly reaching the last of its supply of credibility and authority with citizens, as is consistently demonstrated by numerous studies and surveys. We believe the two dilemmas are directly connected.

No one seriously argues that journalism alone can restore public life's vigor, but we do argue that journalism done with an additional dimension can begin to rebuild the civic capital that is necessary fuel for the revitalization of public life. (It also cannot be overlooked that revitalization of public life is central to the future of journalism, for if people are not interested in public life they have no need of journalists or journalism.)

The narrative of a community, the stories it tells about itself, are joint narratives, publicly produced. Journalism is only half of the equation, and the journalism in a community can be no better than the civic story the community is itself producing.

But it is also true that a community bent on building civic capital needs a public repository for that capital, a place where the knowledge, the people, and the encouragement that success breeds—the accumulated experience of a community learning to make itself better—can be drawn on.

So one of our experiments in public journalism at the *Wichita (KS) Eagle* involves figuring out how to tell this complex and broad story of civic learning that has such intimate importance to citizens (many of whom are newspaper readers) and large importance to the community.

So far, we think the answer lies in a combination of micro and macro approaches:

> **Micro:** a willingness to build a trove of "small" stories, recognizing that (in traditional journalistic terms) they are small, but valuing them as newsworthy for what they represent of the accumulative public narrative.
>
> **Macro:** informed by the micro aspects, putting ourselves in the posture, philosophically and practically, to report on that broader public narrative in ways that have authority and resonance.

Both approaches deal with real news. In fact, citizen re-involvement mushrooming around the country may be one of the biggest untold news stories in decades. Many of the tenets of present journalistic practice dictate that such events, whether micro or macro, are not really news. That's a reflex public journalism seeks to change.

Central to the idea of re-engaging people in public life is perceiving of people not as consumers, or an audience, or spectators at the event of public life, but as citizens, potential participants. That change of mindset will automatically change the way we do some things.

What About Independence?

Such a philosophy can be said to endanger a newspaper's independence only if one believes that journalistic independence is grounded in journalistic detachment. We argue that it is not.

Public journalism does require a step away from traditional detachment—the idea that journalistic objectivity requires our indifference to the consequences of the way we present life's narrative.

Most journalists, hearing our critique of detachment, take not a step but a mental leap: If we're not talking about detachment, they say, then we must be talking about attachment; and if we're talking about attachment, then we must be talking about abandoning such indisputably important and useful roles as watchdog, outsider from government, independent observer, uninvolved-and-thus-credible source of information.

Some recent experiments under the name of public journalism, unfortunately and avoidably, have left themselves open to criticism because they have abandoned one or more of those ideals. But that need not be the case.

For true professionals in any field, neither independence nor objectivity are the same as detachment.

To illustrate: Dr. Jonas Salk, after years of careful experimentation, discovered a vaccine for polio. As a professional scientist, he was required to be objective about his data. Failure to do so would have had severe consequences: He might have reached wrong and delaying conclusions and his experiments were subject to challenge if they could not be replicated by other scientists. But he was hardly detached; he cared very much whether or not he found a vaccine, and his efforts, from beginning to end, sought that specific outcome.

Public journalism seeks the outcome of public life going better because people, with our help, become re-engaged in it. Seeking to manipulate events in order to reach that goal can only produce wrong and delaying consequences.

Most of the traditions and conventions of journalism serve us well and cannot be abandoned without severe consequences for the profession and for public life. But acting on those traditions and conventions with no overriding goal other than purveying information has contributed to the twin dilemmas of public life and journalism. Public journalism seeks to add the dimension of an overarching goal.

Doing journalism in ways that move toward that goal reinforces rather than risks our independence—real and perceived—from government and other institutions, for it relies on the fundamental of democracy that gave journalism its independence in the first place: self-determination.

In other words...

To survive, and certainly to flourish, the practitioners of civic journalism must be patient under criticism and yet show results that inspire imitation by news media not yet initiated into the new journalistic forms. They must show that the new forms do not threaten but, in fact, enhance the credibility of an independent journalism that can be embraced by a wide spectrum of the public. They must answer the fears that will certainly come—and ironically, from both the Left and the Right—that civic journalism's wish to empower the citizenry risks indoctrination.

Edmund B. Lambeth. (1994). Reviewing Clifford Christians, John Ferré, & Mark Fackler, *Good news: Social ethics & the press.* In *Media Development,* 28 (4): 50.

Re-imagine the newspaper as a complex support system for public life. This is a risky thing to do. But newspapers accept all kinds of risks already. When they send out people to cover institutions, they run the risk that those people will become too close to their sources. So the question becomes: What new forms of risk should the newspaper be willing to suffer to reconnect itself to people's lives?

Jay Rosen. (1991, October). To be or not to be? *ASNE Bulletin,* 735, p. 18.

Public journalism is nothing more than the conviction that journalism's business is about making citizenship work. In practice, there is only the pioneering, sometimes contradictory work of dozens of very loosely connected editors and reporters.

Arthur Charity. (1995). *Doing public journalism.* New York: Guilford, p. 9.

(A) paper doesn't necessarily do public journalism by adding bells and whistles like community forums. The first and foremost way of making a story more "public" is by adjusting the reporter's own attitude and style. To bring this off both reporters and editors have to be so thoroughly familiar with the different styles of public and traditional journalism that they can go back and forth between them with ease. The (Norfolk) *Virginian-Pilot* teaches this lesson by assigning its reporters (when time permits) to write two versions of the same story: first the "public" version, to actually go into print, and second, a traditional version.

Arthur Charity. (1995). *Doing public journalism.* **New York: Guilford, pp. 45-46.**

I sometimes wonder if the idea of public journalism can survive its worst examples, which are doubtless still to come. The only antidote, I believe, is that a nuanced understanding must be spread to more and more of the working press, so that journalists can apply high standards to anything they hear presented as public journalism. This is one reason the poor quality of the debate today is so troubling. It is based on a crude caricature of an idea that needs to be grasped at its deeper levels if it is to avoid turning into mush.

Jay Rosen. (1996). *Getting the connections right: Public journalism and the troubles in the press.* **New York: The Twentieth Century Fund Press, pp. 51-52.**

(Public anger at journalism) comes from . . . the public's sense that it is not *engaged* in politics, public life, or the discussion that goes on in the press. The media establishment seems to talk *at* people rather than with or even to them. When anchormen travel to the site of a flood or bombing or hurricane, when correspondents do standups from the campaign trail or the White House lawn, they usually seem to be part of a spectacle, competing to hold our attention for a moment, rather than part of a process that would engage us in solving or even considering shared problems. Politicians seem to dance above the real concerns the public has, rather than doing anything serious to cope with them. The public therefore comes to view the media largely as an irritant, which can be resented or ignored. And it comes to view politicians as mere diverters or entertainers, on a par with the other celebrities competing for our attention on TV each night. There is little sense of the media as a crucial tool for understanding the forces shaping lives, or of politicians as partners through whom we can resolve issues that affect all of us.

James Fallows. (1996). *Breaking the news: How the media undermine American democracy.* **New York: Pantheon, pp. 240-241.**

Public journalism starts with a state of mind . . . it's very very important that we start with the state of mind and not with the process. It means recognizing that every story, everything we do, is engaging the public (in citizenship). . . .

There's a danger if you put the process ahead of the state of mind. Corporate mandates and corporate journalism have led to this sort of problem, in that ideas have not been thought through at the top level. It's been management saying "ready-fire-aim."

Rick Thomas. (1996, May 4). Solving the public journalism puzzle, panel discussion at Society of Professional Journalists Region Three Conference, Macon, Ga. (Thomas is former editor of the Macon *Telegraph*, where public journalism projects "Our Children at Risk" and "The Wishbook" were carried out.)

A First Amendment Perspective on Public Journalism

Paul McMasters
The Freedom Forum

As the larger society struggles to keep its bearing in what has been called a "culture of chaos," the politics of identity, victimization, and empowerment elevates the interests of the individual and group. An already fragile sense of national purpose threatens to fragment. The common ground continues to shrink and shift. In such a milieu, it is only natural that the press itself would experience unease. So it finds itself engaged in a spasm of self-examination that at times borders on self-flagellation.

One of the better impulses produced by this self-examination is "public journalism." There are a number of reasons that this movement has won over so many so quickly. The perception that journalism is in a deepening crisis is palpable. Public journalism advocates offer hope for a rescue. They also offer some very helpful and necessary insights into confronting the criticisms plaguing journalism and journalists. Overall, the cause is helped considerably by the fact that among the proponents of public journalism are some of the best and brightest in the business, professional and academic; they are effective and persuasive voices for change and correction because they speak from a serious and sincere commitment to improving journalistic practices.

That said, it would be foolish at this stage of its existence for anyone to declare public journalism the salvation of journalism, just as it would be folly to declare it an unadorned menace. There are, however, a number of questions that would occur to any good reporter and that should be addressed before this approach gets too deeply embedded in the journalistic psyche.

Some Fundamental Assumptions

A fundamental assumption of the public journalism movement is that democracy is disintegrating. Certainly, the evidence is troubling, significant, and accumulating. But does it prove that public life is more in danger now than it was during, say, the Civil War, the world wars, the Cold War, or the Vietnam War? It is important that we get this right, in context, and in perspective before journalists accept sweeping changes in the way they perceive and go about fulfilling their role in a democratic society.

Another assumption of the movement is that the press is in peril of extinction. Again, the problems and challenges are significant, but hasn't it ever been thus? To concede that the press has problems is not to say that those problems are unprecedented or even unequaled.

In the preface to *Public Journalism & Public Life*, Davis "Buzz" Merritt dismissed those who question these two assumptions with this sentence: "Little time and effort will be spent here trying to persuade you otherwise" (1995, p. xii). The fact remains that the pronouncement that the press is expiring and democracy is dying is a rather bold one. If it is important enough to found a movement on, it is important enough to explicate.

This is, after all, risky business, diagnosing the ills of the larger society and prescribing its treatment by focusing on the fever afflicting only one of its institutions. But, for the moment, let's accept these assumptions at face value and ignore other factors possibly contributing to the decline of both public life and the press—changing society, changing technology, or changing cycles. We still must confront a third issue: whether the problems of democracy and journalism are inextricably—or even materially—entwined. It would seem that far too much is on the line for public journalism advocates to be incomplete or presumptive in their statement of the problems and solutions, or ambiguous in defining them.

Interestingly, in its short life, the public journalism movement has acquired many names but not one single working definition. That's partly purposeful: Many of its proponents argue that to define is to confine. This is an evolving movement, they say. It needs room to breathe and to find itself. Perhaps so, but that sort of ambiguity tends to feed the fears and suppositions of its detractors as well as those who await persuasion. It also provides an opening for those who see public journalism as a vehicle for separate agendas, some of which may not be all that friendly to good

> The pronouncement that the press is expiring and democracy is dying is a rather bold one. If it is important enough to found a movement on, it is important enough to explicate.

journalism.

One of the earliest and leading exponents of public journalism, Jay Rosen, associate professor of journalism at New York University, said, however:

> Those who are pushing this movement forward don't know exactly what they're doing. I'm afraid I have to insist on that point. We're making it up as we go along. We proceed by experiment and reflection, and it's hard to say at this stage whether any of the experiments are really working. (1995, p. 7)

This sort of theoretical approach, an understandable necessity in academe, can suffer mightily in the migration to the nation's newsrooms, where reality is rendered on deadline. In that environment, there are hard consequences to ambiguity and experimentation; they could greatly exacerbate the troubles public journalism proposes to ameliorate.

In response to Professor Rosen, the skeptics probably will have to insist on this point: "If we are to be converted, then public journalism's proponents must make up their minds whether this movement is a technique or a theory, a practice or a philosophy, mere anarchy or a new order, an elaboration on what already exists or a radical revolution." In other words, there is a great need for some assertions about whether the problems are systemic (basic flaws requiring radical measures) or systaltic (cyclic issues requiring restrained responses). Until these matters are resolved, there will be a justifiable skepticism among some journalists as well as the public.

Which brings us to a First Amendment perspective.

A First Amendment Perspective

There appears to be a growing sentiment in some academic and legal circles that the First Amendment is either an interesting relic or an irritating irrelevance. One only has to review the recent writings of such acclaimed scholars as Catharine MacKinnon, Cass Sunstein, Stanley Fish, Mari Matsuda, Richard Delgado, and others to see that the First Amendment is viewed as the problem rather than the solution. There appear to be traces of that sentiment in the debate and dialogue over public journalism. Not that there are any expressions of hostility toward the First Amendment; it's just that it doesn't come up much.

Clearly, the First Amendment protects the press, no matter how it chooses to express itself or perform its job. But if the press fails to distinguish its role from that of ordinary citizens or community leaders or elected politicians, it jeopardizes the public support and tolerance that keep its constitutional mandate in place. It is not in the exercise of its rights that the press garners its support, but in the exercise of its responsibilities. A free press's independence makes it credible and its credibility makes it indispensable to democracy. This is a necessary formulation for the Jeffersonian principle of an informed citizenry to be realized.

> It is not in the exercise of its rights that the press garners its support, but in the exercise of its responsibilities.

Whether public journalism proposes to tinker with the current journalistic imperative or to jettison it in favor of an overhaul, the constitutional franchise of a free press must be kept foremost in mind. Some of the proponents of public journalism offer assurances that this is not about the First Amendment but about the press adopting new, broader values than before, and that those values may well require journalists to shed their traditional role as observers and informers and become activists and facilitators. "Public journalism is about forming as much as informing a public," said Jay Rosen (1995, p. 7). The First Amendment adventurism implicit in such statements sounds a warning for proponents and critics alike to proceed carefully. Some cautions to heed:

Press practice will define public journalism. No one, least of all those who have articulated the concept and need, can be responsible for all the ways public journalism will be translated into reality, but that won't make the damage to press credibility or the threat to its franchise any less. There will be opportunists who hijack it for a joy ride, publishers who use it as a marketing tool, editors who cite it to justify neglect of more traditional reporting, and reporters who go along with it to get ahead.

Money buys trouble, too. Public journalism is expensive. It requires editors, reporters, and support staff with specialized skills. That can absorb precious resources needed for the beats, investigatory reporting and projects, research and development, and training. Perhaps that is why we are seeing the enthusiasm for this movement result in direct funding of projects in the newsroom. Between 1993 and 1996, the Pew Center for Civic Journalism contributed hundreds of thousands of dollars in grants ranging from $5,000 to $61,000 to fund 34 projects in 24 cities. Among the costs picked up: polling, town hall meetings, focus groups, travel expenses for reporters, rent for an apartment for a reporter to live in a high-crime neighborhood, and the salary of a newsroom coordinator who functions much like a community organizer (Shepard, 1996, p. 28). There always is the danger that such money will raise the priority of the project, influence the development of the project, or move the coverage "beyond" the news.

Just don't sit there, do something. There is a heightened potential for more of the bad journalism that provided the impetus for public journalism in the first place. Public journalism, as it is described and, in some cases, practiced, requires patience and a long attention span on the part of editors and reporters—and often on the part of the readers and viewers. It cannot be rendered in black and white; it must be nuanced. But the temptation to hype or to simplify is great. It is not an event or a score or an outcome, but an unfolding process. Done badly, it can be deadly dull— or deadly dangerous.

Just don't sit there, get the public to do something. Informing the public can become secondary to influencing the agenda. The press has to get the public to act, and—although most advocates decry this—to act in a certain way. In other words, journalists should not be content if citizens elect to not attend a meeting, sign onto an agenda, or disagree with an agenda produced by a poll, focus group, or town hall meeting. The public journalism goal is not so much to inform the public in a way that they will want to participate, as it is to get them to participate so they will want to be informed. Here is the way Jay Rosen put it: "Traditional journalism believes that people need to be informed so they can participate effectively. In public journalism, we believe people have to participate effectively so they'll want to become informed" (1995, p. 7).

> The journalist, of all persons, should instinctively identify with the impulse to stand aside, observe, report, tell the story, then let fellow citizens do the rest.

Disconnecting with detachment is not the same thing as connecting with the people. Contrary to what some advocates of public journalism imply, detachment as practiced by good journalists doesn't make them cynics. The only values that should show in newscasts and on news pages should be journalistic values. The journalists who cover democracy's parade are on duty and as such deliver a unique perspective. If they join the parade, they lose that perspective, and their readers and viewers lose a special and necessary insight. Those losses are compounded when journalists form the parade or lead it. Who, then, is left to observe and report—even, occasionally, to rain on the parade? The journalist, of all persons, should instinctively identify with the impulse to stand aside, observe, report, tell the story, then let fellow citizens do the rest. "Like it or not, part of the job of a great editor is to listen to public desires—and then, if necessary, act against them," said David Remnick (1996, p. 42). Journalists are not any more the cynic or less the citizen for fulfilling that role.

Some problems get lost in the shuffle. Today's journalism is rife with such problems as sensationalism, artificial balance, episodic reporting, unfairness, negativity, cynicism—the list goes on. Even if public journalism is practiced as its proponents wish, there is no guarantee that news coverage and news judgments won't continue to suffer from those flaws, especially if attention and resources are diverted to polling, focus groups, town hall meetings, and agenda-setting.

The P.C. newsroom is the P.J. newsroom. If public journalism is adopted for the wrong reasons or put to the wrong uses, then more will have been lost than gained. It does not make sense to believe that the editors and reporters who commissioned the polls, convened the focus groups, organized and moderated the community meetings, and helped bring forth an agenda and a set of solutions won't have a vested interest—or a particular perspective—when it comes to covering the project as a story. Even if they don't, they likely will be perceived as such by both those who have joined the agenda and those who stand outside it. Either way, the press and its role are compromised.

History and context count for something. Many of the problems spurring the public journalism initiative are not new. In fact, it's almost depressing how they parallel complaints and charges contained in the Hutchins Commission report in 1947. It is instructive to remember how similar criticisms in the 1960s and 1970s spawned a frenzy of remedies and responses in the form of press councils, ombudsman posts, and press reviews. Journalism and journalists must not fall prey to a panic created by generalizations and simplifications about stand-ups and spectacles and sensationalism, when enormous amounts of good journalism are produced every day, when unknown, ink-stained wretches in villages and boroughs across the land connect materially with the public. The press deserves every welt the critics' lash inflicts, but it should not let itself be stampeded into solutions not fully developed or defined.

Threats to the Franchise

The list of threats public journalism poses for the press's First Amendment franchise is too long to ignore or to dismiss too quickly. Public journalism could change journalism for the better. Or it could encourage the journalist and the ordinary citizen to become so connected that there is no distinguishing the one from the other, whereupon the First

Amendment justification for treating the journalist any different than anyone else will fade.

Unique protections for a free press were written into our Constitution to ensure a constant, credible, and independent flow of information from the government to the governed and from the governed to the government. If the press becomes an active agent of either or both, then it is not conveying information, it is conveying propaganda, because it is not a disinterested party. In the last few years, we have seen some very good journalism carrying the label of "public journalism." We've seen the readers, viewers, and journalists greatly energized from the discussion and debate over public journalism. That is good. What is not good is the tendency of both sides in this debate to paint the issues with too broad a brush or to confuse criticism with opprobrium. It is hoped these reflections have not stumbled into that thicket.

> Public journalism . . . could encourage the journalist and the ordinary citizen to become so connected that there is no distinguishing the one from the other, whereupon the justification for treating the journalist any different than anyone else will fade.

Thomas Jefferson and James Madison—as well as the proponents and opponents of public journalism—agree that the press is absolutely essential to democracy. But its value rests largely on its independence, its detachment, its need to report from a vantage point above and beyond the fray (but not beyond the news) in order to inform the citizenry. There needs to be some distance between the journalist and what he or she covers, just as there needs to be detachment and distance between the surgeon and patient, the lawyer and client, the scientist and the experiment, the priest and parishioner, the writer and the work. Detachment does not mean not caring about democracy. It means, in the case of the journalists, to care enough to understand that the American people will remember their place and role as citizens if they remember their place and role as journalists.

The one defining value that public journalism proposes to abandon is the First Amendment-protected tradition that all the editorial campaigns, political rhetoric, and community activism in the world won't work permanent and positive change unless the people first have been factually informed from a credible source. The best public journalist, it would seem, is the one committed to informing the public rather than reforming journalism. Journalists should take care not to cast themselves as the great hope and salvation of democracy. That might relieve citizens and community activists of an important responsibility and encumber the press with the role of saving democracy rather than serving it.

References

Merritt, D. (1995). *Public journalism & public life: Why telling the news is not enough*. Hillsdale, NJ: Lawrence Erlbaum Associates.

Remnick, D. (1996, Jan. 29). Scoop. *The New Yorker*, p. 38-42.

Rosen, J. (1995, Nov. - Dec.). What should we be doing? *IRE Journal*, p. 7.

Shepard, A. C. (1996, April). The pew connection. *American Journalism Review*, p. 25-29.

In other words...

The resolution of Watergate was an extraordinary moment in U.S. history. It was also a pivotal moment in journalism and in public life, for the initial reaffirmation quickly deteriorated into an era just as threatening to public life as had been the election of the Nixon crowd.

What should have been a plateau from which the profession moved on to even greater heights turned out to be a peak. We viewed all below us as territory ready to be subjected to a trans-mogrification, in all that word's negative aspects: the journalist as folk hero, the astute political analyst as media star. . . .

Inevitably, in the post-Watergate years journalism's toughness—put another way, its chronic cynicism—began to approach its useful limits: debate as confrontation; campaigns as horse races; compromise as caving-in; intellectual growth as waffling; reticence or lack of knowledge as cover-up; conflict as the most valued journalistic coin. In short, public life as spectacle.

Davis "Buzz" Merritt. (1995). *Public journalism & public life: Why telling the news is not enough.* **Hillsdale, NJ: Lawrence Erlbaum Associates, pp. 58, 60.**

I think before we can have a good dialogue and debate about public journalism we're going to have to do some things. Either the advocates or somebody is going to have to tell us whether public journalism is a technique, or a theory, a practice or a philosophy, a new method or a new order, an elaboration on what already exists, or a radical revolution. I think a lot of them would like to see a radical revolution, and I guess I'm prepared to join that revolution if somebody will just make it a little more clear what it is and where I'm following. I don't know if it's possible, but I think it's needed if we're going to be able to talk about it in a meaningful way.

Paul McMasters (1996, May 4). In panel discussion at Society of Professional Journalists Region 3 Convention, Macon, GA. (McMasters is First Amendment Ombudsman at the Freedom Forum and past president of the Society of Professional Journalists.)

Public journalism, whatever you may call it, isn't a formula. It's not a new color weather map. It's not what is commonly thought of as advocacy journalism. It's not nostalgic for any alleged golden age of journalism or democracy. It's not about simply giving people what they want. Rather it's a pragmatic recognition that people flooded with contextless, fragmentary, episodic, value-neutral information can't make effective work of their decision making.

Davis "Buzz" Merritt. (1994, Summer). Quoted in The emerging electronic democracy. *Nieman reports*, p. 54.

One who wishes to [increase the extent and quality of civic participation] is not merely a watchdog that barks and occasionally bites, but a public policy professional that identifies and fairly assesses the competing values and approaches to complex policy issues. None of these skills and sensibilities is completely foreign to news media operations as we now know them. But, to be successfully developed and deployed, they require a depth of ability and financial commitment that we have not yet seen from media conglomerates heavily oriented to the bottom line.

Edmund B. Lambeth. (1992, Fall). The news media and democracy. *Media Studies Journal*, 6 (4): 166-167.

(I)f journalism took the need for innovations seriously, its offerings could change as rapidly and richly as, say, those in the computer software industry. These are, after all, energetic and creative people. When competing to be first and best at a set task, they can reveal phenomenal resourcefulness and daring. The problem lies with the task that is set. Too often it amounts to being the first to detect the blood in the water around a wounded politician or being the best with a one-line summary of the events of the past week. No one who has seen a pack of journalists descend on Little Rock (during the Whitewater investigation) or watched them jostle for position at news conferences can think they are lazy or undetermined. They are merely misdirected.

If they recognized that their purpose was to give citizens the tools to participate in public life, and recognized as well that fulfilling this purpose is the only way journalism itself can survive, journalists would find it natural to change many other habits and attitudes. . . .

James Fallows. (1996). *Breaking the news: How the media undermine American democracy*. New York: Pantheon, p. 262.

McMasters and Merritt Debate the Merits of Public Journalism

Paul McMasters: The First Amendment doesn't get mentioned very much in discussions of public journalism. And I think it's at the heart of the whole discussion. Whether or not public journalism, in all of its manifestations, observes and honors the First Amendment is an important question for all of us.

And I guess that's one of the things that troubles me the most. I fear . . . that in our passion for connecting with other citizens, in our role as journalists, we blur the distinction. The citizen has a role and the journalist has a role. That's the reason those 45 words of the First Amendment carved out a special niche of all the professions for journalists. That imposes a special obligation on journalists, and that's why I get real nervous when people start saying "detachment" is a bad thing.

I don't think detachment is a bad thing between a surgeon and her patient. I don't think detachment is a bad thing between scientists and their experiments. I don't think it's a bad thing between a priest giving advice to a parishioner. I don't think it's a bad thing between a lawyer and a client. It does not mean they do not care. In fact, I think it means they care enough to back off and do their job and let the emotions come later. And I don't think it's a bad thing for a journalist to do her or his job and then back off and be a citizen in another context.

I think it's the height of citizenship to practice some distance between the subject that you're covering and what winds up in the newspapers. You want to get passionate, you want to be a good citizen, you want to make connections, do it on the editorial pages, do it with the publisher going out there and making those connections. But don't compromise your editor and reporter by putting them in a public meeting that you've convened to decide on an agenda that everybody should adopt.

Buzz Merritt: The First Amendment, to my mind, doesn't require us to be detached or attached; it doesn't require us to be truthful, it doesn't require us to be honest; it doesn't require us to be responsible. The only thing it requires us to be is to be free. And what we make out of that is another matter. Paul will probably disagree with that.

McMasters: No. I wish I'd said what you just said, Buzz, because you're absolutely right. The First Amendment does provide those protections to do just about anything we want. I don't think the public can support us or our First Amendment rights if it doesn't see us performing our special role.

Merritt: I agree with that. Absolutely. They have to see that we have value that's important to them, not just value that's important to us. . . .

I want to say a word about detachment, because I think this is a place where Paul and I probably are pretty far apart. I make a distinction between detachment and objectivity. And I'm assuming for a minute that a certain kind of journalistic objectivity does exist, that there is such a thing, and that it's a good thing (and I would agree with both of those points). That's not to me the same thing as detachment.

To use the scientific metaphor, here's where I think we'll probably disagree. Jonas Salk developed the polio vaccine. He was a scientist. And as a scientist he had to be objective with his data. He had to understand properly what the data were telling him, or else he would have reached false conclusions, and failed in what he was trying to do. Also, because he was a scientist, he had to respect the data and be objective in evaluating the data because other scientists, under the scientific protocols, had to be able to replicate what he did and to come out with the same result. That's what the scientific method is about, part of it. So he had to be objective. And he was a professional scientist, he could be objective. But he was not detached. He cared very much whether he found a polio vaccine. He didn't just go into the lab one day and say, "Well, I wonder what I can find today and if it might be of some help to somebody." He went in there to look for a specific thing. He was not detached from his ultimate goal.

And that's the distinction I make between detachment and objectivity. I say that public journalism includes objectivity insofar as journalistic objectivity can exist, but that as journalists we do need to care about whether public life goes well. That does not mean our dictating how it ought to go or how we ought to get there. But the fundamental of public life is that it's public, and that people are engaged in it, and so it's our job as journalists to do our job in ways that reengage people in public life, so they can make decisions about what's going on.

Paul McMasters, & Davis "Buzz" Merritt. (1996, May 4). In panel discussion at Society of Professional Journalists Region 3 Convention, Macon, GA. (McMasters is First Amendment Ombudsman at the Freedom Forum and past president of the Society of Professional Journalists; Merritt is editor and senior vice president of the Wichita (KS) Eagle.)

Communitarian and Environmental Journalism

Lee Wilkins
University of Missouri

Twentieth-century journalism has its roots in the assumptions and frameworks of the enlightenment. But as critics from Herbert Marcuse and the Frankfurt School, to rhetoricians such as Kathleen Hall Jamieson (1992), and working journalists such as E. J. Dionne (1991) have asserted that enlightenment foundation is the root of many of the contemporary profession's problems, as well as its successes.

In their book *Good News*, Christians *et al.* (1993) suggested communitarianism as the next appropriate philosophical base for journalism in the 20th century. Although the authors posit their communitarian alternative as a part of a journalistic dialectic, it is just as appropriate to place the philosophical movement in a psychological and developmental perspective. If one conceptualizes modern democracy as the historical expansion of rights to increasingly large numbers of people (Burns & Burns, 1991), then as that movement culminates, those people who now have rights become preoccupied with other questions.

Developmental psychologist Abraham Maslow (1954), in his hierarchy of human needs, made much the same point about individual development. As people fulfill their physical needs and needs for security, other needs begin to emerge. Maslow characterized the next level of needs as the need for belongingness—or the need to function first as a part of an intimate group and then as part of more distal associations. Other developmental psychologists, in different language, have noted much the same phenomenon. As people become more sure of who they are as individuals, they discover that part of successful individual functioning is a successful effort at living together. It is an effort at creating and maintaining connections.

Some communitarian philosophers have been reluctant to link conceptions of community with human psychological development. Yet, in spite of this reluctance, the rhetoric of one of the movement's leaders, Amitai Etzioni (1993), made this point. Communities begin, and sometimes end, with families. But they are essential to who we are as people.

Later, as we mature, we hone our individualized version out of the social values that have been transmitted to us. As a rule, though, these are variations on community-formed themes. Thus, many Americans are more socially concerned and active than other nationalities, not because of differences in genes or basic human nature, but because social concern and activism are major elements of this country's moral tradition. If we were living instead in traditional Korea, the same energy would be dedicated to, say ensuring that we conducted ourselves properly toward numerous relatives. That is, the mainspring of our values is the community or communities into which we are born, that educated us (or neglected to educate us), and in which we seek to become respectable members during our adult lives. (p. 31)

Whether one asserts that community arises from some element that is basic human nature, or whether one prefers a more strictly intellectual and philosophical genesis, the result, in ethical terms, is the same. "In communitarianism, persons have certain inescapable claims on one another that cannot be renounced except at the cost of their humanity" (Christians *et al.*, 1993, p. 14). Political theorists such as Davies (1963) and Burns (1971) have noted that this human capacity for, and sometimes need of, community can help explain a great deal about certain sorts of political activity—from revolution to more traditional forms of political behavior.

Christians *et al.* (1993) suggested that community precedes individuality. And, in a purely biological sense, nothing could be more correct. People are part of a group—in utero—before they are born. But, once we emerge from the womb, at least if the fields of developmental psychology and political psychology are correct, human beings spend a great deal of time learning to balance the twin pulls of connection and control. As Carol Gilligan (1982) has noted, control speaks the language of rights, connection the language of responsibilities.

> " Once we emerge from the womb, at least if the fields of developmental psychology and political psychology are correct, human beings spend a great deal of time learning to balance the twin pulls of connection and control. "

The political questions that have preoccupied democratic societies (and still preoccupy the emerging democracies of the former Soviet Union and Eastern and Central Europe) evolve around the issues of control: Who shall be the government, how shall laws be enacted and enforced, what are the boundaries between individual acts and government oversight? Enlightenment philosophy, with its focus on the individual and on the role of the modern state, is well-equipped to help societies find answers to these sets of questions. Traditional democratic theory, beginning with Hobbes and continuing at least through Rousseau, has focused on this set of questions, reflected on them, and suggested answers that have been adopted in a variety of nations since about 1500. Adoption, however, is not equated with perfection. It suggests instead that culturally and historically bounded answers to these political questions have allowed societies to develop to the point where other questions can begin to surface.

Contemporary democracies, having found several sets of answers to the nested questions of rights, have shifted their focus from the granting of rights to the admittedly imperfect allocation of them. In large part, this shift in focus has emerged from the 20th-century work of governing, although there are no clear historical antecedents, such as the role of government in the common defense or Lincoln's analysis of the virtues of union. Democratic culture, particularly in the United States and in Scandinavia, has begun to focus on questions of justice: the outcome of apportionment of rights within a society. Attention to justice, however, demands a different quality of analysis. It must focus on society as a whole. Unlike a Marxist analysis, which asserts that society's constituent groups cannot ever hope to agree, communitarianism asserts that collective thinking, because it is as much a part of human beings as individualistic thinking, is possible. In a political-psychological sense, the nurture of community—the fulfilling of the need for belongingness on both an individual and society level (Davies, 1963)—represents the next step in both individual and societal political development.

The intellectual institutions that support the more practical ones also must seek a different balance. As Westin (1992) has noted, part of contemporary philosophy's problem with issues such as abortion and the environment is that it seeks to apply an ethical language of prioritizing the rights of various stakeholders when what is more appropriately called for is a discussion about the connections between and among values and groups that such practical ethical problems raise. By focusing on connecting values rather than prioritizing rights, Westin asserts that it is possible to recast the debate on certain practical ethical problems in alternative frameworks that, instead of dividing stakeholder groups and apportioning "wins" and "losses" among them, seek to build both community and consensus: "Here the pragmatic impulse is to integrate, interweave, and combine values, seeing the 'conflict' of values as an occasion to work out better forms of coexistence rather than to elevate one set of values over another" (p. 29). This emphasis on the need for connection—to both intellectual ideals and to the people who represent them—owes much to feminist thinking, particularly the developmental work of scholars such as Gilligan (1982). However, it is crucial to note that this emphasis on connection and values also is grounded in more than 500 years of debate about the role of the state and of politics in human affairs. Connections have always been with us. But in our intellectual and rhetorical preoccupations with rights, contemporary thinkers too often fail to acknowledge that rights are merely a means to an end: the creation and maintenance of civil society.

> **In our intellectual and rhetorical preoccupations with rights, contemporary thinkers too often fail to acknowledge that rights are merely a means to an end: the creation and maintenance of civil society.**

In order to operationalize the possible, society's institutions need to become more focused on questions of connections and justice and less focused on questions of rights. This change represents a shift in degree rather than an abandonment of one particular set of questions. Journalism, as one of society's major institutions, must follow suit. "Nurturing communitarian citizenship entails, at a minimum, a journalism committed to justice, covenant, and empowerment. Authentic communities are marked by justice; in strong democracies, courageous talk is mobilized into action" (Christians *et al.*, 1993, p. 14). Philosopher Jurgen Habermas made much the same point when he asserted social order and social action were made possible through communicative action in the public sphere (Baynes, 1992). Habermas based his model of communicative action on "the culturally transmitted and linguistically organized stock of interpretive patterns" (p. 82). He theorized that people did political work through communicating about their unique mental vision of reality with their fellows.

This chapter attempts to operationalize the philosophical shift communitarianism and Christians *et al.* (1993) demand. It asserts that while some traditional political questions remain permeable to the thought processes and rhetoric of the Enlightenment's focus on rights, others demand a different sort of thinking. Environmental journalism, because it must consider issues of community and collectivity as well as more traditional political concerns such as the granting and preservations of rights, provides an ideal base from which to operationalize a communitarian world view in a real professional setting. Further, by thinking of communitarianism as an expected developmental outcome of Enlightenment thinking, environmental reporters can retain and do their jobs in a profession that will move more slowly on this philosophical issue than will satisfy many academics.

This chapter first outlines the central philosophical frame that traditional environmental coverage employs. *Framing*, as the term has been adopted in mass communication research, is shorthand for the consistent pattern of journalistic selection and emphasis of particular features in various stories:

> To frame is to select some aspects of a perceived reality and make them more salient in a communication text, in such a way as to promote a particular problem definition, causal interpretation, moral evaluation and/or treatment recommendation for the item described. (Entman, 1989, p. 52)

Further, journalists often select various frames unconsciously, either as a process of routinization of the unexpected (Tuchman, 1978) or as the result of various psychological processes (Stocking & Gross, 1989). This chapter then suggests alternate frames, founded in a more communitarian world view, that environmental journalists also could employ. It concludes with a projected application of this new framework to a real-world environmental problem: the long-term storage of high-level radioactive waste.

The Environment As a Collective Tragedy

NBC's February 5, 1990, account of former President George Bush's response to global warming is typical of many environmental stories. Bush was characterized as having to respond to dramatically opposing demands. "George Bush the environmental president ran into strong opposition today from George Bush the champion of free enterprise," broadcaster John Cochran began his news report. Even though Bush was speaking to an audience primarily of scientists, the media framed Bush's speech as an uneasy truce between economic development and environmental protection. Then, two scientists who wanted Bush to take more direct and emphatic action were quoted. They were supported in their on-camera appearance by former Colorado Senator Tim Wirth, who said: "Well, we haven't seen any White House effect. We used to get a whitewash effect, now we just sort of get a timid effect." Cochran also noted that Bush's speech appeared to contradict his public stands in the 1988 presidential election campaign. The story closed with a statement that Bush's words were not enough to reassure environmental interests.

The NBC report is fairly typical of media coverage of the environment and science (see, i.e., Singer & Endreny, 1993; Wilkins & Patterson, 1991). The story was framed to emphasize political drama and contradiction, the apparent inability of large institutions to respond, and meaning couched only in expert statements. In many environmental news stories, humanity seeks to control or act on the natural world. Political officials, and to a lesser degree scientists, are the arbiters of those actions. Policy choices are seldom outlined. The news values emphasize conflict, competition, insoluble problems often grounded in competing claims about rights, and institutional power.

> **The tragedy of the commons suggests that people will act in such a way that rights will always trump responsibilities when collective goods are involved.**

Although it is never specifically mentioned, environmental stories such as this NBC report reflect a philosophical understanding: *the tragedy of the commons.* This political concept asserts that people and institutions will promote self-interest to the extent that collective goods—such as lower crime rates or environmental preservation—always will receive less political attention (Hardin, 1968). The tragedy of the commons asserts that when collective societal goods are at issue, political and interpersonal systems are unable to respond because individual actors (including institutions) are motivated to act only out of narrowly defined and immediate self-interest. It is a system in which history, communication, and connection play a secondary role to individual autonomy, self-interest, and rights.

In philosophical terms, the tragedy of the commons suggests that people will act in such a way that rights will always trump responsibilities when collective goods are involved. The tragedy of the commons reflects an Enlightenment world view in which political institutions are structured to decide and adjudicate differing claims about individual rights. In this structure, the community itself has little political voice.

Alternative Values for Environmental News

Gans' (1979) outline of *values in the news* is one of the most influential in mass communication. Emerging as it did from the 1960s and from the discipline of sociology, Gans' discussion of moral-disorder news and of the eight enduring values in the news—responsible capitalism, small-town pastoralism, ethnocentrism, altruistic democracy, individualism, moderatism, leadership, and social order—has been widely cited and applied to a variety of news stories, including environmental news.

Gans used the word *values* to illustrate how journalists frame specific stories, and he did not address any underlying philosophical or ethical issues his use of the term raised. His call for multiperspective news also focused primarily on the issue of sources and story content rather than on addressing the thematic and ethical content of news accounts. Gans' description of values in the news is Enlightenment-centered, reflecting a journalistic reality that draws from the same philosophical base.

Scholars in different disciplines, however, note other values emerging in American culture at about the same time Gans (1979) was writing. Environmental historian Samuel Hays (1987), in fact, has characterized the post-World War II environmental movement by the emergence of three central values that have defined how citizens and politicians have come to view the environment.

As the country became more affluent, its citizens and government became concerned with *health*. Out of this concern arose governmental entities such as the Environmental Protection Agency, the clean air and water acts, and a plethora of state and local agencies with similar caches. Indeed, the health issue has dominated many environmental debates, as the works of Krimsky and Plough (1988) and Singer and Endreny (1993) suggest.

As the country became more suburban, citizens became more concerned with *beauty*. This concern, which certainly predates World War II on the East Coast, was also the result of the suburban lifestyle, where newly affluent and mobile residents wanted someplace to travel to on the weekends. They visited the natural environment, and the development of state and national parks as well as many preservation movements—including those that populated the natural world with animals—owe at least some debt to the impetus of beauty.

The same suburban population, working sometimes with government, sometimes with industry, and sometimes in opposition of both institutions, sought a *permanence* in the natural landscape. The American wilderness movement, which does not have a ready parallel in any other developed country, and a host of environmental preservation organizations, responded to this value. In one interpretation of the value of permanence, individual citizens merely wanted to ensure themselves and their children of a continuing place to visit. In other interpretations, permanence reflected a concern with questions such as preservation of the planet's gene pool or preservation of a continuing resource base to be exploited in various ways. The value of permanence allowed a wide array of interpretations, but it was a value nonetheless.

These three values have minor areas of overlap with those Gans (1979) suggests. For instance, the value of beauty remains connected to a pastoral setting and an escape from urban life in the American psyche. However, the other values outlined do not find as ready a parallel in Gans' work. More importantly, beauty, health, and permanence all involve issues of community and connection. Beauty and permanence, for example, are collective goods. Debate in the United States over the establishment first of a national wilderness act and then of various wilderness areas focuses on the question of preservation of a collective good in the face of individual property rights. In such a debate, the language of responsibility is placed on a more equal footing with the language of rights.

The same can be said for discussion of recent environmental regulations such as the clean air and water acts as well as the adoption of community right-to-know acts. Specifically, community right-to-know acts attempt to find a way to place individual geographical communities on an equal footing with business and industry, even over issues such as proprietary information. Although the legislation itself is framed in terms of "rights" talk, the events that spurned it, for example the role of industry in the Bhopal chemical disasters, are also laced with discussion of responsibility (Wilkins, 1987). In legislative form, community right-to-know acts raise issues of justice as well as those rights; they acknowledge a debt to community as well as to the individual.

While historians can provide applied ethicists with a post hoc understanding of emerging cultural values—and their link to a more communitarian world view—environmental scientists also have promoted an understanding that emphasizes community. Aldo Leopold (1949) provided one of the earliest and best articulations of this sense of community:

> An ethic, ecologically, is a limitation on freedom of action in the struggle for existence. An ethic, philosophically, is a differentiation of social from anti-social conduct. These are two definitions of one thing. The thing has its origin in the tendency of interdependent individuals or groups to evolve modes of cooperation. The ecologist calls these symbiosis. Politics and economics are advanced symbioses in which the original free-for-all competition has been replaced, in part, by cooperative mechanisms with an ethical content. . . . Obligations have no meaning without conscience, and the prob-

lem we face is the extension of the social conscience from people to land. . . . A land ethic, then, reflects the existence of an ecological conscience, and this in turn reflects a conviction of individual responsibility for the health of the land. Health is the capacity of the land for self-renewal. Conservation is our effort to understand and preserve this capacity. . . . A thing is right when it tends to preserve the integrity, stability, and beauty of the biotic community. It is wrong when it tends otherwise. (pp. 238-261)

Leopold's vision, although it was written before *communitarianism* was coined, shares significant elements of communitarian thinking. Leopold's land ethic is *holistic* and focuses on obligations (responsibilities) as well as rights. Perhaps most importantly, Leopold's conceptualization links politics, economics, humanity, and the natural world in a way that is essential for environmental literacy (Orr, 1991). The balance among these competing biological, political, and social interests may be considered a precursor to discussions about justice. Leopold's land ethic is not best-served, he argued, by a discussion of rights without an acknowledgment that rights have limits, particularly when the natural world is involved.

The land ethic also highlights the concept of *cooperation*, with an admittedly biological slant. The biological components of ecosystems must rely on each other—cooperate—for the entire system to continue to function. But human beings can cooperate with each other as well; cooperation is one of the essential ingredients of community. Political scientist Robert Axelrod (1984), in his effort to understand winning strategies in computer games, learned that the simple strategy of tit-for-tat, in which the initial move was always cooperative but in which subsequent moves depended on the responses of others, was most successful. Cooperative players developed robust communities that consistently won the game. Axelrod's experimental work provides a mathematical proof that the tragedy of the commons is not inevitable when a collective good (two players amassing the maximum number of points) is at issue. The tragedy of the commons is only one possible outcome; cooperation is another. The key to cooperation, Axelrod learned, was clear communication between players and the ability of different players to learn—or acquire a historical sense—of the results of a variety of moves.

The combination of an emphasis on permanence, Leopold's (1949) vision of a land ethic, and Axelrod's (1984) experimental work, all suggest that environmental values include consideration of the future in decision-making. Speculation about future impacts—or consequences—has always been involved in thinking about justice in a philosophical sense, beginning with Mill's utilitarianism and continuing through Rawls' (1971) theory of justice and Jonas' (1984) more recent work. Communitarian philosophers have suggested much the same thing: that the continuance of a community demands an acknowledgment that the future is important in political and social decision making. As Etzioni (1993) noted:

> Our commitment to a shared future, especially our responsibility to a shared environment, is a case in point. We are to care for the environment not only or even mainly for our own sakes (although we may desire some assurance of potable water, breathable air, and protection from frying because the ozone layer is thinning out). We have a moral commitment to leave for future generations a livable environment, even perhaps a better one than the one we inherited, certainly not one that has been further depleted. (pp. 10-11)

While these insights have emerged from different disciplines, some of them post hoc and without thorough philosophical grounding, the values emerging from work on the environment do share much with the communitarian point of view. Further, just as Gans' (1979) Enlightenment-oriented values in the news were of practical use to journalists, the values of health, beauty, permanence, responsibility to the whole, cooperation, and analyzing long-term consequences can provide an alternate value frame for journalists covering environmental issues. That alternate frame, further, is one that reflects in quite specific ways communitarian—as opposed to Enlightenment—thinking. It is a practical framework that operationalizes communitarianism. It is also central to note that these values work in tandem—they are themselves connected.

> **Just as Gans' Enlightenment-oriented values in the news were of practical use to journalists, the values of health, beauty, permanence, responsibility to the whole, cooperation, and analyzing long-term consequences can provide an alternate value frame for journalists covering environmental issues.**

The role of the alternative framework in environmental stories would not be to determine which of the values should predominate—as rights-based thinking would suggest—but rather to give voice to a variety of values, thereby helping to create alternative visions for a community of interests. Environmental journalism that employs such a frame would of necessity forsake some of the drama of conflict for the drama of community-building and synergy.

What follows is some discussion of how this alternative framework could be employed in covering one of the more significant environmental issues of the early 21st century.

Covering the Cleanup

Storing high-level nuclear waste is an environmental problem with its roots in the Manhattan Project, more than 50 years ago. At a time when it was necessary to win a war, and when the country knew little about the implications of anything nuclear, a series of policy decisions were made that began the Cold War—and hence generated dangerous waste—and the nation's initial experimentation with nuclear power generation. Then, neither nuclear power nor nuclear bombs production was considered an environmental issue, although a few people and even fewer organized groups raised questions about the long-term issue of waste disposal.

In the ensuing two decades, the nation learned much about things nuclear. Among the most salient facts learned are that even minute quantities of some kinds of high-level waste—for example, plutonium—are deadly for 50,000 to 240,000 years; that nuclear power plants have a long but limited life expectancy; and that disposal of high-level nuclear waste was going to be expensive both financially and politically.

By the end of the 1970s, and particularly after the Three Mile Island incident, disposing of nuclear power-plant waste—and to a less-discussed extent, the waste from the nation's nuclear arsenal—had become a signal environmental issue. Based on current technology, the waste represented an expensive collective good that no single group in society wanted.

Beginning in the late 1970s, Congress began the nuclear-waste siting process—a political process that was designed to find technical solutions to the difficult and complex scientific questions raised by storing high-level waste until it becomes less toxic (about 20,000 to 25,000 years, depending on the elements involved) and the no-less-difficult political questions of devising a process for placing the waste somewhere in the United States.

By 1987, three potential storage sites were proposed in different parts of the United States. In that year, President Ronald Reagan proposed and Congress passed a law that designated Yucca Mountain, Nevada, as the nation's high-level nuclear-waste site. Yucca Mountain is across a state highway from a nuclear testing range, the site of both above-ground and underground atomic bomb testing. It is about 100 miles north of Las

Vegas, in a state with relatively few electoral votes, and in a region of the country—the West—where the federal government already owns and controls a great deal of land.

All of this, of course, has been news, although it has been only recently that the "story" of Yucca Mountain—its location, the debate over science involved in creating a cavern to store high-level waste, and the potential interaction of so much radioactive waste confined to a relatively small area, the expense that the taxpayers, more than $1 million per day and $4.2 billion in total, all do the necessary work to see whether Yucca Mountain can become the first deliberately created nuclear waste dump—has received more than sporadic national attention.

It is self-evident that Yucca Mountain, and the issue of how the country plans to dispose of high-level nuclear waste generated by atomic bomb production and by spent nuclear fuel, will continue to be an important news story well into the next century. Contemporary coverage has focused on the expense of the project, the apparent political dilemma that confronts Congress as well as

> **By recognizing more than one sort of authority in dealing with the future, and by framing similar questions to all stakeholder groups, journalists could aid the process of equalizing the power differential between stakeholder groups, which contemporary journalism only seems to reinforce.**

local governments at several levels, and the emergent science of nuclear-waste storage. All are newsworthy. But a communitarian definition of news might well uncover angles that traditional journalism has not.

First, the Yucca Mountain story should prompt journalists to cover the future as well as the present (Wilkins, 1990). Few stories have as prominent a link to the future, and to the environmental value of permanence, as does storing high-level nuclear waste. Journalists using a communitarian frame could and should investigate such questions as long-term costs for taxpayers and for other stakeholders such as utility companies, long-term implications for land-use planning and economic health for the state of Nevada, and long-term implications for people living in the area.

Further, these stories would tend to be differently sourced from more traditional news stories. Journalists employing a communitarian frame could be expected to ask and accept as authoritative not only traditional sources such as government and business officials, but also ordinary people who would have to deal with long-term consequences in their daily lives and in the lives of their children. By recognizing more than one sort of authority in dealing with the future, and by framing similar questions to all stakeholder groups, journalists could aid the process of equalizing the power differential between stakeholder groups, which contemporary journalism only seems to reinforce.

Addressing the environmental value of permanence also would allow journalists to ask critical questions of scientific expertise involved in the project—such as those asked recently by scientists who suggested that the storage of so much high-level waste in such a small area could lead to potentially lethal chemical reactions. It also would allow journalists to ask policy makers how they have explored the potential impacts of technological changes on the waste repository in the relatively near-term future of the facility—the next 200 to 500 years. Both such stories would allow journalists and their readers and viewers to develop a more contextually rich and holistic understanding of both the problem of long-term storage as well as the implications of a variety of potential solutions. Different points of view from those currently covered by journalists also would be incorporated into such stories.

Using the environmental values of health and beauty, journalists also could explore the impact of high-level storage on the land itself. Nevada residents have a stake in their landscape in a sense that Leopold (1949) would have understood. Using a communitarian frame allows journalists to exploit another professional dictum: Localize the national. By exploring the impact on the land, journalists would be able to localize the Yucca Mountain story to many other regions of the country, particularly those where waste is temporarily stored at operating nuclear power plants or at repositories such as the Hanford, Washington, nuclear reservation.

Just as journalists would be able to localize this national story, so would they be able to cover health issues, such as radiation exposure, which has received relatively little notice regarding high-level waste storage, but has been extensively covered in other areas—for example, in the treatment of some cancers.

But it is in focusing on the issue of cooperation that journalists, through the response of the viewers and readers, stand to contribute to the long-term health of the body politic. Covering Yucca Mountain as an issue that demands cooperation, and seeking out comment and insight from a variety of sources on the origins and impact of cooperation, could significantly help both decision makers and their constituents reframe this environmental Gordian knot. An emphasis on cooperation, for example, would help local political decision makers view the repository as not just an imposition on the state of Nevada, but rather as a collective problem in need of a solution. Exploration, in the form of news stories and policy discussions, of alternatives such as high-level waste reprocessing requires a cooperative rather than conflict-oriented approach (Nuclear Waste Technical Review Board, personal communication,[1] May 23-24, 1995). But the goal of such coverage would be to expand both understanding of the issue and the potential policy debates surrounding the question, and to empower the stakeholders in a process that is clearly going to affect those living now, as well those living in the millennia to come.

Conclusions: An Addition, Not a Subtraction

Westin (1992), in his discussion of the impact of pragmatic thinking of ethical theory and reasoning, suggested that one reason to employ a pragmatic framework when doing ethics is because it allows autonomous moral actors to employ multiple values in doing ethical reasoning, rather than to attempt to find the single value or rule that supplants all others. What Westin calls for is a process of ethical negotiation rather than rule development and adherence. "Ethical thinking ought to move him beyond insistence on all-or-nothing choices and all-or-nothing principles" (p. 33).

Communitarian journalism requires much the same effort. It seeks to expand the sort of values that journalists can bring to bear in their work, and to employ those values in the widest variety of ways—from the questions asked to the sources interviewed. The assertion is not that communitarian thinking should supplant the traditional journalistic approach in all cases, but rather that, in some issues, a communitarian world view is much more likely to produce high-quality professional work than a more Enlightenment-centered approach. This chapter has tried to suggest specific ways in which communitarian thinking could improve and enrich the coverage of environmental issues, particularly in contrast to contemporary coverage.

In adopting a communitarian stance, the ethical journalists must seek to emulate the sort of ethical reasoning Gilligan (1982) proposes for the highest level of moral development. Ethical journalists must learn to cover stories speaking the language of two sets of values—the Enlightenment values of rights and roles and the communitarian values of connection and responsibility. Only through speaking these two moral languages can contemporary journalism fulfill its political mission, one means to the end of democratic governance.

Notes ───

[1] The author was a panel member consulted by the board on the question of whether risk perception should be integrated into the requirements for developing an environmental impact statement about—and ultimately making a siting decision on—Yucca Mountain.

References ────────────────────────────────────

Axelrod, R. (1984). *The evolution of cooperation.* New York: Basic Books.

Baynes, K. (1992). *The normative grounds of social criticism.* Albany: State University of New York Press.

Burns, J. M., & Burns, S. (1991). *A people's charter: The pursuit of rights in America.* New York: Knopf.

Burns, J. M. (1971). *Leadership.* New York: Knopf.

Christians, C., Ferré, J. P., & Fackler, P. M. (1993). *Good news: Social ethics and the press.* New York: Oxford University Press.

Davies, J. C. (1963). *Human nature in politics.* New York: Wiley & Sons.

Dionne, E. J. (1991). *Why Americans hate politics.* New York: Simon & Schuster.

Entman, R. (1989). *Democracy without citizens.* New York: Oxford University Press.

Etzioni, A. (1993). *The spirit of community: Rights, responsibilities, and the communitarian agenda.* New York: Crown Publishers Inc.

Gans, H. (1979). *Deciding what's news.* New York: Vintage Press.

Gilligan, C. (1982). *In a different voice: Psychological theory and women's development.* Cambridge, MA: Harvard University Press.

Hardin, G. (1968). The tragedy of the commons. *Science, 162,* 1243-1248.

Hays, S. (1987). *Beauty, health, and permanence: Environmental politics in the United States, 1955-1985.* New York: Cambridge University Press.

Jamieson, K. H. (1992). *Dirty politics.* New York: Oxford University Press.

Jonas, H. (1984). *The imperative of responsibility: The search for an ethics in a technological age.* Chicago: University of Chicago Press.

Krimsky, S., & Plough, A. (1988). *Environmental hazards: Communicating risks as social process.* Dover, MA: Auburn House.

Leopold, A. (1949). *A Sand County almanac.* New York: Oxford University Press.

Maslow, A. H. (1954). *Motivation and personality.* New York: Harper and Row.

Orr, D. (1991). *Environmental literacy.* Bloomington: Indiana University Press.

Rawls, J. (1971). *A theory of justice.* Cambridge, MA: Harvard University Press.

Singer, E., & Endreny, P. (1993). *Reporting on risk.* New York: Russell Sage Foundation.

Stocking, H. S., & Gross, P. H. (1989). *How do journalists think? A proposal for the study of cognitive bias in newsmaking.* Bloomington, IN: ERIC Clearinghouse.

Tuchman, G. (1978). *Making news.* New York: Free Press.

Westin, A. (1992). *Toward better problems.* Philadelphia: Temple University Press.

Wilkins, L. (1987). *Shared vulnerability: The media and American perceptions of the Bhopal disaster.* Westport, CT: Greenwood Press.

Wilkins, L. (1990). Taking the future seriously. *Journal of Mass Media Ethics, 5*(2), 88-101.

Wilkins, L., & Patterson, P. (1991). *Risky business: Communicating about science, risk, & public policy.* Westport, CT: Greenwood Press.

In other words...

The creativity and ideas are not coming from young people, they're coming from veterans who have seen the failings of traditional journalism and American democracy.

Frank Denton, editor of the *Wisconsin State Journal*. (1994, September), quoted in *Presstime*, p. 30.

The voices in American journalism for too long have been too monotone and monochromatic, coming most often from white male authority figures. The language of journalism has the flexibility to be more inclusive if journalists will expand their reporting strategies and let the voices of the young and the poor and the old be heard. I agree here with Jay Rosen. A goal of journalism must be to improve the nature of public conversation on issues of concern, to define problems, sharpen arguments, and seek common ground. The adaptation of traditional forms (such as oral history) and the creation of news ones (edited transcripts of town meetings) will model modes of public discourse that will revitalize democratic feelings and impulses.

Roy Peter Clark. (1995, Spring), in *The American conversation and the language of journalism*, quoted in Nieman Reports, p. 34.

The first question a reporter ought to ask himself or herself when writing a story isn't "What goes in the lead?" but "What are the values that ought to guide this story?" Does this way of telling the story promote democratic talk, or work against it? Is this what's really at stake to John and Jane Doe, or not? A good reporter should be as intimately conversant with the public's values on crack [cocaine] (or any other issue) as with the crime and medical statistics, the police, or the leaders of the community. Any reporter who fails to see this isn't "telling the story as it is"; he or she is allowing the values for which thinking to be chosen by default.

Arthur Charity. (1995). *Doing public journalism*. New York: Guilford, p. 59.

A popular reportorial device—thought to engage readers and make the news personal to them—is to sort out "winners" from "losers." ... The journalistic notion is that it is a service to citizens because each can quickly decide whether he or she "won" or "lost."

Actually, that approach is a disservice. It is a disservice to citizens because it vastly oversimplifies a complex situation. It assumes citizens are one-dimensional in their interests, and encourages them to be so. Even more distressingly, it is a disservice to the essential democratic values of consent and compromise. It sends the message that the process of deliberation will inevitably make some people "winners" and some "losers" when, in fact, the nature of consent is that trade-offs are made at many levels and "wins" and "losses" are not clear cut. The overriding consideration is whether the process of consent has produced something that ultimately will be good for the society.

Journalists can do something about that destructive habit—both the political system's and journalists' own. We can help citizens become a public by helping them see things from a public point of view, but journalists cannot do that from our own cultural perspective of aloofness if we do not ourselves see things from a public point of view.

Davis "Buzz" Merritt. (1995). *Public journalism & public life: Why telling the news is not enough.* **Hillsdale, NJ: Lawrence Erlbaum Associates, p. 100.**

Journalists are professionally uncomfortable in the world of values, where most ordinary people live. There is no journalistic vocabulary or protocol for dealing with values, and the carefully maintained culture of distance makes the development of one difficult, if not impossible.

Davis "Buzz" Merritt. (1995). *Public journalism & public life: Why telling the news is not enough.* **Hillsdale, NJ: Lawrence Erlbaum Associates, pp. 102-103.**

(T)he goal of traditional journalism is to remain properly detached, whereas the goal of public journalism is to become properly attached.

Davis "Buzz" Merritt. (1995). *Public journalism & public life: Why telling the news is not enough.* **Hillsdale, NJ: Lawrence Erlbaum Associates, p. 117.**

Public journalism tries to put "what matters to citizens," "the choices the community faces," and "the discussions that need to occur" in place of "what political professionals are telling and selling" and "who's up and who's down."

Jay Rosen. (1994). Public journalism: First principles, in Jay Rosen & Davis Merritt, Jr. *Public journalism: Theory and practice.* Dayton, Ohio: Kettering Foundation, p. 16.

The Problem of Compassionate Journalism

Deni Elliott
University of Montana

Like Mom and apple pie, no one can find fault with the ideal of compassion. But, if compassion involves acting in the interest of a particular individual in need, compassion is an ideal only for individuals who are working on their own time. Acting in the interest of particular individuals in need is not morally acceptable for a social institution or for an agent working on behalf of a social institution.

Here I will discuss how compassionate action on behalf of particular individuals creates ethical problems for the social institution of journalism and how that action can keep news organizations from delivering the news.

Moral Responsibility Defined

What it means for one to act in a morally responsible way is that the person or institution meets the minimalistic moral dictate: "Do your job and don't cause unjustified harm." This dictate threads through the major Western moral theories regardless of their subtle distinctions; it also binds major moral traditions of the East and West.

"Do your job" means one should meet all role-related responsibilities. Every legitimate role carries with it definable responsibilities and privileges. This is true for formal professional roles such as journalist, professor, or lawyer. The journalist has the special role of providing citizens with information they need to know for self governance; the professor has the special role of teaching thinking skills and a body of knowledge to postsecondary students; the lawyer has the special role of serving as a knowledgeable advocate for individuals who encounter the judicial system. The special privileges of journalists include being able to ask questions of individuals that would be, by convention, out of line if others asked the same question; the professor can judge the quality of students' work and can significantly impact students' lives through evaluation; the lawyer can keep secrets on behalf of the client that would be illegal for others to keep.

"Do your job" also means that one should meet all role-related responsibilities within informal, non-professional roles, such as parent, life's partner, friend, student, or citizen. "Do your job" is some of what is found in the deontological precept that morality is based on one's intentionally acting out of a sense of duty.

The second half of the moral dictate required for minimal moral responsibility, "Don't cause unjustified harm," is consistent with the deontological moral tradition as well in that when harm is caused, it can often be justified that one acted as one's duty required. The law enforcement officer who causes pain to a suspect and deprives him of freedom through a legitimate arrest is undoubtedly doing the right thing from a perspective of duty ethics.

The consequentialist would not disagree about the correctness of the law enforcement officer's actions. The officer has acted in a way that promotes social utility. As long as the principles of justice were upheld—the suspect has been awarded due process—then the arrest, while harmful to the individual, is consistent with acting in regard for the greatest good for the greatest number.

The moral dictate, "Do your job and don't cause unjustified harm," is also consistent with virtue ethics. Of course, virtue ethics would expect more than this minimalist morality. But, a good person doing well, from a virtuous perspective, would, at least, be morally required to meet his or her moral responsibilities and do so in a way that did not impinge on others in an unjustified way.

This statement of basic moral responsibility is also in line with Eastern philosophies. The sense of persons acting appropriately when they are acting in harmony with self, the spirit, and nature (a basic tenet of Buddhism), fulfills their mission in the world (do your job) and does so in a way that keeps forces in harmony (does not cause unjustified harm).

From an examination of the moral dictate within virtue and Eastern theories it becomes clear that one may, and often should, do more than that which is dictated by minimalist morality. Doing more makes a person morally praiseworthy. But, persons are morally blameworthy if they fail to meet their moral responsibilities. They are morally blameworthy if they fail to do this, regardless of the good things that they may be doing in addition.

The Moral Dictate Applied to Journalism

The job of the journalist in democratic societies is to tell people what they need to know so that they can participate in self-governance. Some justified harm is necessarily caused by journalists doing their jobs. People—including innocent people—are harmed when journalists expose corrupt public officials. But this harm caused is justified by the citizens' need to know important information about their government. However, harm caused becomes less justified the further the story is from the job of journalists. For example, a feature story on how a child genius fared as an adult may well cause harm if the publicity is unwanted. This harm cannot be justified by appeal to the social mission—the job—of journalism. Citizens do not have a need to know the fate of a private individual, except in extraordinary circumstances. The harm, in that case, is unjustified.

> **Compassionate reporting results in unjustified harm when news organizations participate in the same kind of institutional unfairness they are often seeking to expose.**

Unjustified harm can also be caused when a news organization promotes the cause of an individual in need. The harm is caused to others in like situations who cannot get like assistance. The harm is also caused to the consumers of news. Compassionate reporting results in unjustified harm when news organizations participate in the same kind of institutional unfairness they are often seeking to expose. Consumers are harmed—indeed deceived—when they are led to believe that such cases of need are extraordinary; citizens are harmed when they are given dramatic stories of individual distress rather than the stories that could lead to changes in public policy. In this respect, compassion gets in the way of journalists doing their jobs.

Examples of Compassionate Reporting

A cute, White, 6-year-old girl from the suburbs of Portland, Maine, Norma Lynn Peterson, was introduced to the community as she prepared for a fund-raising potluck supper on her behalf (Elliott *et al.*, 1991). Norma Lynn needed a liver transplant; she was on the list as a candidate at the Pittsburgh transplant center. Relatively speaking, she was in pretty good shape.

As a result of coverage by the three network affiliates and the newspaper, the Portland community opened its hearts and checkbooks to Norma Lynn. Five months after the initial coverage, Norma Lynn had a new liver, more than $100,000 in private donations, free air ambulance service to and from Pittsburgh, a camcorder, and a purebred puppy.

A Dartmouth biology professor, Cristopher Reed, needed a bone marrow transplant to combat leukemia. News media were quick to respond with front page and top of the hour stories about the popular professor's desperate search for an unrelated donor. Several hundred people showed up to be tested for the possibility that their marrow might match that of the sick professor, each with the $75 in hand that the commercial marrow bank required to check for a suitable match. No local match was found for Christopher Reed, who soon died from his illness, but the marrow bank had hundreds of new potential donors to add to its computer list.

The Burlington (VT) *Free Press* covered the story of Sue Jackman, a vivacious 30-year-old wife and mother who needed a bone marrow transplant to combat breast cancer (Elliott *et al.*, 1991). Finding a donor was no problem in this case, as this was to be an autologous transplant: Jackman would be both donor and recipient. The problem was a balky insurance company. Her insurer, Blue Cross/Blue Shield of Vermont, called the treatment "experimental" and refused to pay. Within two months of the news coverage, Sue Jackman had received $20,000 in private donations and the insurance company had been pressured into becoming the first in the Blue Cross/Blue Shield family to cover bone marrow transplant for the treatment of breast cancer.

A *Houston Chronicle* reporter, Dianna Hunt, wrote an article on the problems that pregnant women have accessing drug treatment. In the process of doing the story, Dianna championed the case of "Bridget," a cocaine addict in her eighth month of pregnancy. Repeated calls by Dianna Hunt to hospital administrators, social workers, and a judge resulted in an inpatient placement for the pregnant addict (Elliot, 1990).

On the surface, these sound like success stories, the kind of stories that news organizations like to point out to prove that they do more than publish just the bad news. But, each of these stories is problematic. Each is an example of compassion getting in the way of journalists doing their jobs.

The journalistic job is to fulfill the unique role that news media play in society. In the United States, as well as in other democratic countries, citizens are given the opportunity to take an active part in running their country. So, the news media's primary social function is to tell people what they need to know for self-governance.

News media can do many things besides meeting their social function. They can supply the comics and advice columns and human interest stories and the sports pages. But no matter how good a job they are doing at these tasks, if they're not telling people what they need to know for self governance, they're not a mass market news publication or program. The basic moral responsibility for news media is that they do this unique job.

News organizations meet their social function well or they meet it badly. How well they're doing their jobs can differ from day to day and from story to story. But getting clear on the primary moral responsibility for news organizations makes it easier to see what is wrong with compassionate journalism.

Norma Lynn Peterson's Liver Transplant

Citizens need to know some things about solid organ transplantation, about when it is indicated and when it is not. Voters need to understand the kinds of problems that result in children's livers dying at such a young age, particularly as many of those problems are genetically based and discoverable prior to birth.

Citizens need to know about how and why extraordinary health-care procedures like organ transplants are funded. They need to know why they are so expensive and need to understand the intense competition among health-care centers that have resulted in 164 heart transplant centers and 114 liver transplant centers nationally, with three or more competing transplant centers in the same city in some instances. Citizens need to know that transplant centers consider financial as well as clinical factors in determining if someone is a suitable candidate for transplantation. People need to know that people who would be candidates for transplant, clinically speaking, are excluded because they lack funding for such extraordinary care.

Citizens need to know how and why allocations of the limited resources of organs are made as they are. Stories are needed to show what can be done to encourage donation at the time of death and they need to know how candidates for transplants use politics, money, and the news media to jump ahead in line and, thus, decrease their waiting time for an organ.

These weren't the stories told in Norma Lynn Peterson's case. In fact, in 2 1/2 hours of television time and several hundred newspaper column inches, readers weren't even told that Norma Lynn's parents had insurance that paid 80% of her medical costs. Nor were they told that when Norma Lynn was recovering from transplant surgery under the glow of television lights and public attention, a 24-year-old woman from Portland became Maine's first recipient of a heart-lung transplant. After the heart-lung recipient died during surgery, her husband prepared to hitchhike home to their 4-year-old daughter. He didn't have the money for bus fare.

Christopher Reed and Bone Marrow Donation

Citizens need to know how bone marrow donation differs from solid organ donation. They need to know that bone marrow donors need to be living donors and that bone marrow, like other blood products, replenishes.

Citizens need to know that unlike the single government-regulated network relating to solid organ transplantation, there are several bone marrow registries internationally, and at least two unrelated registries in the United States. They need to know that potential recipients are charged to search their computer indices for a possible matches. They need to know that bone marrow registries charge between $45 and $75 for potential donors to be typed and added to the computer list and that most of these donations come from media-led community appeals to help a local, needy individual. They need to know that these searches rarely turn up a donor for the local person in need.

> **Stories of human need tend to be reported in a way that is ultimately one sided and heroic rather than critical and thoughtful.**

These, again, were not the stories that New Hampshire audiences were told during the futile fight to save Christopher Reed's life. Like natural disaster stories, the stories of human need tend to be reported in a way that is ultimately one sided and heroic rather than critical and thoughtful.

Sue Jackman and The Insurance Company

Citizens need to know that all medical payers, whether insurance companies, state Medicaid systems, or the federal government, work from a set of limited resources. Some medical care is provided; other medical care is not. Citizens need to know the criteria by which this rationing is done and how to have input to influence those criteria. If insurance companies or other third-party payers are pressured into providing extraordinary need for one person, other people with less visible or public need will be quietly neglected. Some needy people will give up something to help other needy people.

The readers of the Sue Jackman stories weren't told about this. According to the medical director of Vermont Blues Cross/Blue Shield (personal communication, January, 1992), at the current rate that health insurance costs and salaries are rising, by the year 2004 it will cost employers in the state of Vermont more to provide health coverage than it will cost them to pay their workers. That is, the benefits package will be more than 100% of the salary rate. The medical director said that he felt that he had no control over the rising medical costs and an ever-growing list of expensive procedures to cover. Yet, he had the continuing responsibility to keep paying the bills. Consumers of news and medical services need to know that changes in how we fund health care are required by sheer economics. They need to know how to add their voices to the decisions being made.

Bridget, the Pregnant Cocaine Addict

Citizens need to know why treatment is so difficult to access by pregnant cocaine addicts. As with transplantation, they need to know how priorities in social services are determined, why some people get assistance and others do not. As many of these organizations receive funding through United Way or other charitable groups, citizens need to know how well their philanthropic dollar is used when they are approached for the annual fund raiser.

> Telling the policy story is the moral responsibility of the journalist.

This isn't the story Houston *Chronicle* readers got. Instead, they learned what can be achieved by one person in need if a news organization throws its weight behind her.

It's obvious in each of these cases that these "policy" stories would have detracted from the human drama stories. But, telling the policy story is the moral responsibility of the journalist. The death-defying medical miracle stories are the easy stories to tell. They see one sided and narrow in scope. And, they are not part of what it means for journalists to be meeting the primary social function of journalism.

Stories of Compassion and the Problem of Justice

Even if journalists did tell citizens the necessary policy stories, journalists should not tell the stories of individual need. The problem is one of justice.

News organizations can't provide the same kind of coverage for every person in similar need. Even if news organizations were willing to help fund raise for every case, it wouldn't work. Eventually, the philanthropic dollar is used up. Sooner, rather than later, people tire of hearing the same story and stop shelling out. Also, not every ill person or family is constituted to fund raise on behalf of his or her life. That makes death the price paid for privacy.

Individuals need to be compassionate; institutions, like news organizations, need to be fair. There's a subtle irony created when news media act for the benefit of a single individual. In both the Sue Jackman vs. Insurance Company story and in the pregnant drug addict story, journalists were appalled that institutions didn't help these individuals in need.

This journalistic instinct to hold a corporation and a social service system accountable was in line with journalists doing their job. It is hard to justify a government or an agency denying treatment without compelling evidence that the denied treatment differs in kind from that which is being provided.

The journalists' demand for accountability asks, "How can these powerful institutions care for some and leave others to die?"

In a similar way, when news media do the Sue story and the Bridget story and ignore the Luther story because Luther is not an attractive story subject and turn down the Nancy story because a story like that was done last month, the news organization becomes just one more of those powerful institutions that care for some and leave others to die.

Stories of Compassion and Moral Theory Based on Care

There is a danger that such stories of misplaced compassion might be confused as consistent with a moral theory that is based on care rather than justice. The morality of care is thought to be a morality of relationships between specific individuals as contrasted with the morality of rights competing among strangers. But, morality of care does not imply paternalism (or maternalism). According to Gilligan (1982):

> In women's development, the absolute of care, defined initially as not hurting others, becomes complicated through a recognition of the need for personal integrity. This recognition gives rise to the claim for equality embodied in the concept of rights, which changes the understanding of relationships and transforms the definition of care. (p. 166)

Caring does not imply an abdication of professional duties. For example, in speaking of a lawyer who construes her job within a morality of care, Dana and Rand Jack (1988) wrote, "Recognizing her lack of power to control what happens to other people, Carol places boundaries around her feelings of personal responsibility. Her limitation of responsibility allows her to feel care without guilt and pain each time a negative result occurs" (pp. 283-284).

One can legitimately care in the process of doing one's job without interpreting that care as a need to take responsibility for the needs of individuals encountered in the process of doing one's job. Institutions can express care and compassion by going beyond their social function to offer special assistance to everyone in like need.

Unique disasters that affect the community at large like earthquakes and floods give news organizations opportunities to rally behind a community cause and to broadcast need and deliver assistance in special ways. Every person affected has an equal chance of reaping the benefits of newsroom intervention. But rallying around an individual's cause produces questionable reporting and lousy public relations. It leads the community ultimately to seek that the news organization is no less unfair than the system it seeks to expose.

References

Elliott, D. (1990). Make the choice: Good samaritan or good reporter. *Fineline: The Newsletter of Journalism Ethics,* 1 (11), 1, 8.

Elliott, D. (1994). A case of need. In P. Patterson & L. Wilkins, *Media ethics: Issues and cases,* (2nd ed.), 72-74. Dubuque, IA: Brown & Benchmark.

Elliott, D., Conquest, W., & Drake, R. (1991). *Buying time: The media role in health care.* Videodocumentary. Fanlight Productions, Distributor.

Gilligan, C. (1982). *In a different voice.* Cambridge: Harvard University Press.

Jack, D., & Jack, R. (1988). Women lawyers: Archetype and alternatives. In C. Gilligan, J. Ward, J. Taylor, & B. Bardige (Eds.). *Mapping the moral domain: A contribution of women's thinking to psychological theory and education,* 263-288.

⎡——— In other words... ———⎤

Davis Merritt of the *Wichita Eagle* has described the public news-paper's niche as being "a fair-minded participant in a community that works."

Arthur Charity. (1995). *Doing public journalism.* **New York: Guilford, p. 150.**

Critics of public journalism . . . believe that . . . if a newspaper starts setting agendas, framing issues, forcing candidates and experts to explain themselves in different ways, promoting forums, and spelling out what "the public" wants, it may think it's speaking for ordinary citizens but it will really end up speaking only for itself. Journalism's one protection against arrogance—its one claim on the public trust—is its refusal to get involved. Giving that up, it will inevitably careen down the same slippery slope as dema-gogues and spin doctors. It will end up speaking only for citizens it agrees with, and cheerleading civic action in which it's improp-erly involved.

Actually, public journalism has a golden rule—an ethical line—every bit as sharp as mainstream journalism's rule, and just as easy to elaborate into a code book of professional norms: *Journalism should advocate democracy without advocating particular solutions* . . . public journalists could well argue that the mainstream's rule of noninvolvement is the one that realistically threatens the public. . . . Which form of journalism is really more flawed and dangerous in a free society: the one that sits passively by while people grow di-vided, or the one that finds ways of bringing them together?

Arthur Charity. (1995). *Doing public journalism.* **New York: Guilford, pp. 144, 146-147.**

As most of them realize, journalists do more than furnish us with facts. They frame and narrate the story of our common life. This story needs to provoke and challenge as much as it informs and en-tertains. In every community and about the nation as a whole, there are disturbing and depressing tales to be told. If the press does not commit to telling them, well and often, its demise will be deserved. But there are ways of facing even the darkest facts that leave us open to the task of remaking them. As storytellers, journalists find their deepest challenge here. Without relinquishing their stance as observers and critics, they can try to nourish a particular understanding of American society: not an audience of savvy spectators nor a class of information-rich consumers, but a nation of citizens with common problems, an inventive spirit, and a rich participatory tradition.

Jay Rosen. (1996). *Getting the connections right: Public journalism and the troubles in the press.* New York: The Twentieth Century Fund Press, p. 5.

What ought to be discussed is not whether the press should be "involved" or "detached," but the best kind of involvement, the nature of the press's legitimate influence, the values that lie beneath its own agenda. There is considerable room for debate on these issues, and those experimenting with public journalism welcome the exchange. Not, however, if they have to establish what should be an acknowledged fact: journalism is no daily mirror of events but a story with themes chosen by journalists.

Jay Rosen. (1996). *Getting the connections right: Public journalism and the troubles in the press.* New York: The Twentieth Century Fund Press, p. 14.

Public journalism is controversial, I believe, not because it demands that journalists get involved, but because it lifts their involvement into public view, acknowledging what everyone already knows: the press is a player. It then proceeds to ask: *For what for for whom* should the press be playing? The answers offered are certain public values: civic participation, deliberative dialogue, politics as problem solving, and the cultivation of "democratic dispositions."

Jay Rosen. (1996). *Getting the connections right: Public journalism and the troubles in the press.* New York: The Twentieth Century Fund Press, p. 69.

The proper formulation . . . is not detachment on the one hand or a Hearst-like meddling on the other. That is a false frame. Between the line of total noninvolvement and the line of Hearst's famous "You supply the pictures, I'll supply the war" is a huge and promising middle ground. Public journalism operates in that ground, retaining neutrality on specifics and moving far enough beyond detachment to care about whether resolution occurs.

If journalists are smart enough and professional enough to define some razor-thin line of objectivity and adhere to it, we are also smart enough and professional enough to define a slightly different line without tumbling all the way into the abyss of inappropriate involvement.

Davis "Buzz" Merritt. (1995). *Public journalism & public life: Why telling the news is not enough.* Hillsdale, NJ: Lawrence Erlbaum Associates, p. 116.

Bibliography annotated by Lee Peck and Lynn Waddell

Books

Altschull, J. H. (1995). *Agents of power: The media and public policy* (2nd ed.). White Plains, NY: Longman Publishers.

> Altschull, a professor at Johns Hopkins University, updates his 1984 book to emphasize "the interdependence of mass media and politics in the United States and abroad," focusing on political, economic, and cultural events. The book, in six parts, takes readers from the mission of the American press to "the boundaries that constrain the news media inside the political economy," the author says.

Anderson, R., Dardenne, R., & Killenberg, G. M. (1994). *The conversation of journalism: Communication, community, and news.* Westport, CT: Praeger.

> The authors believe that to cure newspapers' ills—the loss of readership and the public's dissatisfaction with the press—it will take more than a good marketing plan. They suggest that newspapers become the carrier for public discourse, "a medium for conversation among citizens rather than a conduit for professionally packaged information," says John J. Pauly in the book's foreword. The authors say that journalists need to give democracy more meaning in the newspaper and report the public's concerns—not only through reporting but through the citizen's voices.

Bogart, L. (1989). Press and public: *Who reads what, when, where, and why in American newspapers* (2nd ed.). Hillsdale, NJ: Lawrence Erlbaum Associates.

> Bogart addresses newspapers' readership problems by looking at a variety of statistics from the 1980s. He says that throughout history, papers have had the function of defining their communities, but because of changes in values and lifestyles, the function is out of whack. He says that the future of newspapers "depends on the ability of the people who run them to adapt to the changing requirements of the public." Thus, his book focuses on readers and the changes in their habits.

Bogart, L. (1991). *Preserving the press: How daily newspapers mobilized to keep their readers.* New York: Columbia University Press.

> The author gives an account of the Newspaper Readership Project, 1977-1983, which was an attempt to stop dropping newspaper circulation numbers. The project "provided a channel for intense discussion by publishers, editors and other newspaper people of fundamental questions regarding the functions of the press," Bogart says. However, his book should be read as a personal memoir, not as a history, he says.

Carey, J. (1991). A republic if you can keep it: Liberty and life in an age of glasnost. In R. Arsenault (Ed.), *Crucible of liberty: 200 years of the Bill of Rights* (pp. 108-128). New York: Free Press.

> This essay is rewritten from a speech presented in 1991 at the University of South Florida St. Petersburg's lecture series on the Bill of Rights. Carey, a professor at Columbia University's graduate school of journalism, discusses the collapse of governments in Eastern Europe and the help Americans are giving the people from these nations—from writing a First Amendment to managing a newspaper or TV station. He points out, however, the people of Eastern Europe always had "a free public life"—something he says needs to happen in America.

Charity, A. (1995). *Doing public journalism.* New York: Guilford Press.

> Published as a textbook with a teacher's guide, Charity's book explains public journalism and the different philosophies behind the concept. He also gives examples of newspapers that are experimenting with it.

Christians, C. G., Ferré, J. P., & Fackler, P. M. (1993). *Good news: Social ethics and the press.* New York: Oxford University Press.

> The authors discuss their concept of "communitarian journalism," which is grounded in community instead of individualism. They say that the organizational culture of the news business has to change if the content of the news is to change. They acknowledge that news is a business; however, they believe that money shouldn't control it. They envision a corporate culture in which employees have a voice and the atmosphere is more "humanized," thus leading to a situation where a communitarian ethic can develop.

Dahlgren, P., & Sparks, C. (Eds.). (1991). *Communication and citizenship: Journalism and the public sphere in the new media age.* New York: Routledge.

> This book has its roots in a May 1989 colloquium organized by the Department of Journalism, Media and Communication of Stockholm University. Through differing viewpoints, all the essays in this volume address aspects of the relationship between the public and the media in both the United States and Europe.

Dennis, E. E., Gillmor, D. M., & Glasser, T. L. (Eds.). (1989). *Media freedom and accountability.* New York: Greenwood Press.

> This book helped fuel recent debate about the role and responsibility of the press. It contains essays by John G. Merrill, A. H. Raskin, Clifford Christians, Richard Cunningham, Alfred Balk, Lewis Lapham, Henry Geller, John Kamp, David A. Anderson, John R. Finnegan, Kenneth Morgan, William A. Henry III, and the book editors.

Elliott, D. (Ed.). (1986). *Responsible journalism.* Beverly Hills, CA: SAGE Publications.

> Through nine essays, written by different authors, "competing perspectives" on press responsibility are presented, says the editor. Some of the questions explored in the book: Should journalists be advocates or observers? Where should loyalties lie? Who should determine journalistic responsibilities?

Enteman, R. M. (1989). *Democracy without citizens: Media and the decay of American politics.* New York: Oxford University Press.

> Through social science research, the author presents the paths and the obstacles to improving the governmental process. He says the news media fall "far short of the ideal vision of a free press as civic educator and guardian of democracy." He introduces a theory that explains how the media can wield the power to alter public policy but can't harness that power to serve democratic citizenship. In his final chapter, however, Enteman offers suggestions on improving journalism by enhancing citizenship.

Fallows, J. (1996). *Breaking the news: How the media undermine American democracy.* New York: Pantheon Books.

> *The Atlantic Monthly* editor bashes today's media, saying they distort and disdain civic life, make spectacles out of activities and portray the world in a pessimistic light. He says journalists care more about sensationalism than the well-being of their audience. He tracks the demise of journalism beginning with the entrance of television news, which he says made reporters the interviewee instead of interviewer. Fallows said he subscribes to the public journalism theory as one of the possible solutions to the problems in the press.

Fowler, R. B. (1991). *The dance with community: The contemporary debate in American political thought.* Lawrence, KS: The University Press of Kansas.

> The author explains that his book is a journey in "contemporary intellectual history," exploring the developments in American thought as they focus on community. He says interest in community is a trend in current thinking and attempts to show readers the meaning of community in today's world.

Glasser, T. L., & Salmon, C. T. (Eds.). (1995). *Public opinion and the communication of consent.* New York: Guilford Press.

> This book of essays covers the theoretical issues of public opinion and communication, although it tells readers more about the mass media than about public opin-

ion. Contributors have backgrounds ranging from political science to psychology. It is valuable to students and scholars alike, for it provides a good look at current scholarship in this area as well as its history and future. Of special interest is the final section, which explores the relationship between public opinion and mass media within a democratic framework.

Griffin, R. J., Molen, D. H., Schoenfeld, C., & Scotton, J. F. (1991). *Interpreting public issues.* Ames, IA: Iowa State University Press.
The book is a guide to "issue-centered" journalism, explaining how to identify issues, collect information, and clearly interpret the story. A variety of public issues are used as the subjects of chapters.

Lambeth, E. B. (1992). Committed journalism: *An ethic for the profession* (2nd ed.). Bloomington, IN: Indiana University Press.
University of Missouri professor Lambeth offers criteria "by which to evaluate news media leadership and journalistic storytelling." The book also attempts to make a connection between the ethics of journalism and the problems of the larger culture.

Lappe, F. M., & DuBois, P. M. (1994). *The quickening of America.* San Francisco: Jossey-Bass.
The authors ask readers to forget the negative images of today's society. They attempt to "tackle the myths about public life that are blocking Americans' growth and effectiveness in every aspect of our lives, from workplaces and schools to our communities." Chapter 6, "Making the Media Our Voice," explains how citizens and the media can work together to create change. The authors believe that "it's in the relational self-interest of your local paper to reconnect" with the community.

Lauterer, J. (1995). *Community journalism: The personal approach.* Ames, IA: Iowa State University Press.
Penn State assistant professor of journalism Lauterer's book aims to serve as a survival manual/field guide/handbook for both students and professionals studying community journalism. The author, who has 15 years experience working at community newspapering, shares personal anecdotes.

Lichtenberg, J. (Ed.). (1990). *Democracy and the mass media: A collection of essays.* New York: Cambridge University Press.
This book grew out of discussions from 1985 to 1986 by the University of Maryland's Institute for Philosophy and Public Policy Working Group on News, the Mass Media, and Democratic Values. The group met three times and discussed the moral, philosophical, and legal foundations of regulation.

Mathews, D. (1994). *Politics for people: Finding a responsible public voice.* Urbana, IL: University of Illinois Press.
The author, the president of the Kettering Foundation, suggests ways "the people" can become a responsible public. "Working together with others to solve common problems recreates a sense of community that people like," he says. He makes suggestions for things citizens might do to make politics more like "what they want it to be."

Merritt, D. (1995). *Public journalism and public life: Why telling the news is not enough.* Hillsdale, NJ: Lawrence Erlbaum Associates.
The author, editor of *The Wichita (KS) Eagle,* says the relationship between journalism and democracy needs to change, and he makes suggestions on where to start. The three-part book looks at why journalism and public life are bound together—in success and failure; it looks at the author's development as a journalist; and it looks at journalism's future in cyberspace.

Putnam, R. (1993). *Making democracy work.* Princeton, NJ: Princeton University Press.
Putnam studies the importance of a community culture to democratic politics, providing evidence of the connection between newspaper reading and participation in civic life.

Reich, R. B. (Ed.). (1988). *The power of public ideas.* Cambridge, MA: Ballinger Publishing.
Policy making in America is this book's focus, and ideas about what's best for the

public are emphasized. In Chapter Nine, the role of the media in public deliberation is explored; author Martin Linsky suggests that they too can play a role in the process.

Ripley, C. (Ed.). (1994). *The media and the public.* New York: H. W. Wilson.
Ripley compiles numerous essays on various aspects of the media's relationships with consumers including: the role of the media in shaping public policy, by Charles Green; journalism and the public trust, by Dan Rather; and the plugged-in voter, by Jon Katz.

Rosen, J. (1996). *Getting the connections right: Public journalism and the troubles in the press.* New York: Twentieth Century Fund.
A reform movement rising from the ranks of the American press calls on journalists to do more than just report the news. "Public" journalism summons the press to help revive civic life, improve public dialogue, and fashion a coherent response to the deepening troubles in our civic climate—most of which, Rosen believes, implicate journalists. Urging the press to confront the long-suppressed fact that it is a participant in American life and not just a chronicler of events, Rosen argues that the press suffers when the quality of public life erodes. Rosen details public journalism initiatives around the country and responds to critics who call them a fad or, worse, a cynical attempt to "give readers what they want."

Rosen, J., & Taylor, P. (1992). *The new news vs. the old news: The press and politics in the 1990s.* New York: Twentieth Century Fund.
Written during the summer of 1992, these two essays address communication between the public and political leaders. Rosen's "Politics, Vision, and the Press: Toward a Public Agenda for Journalism" argues for "a new public agenda for journalism," an agenda that addresses journalism's role in democracy. Taylor's essay, "Political Coverage in the 1990s: Teaching the Old News New Tricks," argues that it is possible for "the elite media to behave like an elite," but they have to redefine their roles: No longer is storytelling sufficient; the level of public discourse also must be raised.

Rosenstiel, T. (1993). *Strange bedfellows: How television and the presidential candidates change American politics.* New York, Hyperion.
Rosenstiel of the *Los Angeles Times* followed the ABC television network during the 1992 election presidential campaign to see how the media shaped the race; his book reports on what he learned. "What I saw, from the other side of the camera lens, suggests the press has less power to reform politics than many imagine . . . Unlike the fashionable idea of the day, the traditional press are not becoming irrelevant, but their sins are also greater than they recognize and in many ways getting worse," he reports in his introduction.

Schudson, M. (1988). What is a reporter? The private face of public journalism. In J. W. Carey (Ed.), *Media, myths, and narrative: Television and the press* (pp. 228-245). Newbury Park, CA: SAGE Publications.
The author attempts to define what a reporter is by looking at the autobiographies of Lincoln Steffens and Harrison Salisbury. He says that reporting is an occupation invented in the 19th century—"a result of and a contributor to a democratic market society and an urban commercial consciousness." He says it has evolved into a life of its own, however, and "a unique self-consciousness."

Siegel, R. (Ed.). (1994). *The NPR interviews.* Boston: Houghton Mifflin.
This National Public Radio publishing project, edited by NPR's Robert Siegel, contains a variety of interviews aired during 1994. The editor says "this collection maintains one of NPR's knacks for recording and presenting the people of this country. . ." Dozens of interviews on a variety of topics are shared.

Stamm, K. R. (1985). *Newspaper use and community ties: Toward a dynamic theory.* Norwood, NJ: Ablex.
When University of Washington professor Keith Stamm wrote this book, the relationship between newspaper use and the individual's ties with a local community

had "never been a predominant concern of the discipline of mass communication," he says. The author tries to place research from the '80s "in context with historical roots of its major concepts," with the assumption that relationships between the public and newspapers can be understood if they are looked at in "a community framework."

Stavitsky, A. (1995). *Independence and integrity: A guidebook for public radio journalism.* Washington, DC: National Public Radio.

In May 1994, 80 public radio professionals gathered at the Poynter Institute for Media Studies in St. Petersburg, FL, and discussed "the wide range of issues affecting the independence and integrity of public radio journalism," says the introduction of the book, based on the three-day session at the Poynter. The premise is that public radio is public journalism. The book provides the tools to evaluate editorial decisionmaking.

Williams, F., & Pavlik, J. V. (Eds.). (1994). *The people's right to know: Media, democracy, and the information highway.* Hillsdale, NJ: Lawrence Erlbaum Associates.

Ten chapters written by a diverse group of authors address the prospects for "citizen information services" on the information highway. The editors have a vision of how a national information service could "transform the nation's communications infrastructure on an order of magnitude that the telegraph, the telephone and broadcasting have done in earlier times."

Yankelovich, D. (1991). *Coming to public judgment: Making democracy work in a complex world.* Syracuse, NY: Syracuse University Press.

The author elaborates on concepts that have evolved out of his experience with conducting public opinion surveys. He says that "the importance of information in shaping responsible public opinion is vastly exaggerated." He explains why there is "something for everyone (from journalists to average citizens) to do" to help preserve democracy.

Articles

Albers, R. R. (1994, September). Going public: Public journalism unites some publishers and newsrooms in a controversial mission. *Presstime,* 16 (8), 28-30.

Albers explores the pros and cons of public journalism by reporting on experiments being done at several newspapers. She includes results from an industry attitude survey.

Archer, J. (1996, Sept./Oct.). Public journalism from the streets. *The IRE Journal,* 6-9.

Archer proposes that instead of what is called the "new" public journalism, community journalism is simply the established method of "beat" journalism, in which it is the reporters' responsibility to know the issues, news, and stories that are a part of the neighborhood, community, or city that they cover.

Aucoin, J. L. (1996, Spring). Community-connected journalism. *Media Ethics,* 2, 7, 25.

Aucoin challenges some of the principles behind public journalism, saying it should be confined to the editorial pages, not the news section of the newspaper.

Awbrey, D. (1991, September 29). Journalism's future is close to home. *The Wichita (KS) Eagle,* A13.

Awbrey, editor of the editorial pages at *The Eagle,* explains that newspaper readership is down and so is voter turnout. He says that for newspapers to survive into the 21st century, their staffs must help rekindle the public spirit of the American people and stop alienating themselves from their readers.

Balough, M. (1996, January/February). Changing techniques: Austin experiment may alter the way journalists measure populace's mood. *Quill,* 20-22.

Balough, former editor of the Austin American-Statesman, writes about the potential impact of the National Issues Convention on journalism practices held in Austin.

Bare, J. (1992, Fall). Case study—Wichita and Charlotte: The leap of a passive press to activism. *Media Studies Journal,* 6 (4), 149-161.

A report on how *The Wichita Eagle* and *The Charlotte Observer* initiated a process where journalists and the public decided together what the content of the news would be. The two papers allowed citizens to prioritize news items about the 1992 presidential campaign by looking at polling data and other methods.

Barlow, W. (1988). Community radio in the U.S.: The struggle for a democratic medium. *Media, Culture and Society,* 10, 81-105.

Barlow of Howard University says that although community radio has political and economic constraints, "it still has more democratic potential than any other form of mass media operating in the United States."

Beaudry, A. E. (1996, Winter). The civic role in public journalism. *National Civic Review,* 26-28.

Community leaders, civic activists, and public officials need to view civic journalism as a community team sport requiring their active participation. Civic sector/media partnerships for civic journalism are essential tools for achieving any type of community action.

Benfield, R. (1995, Fall). Instant feedback feature makes livelier pages. *The Masthead,* 47 (3), 13-14.

Benfield, editorial page editor of *The Record* in Hackensack, N.J., writes about how his newspaper requests faxed or phoned daily responses to editorials. The experiment has resulted in editorial writers feeling more connected with their community. The newspaper has also gotten response from readers who say they don't have time to write letters.

Bennet, J. (1996, Sept. 24). North Carolina media try to lead politics to issues. *New York Times,* A1, A21.

Bennett, W. L. (1993, Summer). A policy research paradigm for the news media and democracy. *Journal of Communication,* 43 (3), 180-189.

This essay by Bennett, University of Washington political science professor, proposes "a framework to join journalists and communication scholars in dialogue about the conditions that best promote the public dialogue of democracy itself." He says now is a good time for academics and journalists to discuss democracy and social responsibility because journalists are in the process of redefining their roles in society.

Blount, T. (1992, September). In Decatur, Ill., tough times spurred a newspaper to lead the revitalization effort. *ASNE Bulletin,* 743, 11-12.

Blount, the editor of the *High Point (NC) Enterprise,* writes about his experience with "The Decatur Advantage," a program created in the early 1980s by publisher Wayne Schile to help city leaders revitalize Decatur, Illinois, a medium-sized industrial city experiencing high unemployment. Blount was a member of the steering committee.

Broder, D. S. (1990, January 14). Five ways to put some sanity back in elections. *The Washington Post,* B1.

As the midterm 1990 elections approach, *Washington Post* political columnist Broder says that journalists need to do something about "this win-at-all-costs mentality that is undermining our political process." He presents his five-point agenda for improving media coverage.

Broder, D. S. (1992, March). Campaign '92: It's time to replace sloganeering with simple shoe-leather reporting. *Quill,* 81 (2), 8-9.

Washington Post syndicated columnist Broder says that journalists at his paper are allowing "the voters' agenda to set our coverage agenda" for the 1992 political campaign. To find out what that agenda might be, simple "shoe-leather reporting" was and is employed. "We need to become once again `the voice of the people' by letting their voices be heard in the news columns of our paper," he says.

Broder, D. S. (1992, December 27). Voters taking back the campaigns. *The Washington Post,* C7.

Editorial writer Broder salutes people he thinks improved politics during the 1992 election campaign. He commends volunteers in Oregon, Minnesota, and Pennsylvania. He also acknowledges journalists who used the concept of public journalism to empower voters.

Broder, D. S. (1996, January 3). Civic life and shared values remain essential. *St. Petersburg Times*, 13A.
In a restates the need for more civic involvement and a "return to civility in our public discourse." He notes how the movement to improve civic life has gained support from many scholars and political parties. He predicts it will continue to be a popular discussion topic.

Brown, R. U. (1995, August 12). Public journalism. *Editor & Publisher*, 6.
In this editorial Brown argues that the problem with public journalism is that there is no accepted definition. He agrees with *Wichita Eagle* Editor Davis "Buzz" Merritt that journalism should help connect citizens with public life.

Burke, T. (1996, March). People spoke; who listened? Media, candidates find tables turned as issues convention puts citizens center stage. *Quill*, 33-34.
Burke, deputy managing editor of the *Austin American-Statesman*, covers the results of the National Issues Convention held in Austin, Texas. The convention was intended to measure people's political opinions after they had a chance to talk with politicians. While the convention host said the experiment was a success, many journalists questioned were ambivalent. The lack of appearances by politicians and strong opinion polls didn't make for good news fodder.

Byrd, J. (1995, February 5). Conversations with the community. *The Washington Post*, C6.
Ombudsman Byrd believes that newspaper staffs have no business deciding what's good for a community. She says, however, that goals of public journalism may be accomplished without compromising journalism's principles. For instance, "the community decides what to talk about; the newspaper provides the encouragement and the means."

Calamai, P. (1995, Spring). Another link with readers. *Nieman Reports*, 49 (1), 39-40.
Calamai, editorial page editor of *The Ottawa Citizen* in Canada, explains his newspaper's presence on Free-Net, a no-charge local electronic bulletin board. He says this is an easy way for newspaper staffs to link with readers; however, he warns: "The real challenge is to use these new electronic links to confront the intellectual flabbiness that too often passes for thinking in North American society."

Caldwell, B. (1994, March 27). Public's role in coverage increases. *The Oregonian*, D1.
The Oregonian's public editor Caldwell describes the newspaper's coverage of politics and says more changes are in store. He says the paper is trying to focus more directly of the central issues of the 1994 campaign, using some of the principles of public journalism.

Carey, J. W. (1987, March/April). The press and public discourse. *The Center Magazine*, 20, 4-16.
The author looks at "the problem of journalism" today by reflecting on the words of Walter Lippmann's 1922 *Public Opinion*. Although he offers no solutions to the present state of affairs—the relationship between the public and journalism—he asks that readers consider how they might "restore the public to a vital role in American politics and American journalism."

Carey, J. W. (1993, Summer). The mass media and democracy: Between the modern and the postmodern. *Journal of International Affairs*, 1-21.
Carey, often described as today's leading journalism scholar, offers a sweeping view of the evolving relationship between journalism and democracy, from Colonial times through the "modern" era of mass media and national society, to a just-emerging "post-modern" period that he predicts will have much in common with the days of the Founding Fathers.

Case, T. (1993, January 30). Can journalists be joiners? *Editor & Publisher*, 126 (5), 15, 43.
Case reports on "Community Involvement vs. Conflict of Interest: Can Journalists

be Joiners?" a panel discussion at the Society of Professional Journalists' 1992 convention in Baltimore. An editor, Dale McFeatters of Scripps Howard News Service, and two professors, Don Lambert of Ohio University and Louis Hodges of Washington and Lee University, comprise the panel; they discuss whether journalists can safely get involved in their communities and still maintain objectivity.

Case, T. (1994, November 12). Public journalism denounced. *Editor & Publisher,* 127 (46), 14-15.
The author reports that many of the attendees of the October 1994 Associated Press Managing Editors convention do not support the increased use of public journalism, which they see as an abandonment of journalism ideals.

Champlin, C. (1995, Spring). Reading the public from the arts pages. *Nieman Reports,* 49 (1), 30-32.
The author, arts editor emeritus for the *Los Angeles Times,* says that when money gets tight, the arts often suffer—symphonies go bankrupt and dance companies close. Newspapers remain supportive of the arts, however, and "readers of newspapers may rediscover their common cause with the paper, and newspapers struggling to assert their identities amid technological upheavals, may rediscover their strong links to readers."

Charity, A. (1996, January/February). Reluctant sea change: Resources abound for journalists seeking information about public journalism's role. *Quill,* 23-27.
Charity, author of *Doing Public Journalism,* says there's more talk about public journalism than practice. Many journalists are confused about what it is, so he offers lists of ways to learn about it. He gives a run-down of what he considers the "best manifestoes" of public journalism, the "best critical assessments," "best reprints" of public journalism projects, videos on public journalism, best looks at the broader picture, best places to study people, what to watch for in 1996, and "best public journalism organizations."

Charity, A. (1996, Winter). Public journalism for the people. *National Civic Review,* 7-13.
Public journalism has the potential to be an extraordinary organizing force in American culture and is one of the greatest tools for increasing public participation. Charity examines the five basic tasks of public journalism.

The Charlotte Project: A status report. (1992, Summer). *Poynter Report,* 11-18.
The Charlotte Project, an experiment by The Poynter Institute for Media Studies, *The Charlotte Observer,* and WSOC-TV in Charlotte, was created in 1991 to improve coverage of the 1992 election campaign. The article looks at the status of the project in the summer of 1992; voter-inspired issues are the basis for much of the coverage.

Clifton, D. (1994, March 6). Creating a forum to help solve community problems. *The Miami Herald,* C4.
The Herald's executive editor explains the "Community Conversations" readership project, created so the news staff could better understand readers and also could try "community building"—writing stories that illuminate problems but leave the solutions to those who want to seek them. Clifton says the paper doesn't take sides. "We've been carefully taught that 'objectivity' is the altar to which we must genuflect if we are to call ourselves journalists," he says.

Cohn, J. (1995, Summer). Should journalists do community service? *The American Prospect,* 14-17.
Cohn traces the history of public journalism and outlines the controversies surrounding it. Not only does this journalism practice threaten conflicts of interest, he says, it also may undermine newspapers' strength. "The great art of journalism is not in restating what the public already thinks, but in getting the public to think differently."

Conciatore, J. (1994, October 31). NPR election project puts the people's voice on air. *Current,* 13 (20), 1, 6, 15.
Writer Conciatore reports that "reinvesting the power of the democratic process in the voter is the primary goal of public journalism," which the NPR Election Project promotes. At the time of the article's printing, six public radio stations in five cities

had established partnerships with daily newspapers in their cities. Some partnerships also included TV stations. Citizens' issues of concern during the 1994 election campaigns were identified through the project and were reported on.

Conte, C. (1996). Civic journalism: The issues. *CQ Researcher*, 6 (35), 819-826.
Conte examines the question of whether journalists can become involved in solving society's problems without compromising their role as government watchdogs.

Corrigan, D. (1995, July-August). Does "public journalism" serve the public or the publishers? *St. Louis Journalism Review*, 25 (178), 9.
The author reviews the arguments for and against the práctice of holding focus groups with newspaper readers to determine their opinions and to allow them to dictate what and how the news should be covered.

Corrigan, D. (1996, March 18). Press seeks remedy for its failings. *St. Louis Post-Dispatch*, 15B.
Corrigan writes in his editorial that public journalists need to brush up on journalism history; the press has long been criticized for its negativity. The press should also listen more closely its readers who, he says, want objectivity in their news stories.

Craig, D.A. (1996). Communitarian journalism(s): Clearing conceptual landscapes. *Journal of Mass Media Ethics*, 11 (2), 107-118.
This essay sets communitarianism in one context of political theory and public policy, then explores the contrasting ways the term has appeared in three recent books on press theory and practice. Examination of the philosophical roots and practical implications of these works shows communitarian journalism is not necessarily a radical departure from current press theory.

Cunningham, R. (1996). New books provide a sharper focus on public journalism: An essay review. *Journal of Mass Media Ethics*, 11 (3), 184-91.
Cunningham reviews books by Charity, Fiskin, Merritt, and Rosen, noting their contributions to public journalism. He concludes, "It is no longer enough for a journalist to say, 'I am a good person reporting well.' The ethical question now is, 'What more shall I do?'"

Delaney, P. (1995, Spring). How technology spoils reporters. *Nieman Reports*, 49 (1), 27-29.
Delaney, chair of the journalism department at the University of Alabama and former senior editor of the *New York Times*, explains why journalists have to "come to terms with the new age" and have to go back to their real sources—people—if they are going to get back their lost stature and status. "Basic journalism" is the key, he says.

Dennis, E. E. (1995, July 29). Raising questions about civic or public journalism. *Editor & Publisher*, 128 (30), 48-49.
Dennis, executive director of The Freedom Forum Media Studies Center, says journalists should concentrate on defining public journalism and how it fits with the original ideas of journalism before debating whether to practice it.

Dennis, E. E. (1995, Summer). Questions for journalism. *Grassroots Editor*, 36 (2), 8.
Dennis said it is time for public journalism supporters and critics to meet in open debate. The scholar also provides a list of questions that need to be raised about the practice, beginning with how to define it.

Denton, F., & Thorson, E. (1995, March). Does civic journalism work? *Civic Catalyst*, 6, 8.
Denton, editor of the *Wisconsin State Journal*, and Thorson, a journalism professor at the University of Missouri, report on "We the People/Wisconsin," an election-based civic journalism project. Their report says early results from this experiment—which has included town-hall meetings, candidate debates, and citizenship training—have shown that civic journalism can "pull ordinary citizens into caring about candidates and issues—and even into voting."

Dill, S. (1992, September). In search of the public's agenda. *ASNE Bulletin*, 743, 14-15.
Dill, the executive editor of *The Wichita (KS) Eagle*, explains her newspaper's "issue-oriented campaign coverage." She discusses the ups and downs of this kind of cov-

erage and also what the staff didn't get "exactly right."

Edelman, M. (1992, Winter). Constructing the political spectacle. *Kettering Review,* 24-29.
Edelman, a political science professor at the University of Wisconsin, describes how the media create "the political spectacle," a social phenomenon. How the media interpret a story is then interpreted by audiences to fit their respective values. Thus, "the political spectacle does not promote accurate expectations or understanding, but rather evokes a drama that objectifies hopes and fears," Edelman says.

Eisner, J. R. (1994, October 16). Should journalists abandon their detachment to solve problems? *The Philadelphia Inquirer,* E7.
The Philadelphia Inquirer editorial page editor says that if journalists lose their impartiality, they risk destroying their most precious mandate—to independently report the news. The Fourth Estate has "taken a beating in the public's regard," she says, but she questions whether public journalism is the answer to repairing the problem.

Emig, A. G. (1995, Summer). Community ties and dependence on media for public affairs. *Journalism & Mass Communication Quarterly,* 72 (2), 402-412.
Emig reports on a telephone survey showing a connection between people with strong community ties and certain types of media. The survey of 373 people also showed a relationship between the types of media consumed and community processes.

Eveslage, T. E. (1993, February). The social studies and scholastic journalism: Partners in citizenship education. *Social Education,* 57 (2), 82-86.
Eveslage, a professor in Temple University's journalism department, suggests strengthening citizenship education through the cooperation of junior high school and high school social studies and journalism teachers. "Young journalists who see their social studies lessons come to life in the student press, where freedom of expression can effect change, are likely to continue to be active citizens," he says.

Fallows, J. (1994, December). Did you have a good week? The new unit of political significance. *The Atlantic,* 274 (6), 32, 34.
The author argues that journalists report serious news with "the same artificial, short-lived intensity as sports." Public journalism proponent Jay Rosen of New York University is quoted as warning, however, that ordinary citizens realize politics concerns values and choices, not just the ups and downs of "each tactical fight."

Fibich, L. (1995, September). Under siege (public perceptions of mass media). *American Journalism Review,* 17 (7), 16-23.
A NBC/*Wall Street Journal* survey shows that the mass media have become alienated from the public. Of 500 surveyed, only 26 percent had a "somewhat positive" or "very positive" perception of journalists. Meanwhile, 50 percent said they had a negative impression. Criticisms include sensationalism, selective reporting, bias, and inaccuracy.

Field, T. (1995, March 18). In praise of public journalism (Shop talk at thirty). *Editor & Publisher,* 128 (11), 56-57.
Reporters and their editors need to regain ties to their community. They should be accessible to their readers by phone. Journalists have a responsibility to serve their readers by providing a forum for public disclosure, he says.

Finch, J. (1994, December 11). Should press take on the role of referee on public issues? *Richmond (VA) Times-Dispatch,* F2.
Times-Dispatch ombudsman Finch says that Jay Rosen, a New York University communications professor, and Davis Merritt, editor of *The Wichita (KS) Eagle,* are the developers of the public journalism movement, and he explains their belief that "salvation" lies in their concept. He also presents differing views on the movement and tells his readers that the *Times-Dispatch* has "walked around the edges of public journalism" in past months. He asks them to tell him what the role of journalists should be.

Fischer, J. (1994, November 13). This type of project won't solve newspapers' problems. *San Jose Mercury News*, F4.

> *News* staff writer Fischer explains that public journalism is " a newspaper adopting a mom-and-apple-pie issue as a way to do some genuine good and show the public we're in this for something more than money." He writes negatively about the paper's "adopt-a-precinct" project, created before the 1994 election. He gives the example of how voters in one district still stayed home, regardless of the newspaper's involvement.

Fitzgerald, M. (1993, March 27). Community involvement is his credo. *Editor & Publisher*, 126 (13), 20-21.

> The incoming American Society of Newspaper Editors president and editor of the Portland Oregonian Bill Hilliard has been involved in civic activities for many years. The first black president of the ASNE, Hilliard explains that his involvement stems from injustices he suffered while growing up during the Depression in Portland. He does not want others to suffer the same injustices, and, thus, this is the reason for his civic involvement—something many editors avoid.

Fitzgerald, M. (1995, November 11). Decrying public journalism. *Editor & Publisher*, 128 (40), 20.

> Fitzgerald writes of a speech made by *Ames Iowa Daily Tribune* editor Michael Gartner. Gartner, speaking to a Society of Professional Journalists conference, said a newspaper should leave its opinions on the editorial pages. He criticized *The New York Times* and *Washington Post* for printing the Unabomber's manifesto. He said it was "public journalism run amok."

Fouhy, E. (1994, January 10). Toward a new agenda in TV news. *Broadcasting & Cable*, 125, 32.

> The director of the Pew Center for Civic Journalism, a former TV news executive, says local TV stations will survive and prosper in the age of converging technologies because they have their "roots in the community." But, he warns, TV journalists must learn to respond to growing anger among viewers. "It's as if journalists, in their fixation with urban violence, are willing to destroy the sense of citizenship, a value all Americans still hold dear," Fouhy says and suggests journalists start listening to "their customers."

Fouhy, E. (1994, May). Is "civic" journalism the answer? *Communicator*, 38 (5), 18-19.

> The author says local TV stations must do local news even better before they get struck by "the increasing flow of traffic on that superhighway." He suggests TV newsroom staffers change the way they do their "business and the way they define news," and he says civic journalism might be the answer.

Fouhy, E. (1994, Summer-Fall). The dawn of public journalism. *National Civic Review*, 83, 259-266.

> Fouhy explains the civic journalism model and how news organizations across the country are applying it in their communities. He reports on the partnerships that have been created among newspapers, television and radio stations, and the communities that these media serve.

Fouhy, E., & Schaffer, J. (1995, Spring). Civic journalism—growing and evolving. *Nieman Reports*, 49 (1), 16-18.

> The authors—both directors at the Pew Center for Civic Journalism—say public journalism has energized citizens and the press. They cite examples of news organizations that have tried the concept and report successes.

Frankel, M. (1995, May 21). Reporting versus reform. *St. Petersburg Times*, D1.

> Frankel, a former editor at *The New York Times*, says that public journalism wants to solve society's problems but that such activism may compromise a "redefining journalism as a quest for a better tomorrow will never compensate for its poor performance at explaining yesterday."

Frankel, M. (1995, Fall). Journalists should leave reform to reformers. *The Masthead*, 47 (3), 21-22.

> Frankel says the result of public journalism crusading will be "superficial or extremely messy and embarrassing." He argues that newspapers should improve

their coverage of yesterday's events, rather than attempting to mold tomorrow's.

Gale, D. (1995, Spring). Many tune in, but who listens? *The Masthead,* 47 (1), 10-11.
Although radio and television stations do listener or viewer surveys, the information gathered never addresses who is watching or listening to broadcast editorials, says the author, who is with KSL AM/TV in Salt Lake City and presents his editorials on the air. He has to depend on phone calls and letters to determine who is listening, but he says he believes that "thousands are tuned in" and "community leaders pay attention."

Garnham, N. (1993). The mass media, cultural identity and the public sphere in the modern world. *Public Culture,* 5, 251-265.
Garnham, who teaches communications and is the director of the Centre of Communication and Information Studies of Westminister University, writes of the struggle to maintain cultural identity in an increasingly democratized world. Garnham says the mass media are closely tied to these changes, and he offers modernist and postmodernist theories on how to achieve the delicate balance.

Gartner, M. (1995, November/December). Give me old-time journalism. *Quill,* 66-69.
Public journalism can be dangerous, Gartner, the chairman and editor of *The Daily Tribune* in Ames, Iowa and former NBC News president, told attendants at the Society of Professional Journalists president's banquet in 1995. In excerpts from his speech, Gartner says it is not the role of journalists to campaign, but to expose.

Gibbs, C. (1995, March). Big help for small papers: At-risk community papers—and their editors—get help from an innovative volunteer program. *Quill,* 83 (2), 32-35.
Research from The Huck Boyd National Center for Community Media at Kansas State University shows that good community journalism is "essential to the well-being of America's smaller communities," Gibbs reports. Thus, the center sends student journalists to communities to train citizens who want to sustain or start a community newspaper.

Glaberson, W. (1994, October 3). A new press role: solving problems. *The New York Times,* D6.
Times writer Glaberson discusses the pros and cons of public journalism and includes the thoughts of advocates Davis Merritt of *The Wichita (KS) Eagle* and Jay Rosen of New York University. The article points out that more experimentation may be needed before public journalism finds a place in news coverage.

Glaberson, W. (1994, December 12). Fairness, bias and judgment: Grappling with the knotty issue of objectivity in journalism. *The New York Times,* D7.
Through a question-and-answer format, the author interviews Jay Rosen, New York University communications professor and director of the Project on Public Life and the Press, about objectivity in journalism. Rosen says he believes that an objective press must be "in conversation with the rest of the country and the political culture."

Glaberson, W. (1995, February 27). The media business. *The New York Times,* D8.
Glaberson writes about the state of public journalism and how *The Wisconsin State Journal* has contributed to its development. He gives opinions of advocates and opponents to the Wisconsin projects.

Glass, A. J. (1995, September). It's official: most people don't like us any more. *ASNE Bulletin,* 770, 6-7.
A Times Mirror Center for People and the Press survey showed that the public does not think the media care about them. Respondents characterized the media as being more concerned with ratings and money. They also believed the media prevented solutions.

Glaser, L. E. (1994, October 23). New concept in journalism urges advocacy. *The Fresno Bee,* B9.
Bee ombudsman Glaser, just back from a Poynter Institute for Media Studies ethics seminar, shares comments about public journalism made by Poynter senior scholar Roy Peter Clark. "Journalism is valuable if public life remains viable," she reports Clark as saying. She explains the concept to her readers.

Glaser, L. E. (1994, October 30). Media advocacy to push causes step over line. *The Fresno Bee,* B9.

Glaser says that the staff of the *American Journalism Review* considers public journalism "the hottest secular religion in the news business." However, Glaser presents what the opponents of public journalism have to say about the movement. She reports that the *Bee's* managing editor says the paper is not "advocacy based," and she says that she's not comfortable with the concept either.

Glasser, T. L., & Ettema, J. S. (1989). Investigative journalism and the moral order. *Critical Studies in Mass Communications,* 6 (1), 1-20.
The authors, both journalism professors, examine the consequences of "a press that seeks to be both a detached observer of fact and a custodian of conscience." Through interviews with investigative reporters, they examine how news people deal with the tension between objectivity and adversarialism. They also look at investigative reporters' contributions to moral order within the communities they cover.

Glasser, T. L. (1991). Communication and the cultivation of citizenship. *Communication,* 12, 235-248.
Glasser of Stanford University says that "a publicly told story engages others not by informing them but by inviting them to share in the discovery of a world in which they can recognize themselves." Stories reveal understanding, not just facts, thus involving readers in ways a straight report can't. Through this kind of communication, Glasser believes a citizen can be a participant, not just a spectator.

Goldberg, C. (1996, January 8). A new paper accentuates the positive. *The New York Times,* 41.
Goldberg reports on a new newspaper, *The World Times,* that publishes positive news. Based in Santa Fe, N.M., the broadsheet is attempting what some call "New Age journalism."

Greider, W. (1992, Winter). Reporters and their sources. *Kettering Review,* 55-58.
The author, the national editor of *Rolling Stone,* says, "The press communicates much less coherently than it thinks it does." He comes to this conclusion after years in the news business, and he believes that the news media need to reinvent their definition of news and focus on "context and comprehension." Reporters need to explain more and startle less, he says.

Grossman, L. (1994, Summer). The emerging electronic democracy. *Nieman Reports,* 53-57.
Grossman, former NBC and PBS president, moderates a panel of four media professionals who discuss their opinions on the electronic media's ability to facilitate democracy. Panelists include: Matthew F. Wilson, editor of *The San Francisco Chronicle;* Davis Merritt, editor of *The Wichita Eagle;* Leonard Downie Jr., executive editor *The Washington Post;* and Andrew Blau, director of Communications Policy Project, Benton Foundation.

Hallin, D. C. (1992, Summer). The passing of the "high modernism" of American journalism. *Journal of Communication,* 42 (3), 14-25.
An associate professor of communication at the University of California at San Diego, Hallin writes about two themes—the collapse of political consensus and the intensification of economic competition—and explains how these themes are "shaking up the profession of journalism."

Harwood, R. C. (1994, Spring). Is the public ready to decide? *Social Policy,* 24 (3), 13-23.
The author, former ombudsman of *The Washington Post,* believes public participation, not politics, should influence the health care debate and explains why the media should take an active interest by involving the public and working with them to solve issues.

Harwood, R. C. (1994, June 1). Journalists are losing touch with their readers. *St. Petersburg Times,* A16.
Harwood says the press is superficial and incompetent, and the public does not trust journalists. Until the term "reliable source" is redefined, journalists will continue to lose credibility—and readers.

Harwood, R. C. (1995, January 17). Civic Journalism 101. *The Washington Post,* A19.

The detachment of newspapers from their communities, the author says, contributes to the alienation of citizens from public affairs. He says he has some misgivings about public journalism, however. Because the press already has credibility problems, "to anoint ourselves now as leaders of a new American reformation may be a little more than the market will bear," he explains.

Harwood, R. C., & Mermin, D. (1995, March). Tapping the hidden layers of civic life. *Civic Catalyst*, 9.

The authors, who work for the public issues research firm The Harwood Group, report on their firm's research in Wichita, Kansas. Researchers have been listening in on public conversations at "informal civic spaces"; thus, as they move through neighborhoods, they are developing a kind of public-life map. The research suggests that the newspapers which "tap into public conversations and write these kinds of stories will actually help to breathe new life into the civic spaces of their communities. "

Hernandez, D. G. (1996, February 24). Bewildered by the media. *Editor & Publisher*, 11.

In the report "America Struggles Within," the Pew Center for Civic Journalism details the public's belief that the news media have lost a sense of their mission in society. Focus groups have stated that too much of what the news media offer is dirt and gossip.

Holland, R. (1994, December 28). For news biz, a shift to new paradigm? *The Richmond Times-Dispatch*, A9.

The author reflects on Poynter Institute senior scholar Roy Peter Clark's booklet *The American Conversation and the Language of Journalism*, which says that journalists need to dig for details to make their stories real and connect better with their readers. Holland takes this thought one step further, however. He says there is a connection between clear language and "clear motive." He fears public journalism threatens to "muddy the mission of newspapers to the detriment of readers and writers alike."

Hoyt, M. (1992, July-August). The Wichita experiment: What happens when a newspaper tries to connect readership and citizenship? *Columbia Journalism Review*, 31 (2), 42-47.

The author presents examples of newspaper staffs trying "community connectedness," or public journalism, using *The Wichita (KS) Eagle* as his main model. *The Eagle* succeeded in motivating—and mobilizing—readers during the 1992 presidential campaign.

Hoyt, M. (1995, September/October). Are you now or will you ever be, a civic journalist? As the theory moves into practice in more and more newsrooms, the debate gets sharper. *Columbia Journalism Review*, 27-33.

A chronology of public journalism is given, as well as a critical analysis of the practice. Hoyt quotes supporters and critics, practitioners and academics in this piece which attempts to define public journalism and whether it is positive for the industry.

Hudzinski, J. (1996, March 24). Top priority: Staying in touch; reshaping how we cover the news and our community. *Ashbury Park Press*, C3.

The new change facilitator for the *Press* explains how the newspaper is transforming and enveloping the practices of public journalism. He describes to readers what public journalism is, and how their newspaper will change because it.

Isaacs, S. D. (1994, Fall). Out there, new rules are like the old. *Nieman Reports* 48 (3), 53-54.

In 1994, Columbia University's 200 students in the graduate school of journalism set out to discover if "the old rules have changed" by asking their hometown papers questions about weakening of standards. Questions included the following: Can a newsroom employee seek election to the town council? Have newspaper publishers taken to insisting that editors and reporters get more involved in civic organizations? Students discovered that the toughest policies discouraging community involvement still endure at the larger-circulation papers.

Jackson, W. E. (1996, October 8). Polls skew campaign coverage. *St. Petersburg Times*, A13.

Jackson, a political science professor from North Carolina, criticizes public journalism in election coverage, saying the state's newspapers have abdicated their responsibility to fully inform voters. Instead, polls are driving the candidates—and now the journalists, he says.

Jacobs, J. (1994, October 10). So, we'll be taking some responsibility. *San Jose Mercury News*, B9.
The Editorial page writer Jacobs says that journalists aren't quite sure what public journalism is, yet her paper is embarking on a project aimed at getting people to vote in the 1994 election. The paper will deliver free newspapers to residents in an area of town who don't usually get the paper. The residents also will be provided with information on campaign issues, and public forums will be held. The idea is "to see whether giving people lots and lots of information about their choices will increase their political participation," she says.

James Fallows journalist and author. (1996, March 3). *The San Diego Union-Tribune*, G5.
The Tribune offers a question and answer session with James Fallows, journalist and author of *How the Media Undermine Democracy*. Fallows says that public journalism can be misused, but it also creates an internal awareness of how much the media impact their communities.

Jennings, M. (1995, January 29). Being heard doesn't have to be hard. *Dayton (OH) Daily News*, B8.
The Daily News editor explains how his newspaper staff will try to "reconnect" readers with their government. Jennings explains the special projects and stories the paper's editors have planned for political coverage. "We want to make it very hard for you to miss stories about what your government is doing to you or for you," he says.

Johnson, H. (1995, Spring). Shoe leather, shoe leather, shoe leather. *Nieman Reports*, 49 (1), 26.
Johnson, author and journalist, explores the different ways that newspaper staffs try to keep readers—from public journalism to the new technology. He says, however, that the best way to keep readers is to stop alienating them and to "get back to the basics."

Jurkowitz, M. (1996). From the citizen up. Public journalism tries to give people voice. But can this approach to reporting the news be good and do good without compromising traditional journalism? *Forbes Media Critic*, 75-83.
Jurkowitz, umbudsman for the *Boston Globe*, questions the ethical dilemmas arising from public journalism—when and where the news media must draw the line between active community involvement and dispassionate reporting.

Jurkowitz, M. (1996, February 25). Talking back; can "public journalism," a controversial experiment that gives the people a voice in the news, help save democracy in trouble and a press in disrepute? *The Boston Globe*, magazine, 15.
The Globe ombudsman outlines the pros and cons of public journalism and concludes that it may "have to head back to the shop for an overhaul if the 1996 presidential campaign—as seems likely—is driven more by megabucks, wedge issues, and negative ads than by the questions on the lips of voters."

Jurkowitz, M. (1996. May 27). The media's best-kept secret. *Boston Globe*, 17.
Boston Globe ombudsman Jurkowitz discusses the *Globe*'s efforts at a "public journalism" campaign in 1994, and an upcoming one covering the U.S. Senate race between Sen. John Kerry and Gov. William Weld in 1996.

Kelly, M. (1996, Nov. 4). Media culpa. The New Yorker, 45-49.
In this hard-hitting critique of public journalism, Kelly finds fault with North Carolina news media for manipulating the 1996 political campaign by focusing on selected issues and ignoring some that the candidates themselves thought to be crucial.

Kelly, T. (1994, October 16). Community: A hot topic for editors and for you. *Lexington Herald-Leader*, E2.
Herald-Leader editor Kelly raises questions about his paper's future based on the

comment: "If this newspaper isn't the watchdog, nobody will be." However, he worries that if journalists just point out all the things wrong in a community, will they create chaos or actually help?

Kent, C. (1996, January/February). A foray into "hope journalism." *American Journalism Review*, 17.

Kent, editor of the National Media Relations newsletter *Issues & Policy*, writes about the founders of the American News Service, an agency that produces news reports of "'constructed, solution-oriented activities . . . that will inform, intrigue and inspire.'" ANS founders, a husband and wife team, started the news service after the completion of their book *The Quickening of America* in 1994.

Knecht, G. B. (1996, October 17). Why a big foundation gives newspapers cash to change their ways. *Wall Street Journal*, 1, 6.

The Pew charitable trust, a non-profit foundation, is handing out millions of dollars to newspapers that will undertake public or civic journalism projects.

Koch, T. (1994, May). Computers vs. community: A call for bridging the gap between two camps, two tools. *Quill*, 82 (4), 18-22.

The article describes two groups of journalists: academic journalists who are concerned with community connectedness, and news people who are looking at computer-assisted reporting for information and productivity. It is suggested that both groups should listen to each other and combine their insights.

Krimsky, G. A. (1995, September 23). Raising the standards of journalism (Shop talk at thirty). *Editor & Publisher*, 128 (38), 56-57.

Krimsky says the press should return to professionalism and become a public service rather than a customer service. Newspapers should not abandon journalistic standards, he says.

Kruh, N. (1996, Winter). Public journalism and civic appeal: A reporter's view. *National Civic Review*, 32-34.

Rather than relying on experts or public officials to solve community problems, citizens are increasingly becoming involved in arriving at solutions themselves. Public journalism, an accompaniment to this trend of civic renewal, has the potential to open up an entirely new way of developing communities.

Kurtz, H. (1994, June 5). Florida newspapers team up in attempt at voter-friendly coverage. *The Washington Post*, A4.

Post staff writer Kurtz explains the effort of six Florida newspaper staffs who joined to produce "no-nonsense, issue-oriented, voter-driven coverage" of the 1994 election campaign. "The Voices of Florida" project taps into voters' concerns through polls, interviews, letters, and so on, Kurtz reports. However, the article also stresses that if voters are uninformed or "have simply tuned out," can this different kind of coverage make citizens care about the race?

Kurtz, H. (1995, May 19). A foundation of fraud; *The Philadelphia Inquirer* trumpets a bogus charity. *The Washington Post*, D1.

Kurtz writes about *The Philadelphia Inquirer's* controversial acceptance of partial funding for a public journalism project and its upbeat coverage of the charity which donated the money. The charity was later charged with civil fraud by state officials.

Kurtz, H. (1996, June 4). When news media go to grass roots, candidates often don't follow. *The Washington Post*, A6.

The dozens of grass-roots efforts in the 1996 campaign season orchestrated by newspapers and TV and radio stations are part of a growing movement called public journalism that is trying to foster unscripted encounters between the public and the politicians. Candidates have not embraced the movement.

Lamb, D. (1993, Spring). A storyteller's legacy. *Grassroots Editor*, 34 (1), 11-14.

Lamb, a communications professor at the University of New Mexico, calls on Benjamin Harris, publisher of the United States' first newspaper, the nation's first community journalist. She says he left an example that holds up three centuries later—he reflected his community, and "he was helping to create it as well."

Lambeth, E. B. (1992, Fall). The news media and democracy. *Media Studies Journal,* 6 (4), 161-175.

Lambeth, a University of Missouri journalism professor, explains that many news executives are deliberately changing the culture of their news organizations and journalism's standard of performance by seeking solutions to community problems instead of just raising the community's consciousness. Lambeth pursues the questions: How does democratic journalism change and improve? What constitutes improvement?

Lambeth, E. B., & Aucoin, J. (1993, Spring). Understanding communities: The journalist as leader. *Journalism Educator,* 48 (1), 12-18.

The authors explain that if journalism students have an understanding of the communities where they live, they will make better public affairs reporters and also may become active in the struggle to keep journalism's "public service orientation." The article offers community journalism teaching exercises.

Lambeth, E. B. (1994, April). On the page . . . Good news, social ethics & the press. *Media Development,* 50-51.

The author's brief essay on the melding of public journalism and communitarian social and political ideas incorporates discussion about the book *Good News, Social Ethics & the Press* by Christians, Fackler and Ferré. The author advises practitioners of community journalism to withstand criticism and be willing to bear the expensive costs of the practice. Without the commitment, the movement could dwindle into a managerial pandering to readers, the author said.

Lambeth, E. (1996, Winter). *AEJMC Civic Journalism Interest Group News,* 1-4.

The head of the AEJMC Civic Journalism Interest Group writes about upcoming conferences, books and studies concerning civic journalism. Lambeth also invites research papers, conference ideas and attendance to Civic Journalism Interest Group business meetings and conferences.

Lydon, C. (1995, Spring). Talk radio: Finding a different public. *Nieman Reports,* 49 (1), 37-39.

Lydon, who works for WBUR, a National Public Radio station in Boston, discusses his talk show "The Connection," which was launched during the 1994 election campaigns. He says radio talk shows do have value, and talk radio audiences have "a spirit of openness and opportunity, the robust irreverence, the unregulated and sometimes rowdy give-and-take that . . . we deem the essential American sound."

Marks, A. (1995, July 24). `Public journalism' aims to revitalize public life. *The Christian Science Monitor,* 12.

The reporter takes an objective approach to writing about public journalism as a movement sweeping the nation. Listed as reasons for the change include declining readership, fierce competition, and the credibility gap.

Marshall, A. (1995, November/December). Focusing on the rotten barrel. *The IRE Journal,* 9-10.

Marshall, city hall and urban affairs reporter for *The Virginia-Pilot,* defines public journalism as a philosophy of how "stories flow from the civic and political culture of a community." He advocates its combination with investigative reporting techniques to refocus on the corruption or inefficiencies of the system, rather than those of individuals.

McGarvey, R. (1995, September). Community ties. *America West Airlines Magazine,* 54-57.

Amitai Etzioni, a professor at George Washington University in Washington, D.C., answers questions about his belief in communitarianism, a philosophy that revolves around family, values, and country.

Mears, W. R. (1995, September). Let's stop agonizing and get back to doing our job. *ASNE Bulletin,* 770, 11-12.

The *Associated Press* columnist says he thinks people dislike journalists because they cannot trust them. The way to win back that trust is through "simple, objective, accurate, straight-forward reporting," he says.

Mencher, M. (1994, Summer). Reconstructing the curriculum for service to the nation. *Journalism Educator, 49* (2), 71-76.

Mencher, professor emeritus of journalism at Columbia University, says future journalists need to be trained as activists through a journalism curriculum that would have a conceptual base of public service. "All journalism courses would have a writing component," he explains, "and the reporting and writing courses would consist of laboratory prototype exercises and reporting assignments designed to prepare students for community reporting, the reporting that is devoted to empowering the people by conferring legitimacy on certain important issues."

Mendell, D. (1996, March 3). 4,000 register to vote; state lauds `News' effort. *The Dayton Daily News,* 1B.

The author writes about the success of his employer's public journalism project to register voters. *The News* registered more than 4,000 new voters by including registration slips within its newspaper.

Merritt, D. (1993, December 26). Charting path for public journalism. *The Wichita (KS) Eagle,* A15.

The editor of *The Eagle* explains the concept of "reviving public life" through changing the way journalism is done and says he is taking a year off to explore public journalism.

Merritt, D. (1994, October 30). Public journalism: A movement toward fundamental cultural change. *The Wichita Eagle,* A17.

Merritt tells his readers about his leave of absence, taken to write a book that explains the philosophy of public journalism. He says journalism must help make public life improve, but that citizens must help, too.

Merritt, D. (1994, October 30). What role do you play as citizen? *The Wichita Eagle,* A17.

The *Eagle*'s editor asks his readers to become "conscientious citizens." He says that unless citizens learn the art of deliberation, the community will never be able to resolve issues democratically. He asks that readers talk back to the media by writing and calling reporters, editors, TV producers, and news directors.

Merritt, D. (1994, October 30). The road began in Wichita. *The Wichita Eagle,* A17.

Merritt explains the newspaper's "Voter Project," created in 1990 so candidates would address issues citizens cared about. He also explains the paper's "People Project," created in 1992 as a series designed to show how residents could have positive impacts on the community's problems.

Merritt, D. (1995, July 1). The misconceptions about public journalism. *Editor & Publisher,* 128 (26), 80, 68.

One of the leading proponents of public journalism defends the concept and practice against critics and explains how his paper engages in public journalism.

Merritt, D. (1995, Summer). Public journalism—defining a democratic art. *Media Studies Journal,* 9 (3), 125-132.

Merritt says journalism and democracy are naturally intertwined. Journalism should be flexible enough to cover government in a way that facilitates democracy.

Merritt, D. (1995, Summer-Fall). Public journalism and public life (A new paradigm of leadership: models for community renewal). *National Civic Review,* 84 (3), 262-266.

Merritt notes the Times-Mirror poll showed 71 percent of Americans believe the newspaper gets in the way of solving problems. From such negative reactions came the public journalism movement which seeks to reunite readers with the newspaper.

Merritt, D. (1996, July-August) Missing the point. *American Journalism Review,* 29-31.

The ethical debate over public journalism rages on with Merritt attempting to dispel much of the hype and oversimplification of what it means to practice public/civic journalism.

Meyer, P. (1995, November/December). Discourse leading to solutions. *The IRE Journal,* 3-5.

University of North Carolina professor Philip Meyer examines the compatibility of public journalism and investigative reporting. He writes that the former can save the later by "applying to it the discipline of method." Public journalism can also be helpful to investigative reporting as long as it supplements, not replaces scientific methods.

Miller, E. (1993, Winter). The Charlotte project: Did it work? *Poynter Report Newsletter*, 7-8.
With Poynter Institute of Media Studies personnel acting as coaches, *Charlotte Observer* staffers set about changing election coverage with the goal of reconnecting citizens to the process of democracy; Miller reports on the details.

Miller, E. (1994, Spring). Pioneering efforts in Wichita and Charlotte encourage further experiments in 5 cities. *Poynter Report Newsletter*, 3-4.
The article explains how newspapers and their local National Public Radio affiliates were working together with hopes of involving citizens in campaign coverage. The news organizations became involved after a Poynter Institute experiment, which began in 1991, with *The Charlotte Observer* to reinvent election coverage.

Morgan, H. (1994, May). Doing it in Dayton. *Quill*, 82 (4), 29-33.
The article describes the use of computer-assisted reporting at the *Dayton Daily News* for reporting projects that have become public service pieces, giving the newspaper staff a chance to learn from the community.

Morgan, H. (1994, May). Reinventing the wheel: Newsroom organization at the *Dayton Daily News* in Ohio. *Quill*, 82 (4), 34-36.
The newsroom reorganization at the *Dayton Daily News* is explained; reporting teams have four overlapping beats—public life, projects/real life, sports, and private life—while other groups, called producers, handle news trends, news events, and news presentation.

Navasky, V. (1995, Summer). Scoping out Habermas. *Media Studies Journal*, 9 (3), 117-124.
Navasky explores the philosophy of Jurgan Habermas as it applies to journalism. Habermas made a connection between journals and democratic opinion formation. The philosopher concluded that debates and conversations were essential to democracy's success.

Nieman poll finds decline in media quality. (1995, Fall). *Nieman Reports*, 49 (3), 39-42.
George Gallup Jr., former *Atlantic Monthly* editor Robert Manning and 1995 *Nieman* editor-in-residence Louis Ureneck discuss the results of the Nieman Foundation of Harvard University's survey of 500 fellows. The results showed a decline in public confidence in the media, deterioration in journalism quality, and a blurring between entertainment and news.

Oppel, R. (1992, January 12). We'll help you regain control of the issues. *The Charlotte Observer*, A1.
The Observer's editor explains how his newspaper will help citizens decide the 1992 campaign agenda—through intensive polling; thorough follow-up reporting, which includes checking soapbox statements; and reader involvement. He also explains how the newspaper is collaborating with the Poynter Institute for Media Studies in trying this approach to campaign coverage.

Overholser, G. (1995, September 17). Learning from 'Civic Journalism.' *The Washington Post*.
The Washington Post ombudsman questions why the practices of public journalism require a new title. She says applying public journalism practices to traditional journalism would be much simpler since many are resurrected practices. Furthermore, this tact would be more easily accepted than arguing to displace traditional journalism.

Peck, C. (1995, March). The ethics of public journalism: Three views. *ASNE Bulletin*, 44.
Peck summarizes the ethical questions being raised about public journalism from three viewpoints: the proponent's, the traditionalist's, and the public's.

Peirce, N. R. (1992, September). Are newspapers crossing a troubling line in efforts to lead their communities? No: Other groups are inadequate. *ASNE Bulletin*, 743, 5-6.
Newspaper staffers should not compromise their journalistic independence, but

should still devote substantial space in their paper to community issues, says Peirce, a nationally syndicated columnist.

Peirce, N. R. (1994, June 25). Civic journalism: Newspapers and broadcasters are beginning to focus on the concerns of all of us—not just as consumers but as participating citizens. *The Charlotte Observer,* A15.
> The author explains how the concept of public journalism is "spreading coast to coast" and explores the pros and cons of using the public journalism concept during election years.

Peirce, N. R. (1994, July 2). Civic journalism: A new genre. *National Journal,* 26, 1585.
> The article looks positively at the trend of public journalism at newspapers, TV stations, and National Public Radio.

Peirce, N. R. (1994, October 24). Promoting constructive pubic debate: Civic journalism can help define the issues for politicians. *The Philadelphia Inquirer,* A7.
> Urban affairs writer Peirce explains public journalism efforts by several newspapers during the midterm election season.

Peterson, I. (1996, March 4). Civic-minded pursuits gain ground at newspapers. *The New York Times,* D5.
> The author writes about the business side of public journalism. Several newspapers practicing public journalism have shown a slight increase in circulation, but only one study of the circulation impact has been conducted.

Pike, M., Sheath, R., & Carey, J. (1995, March 24). Public journalism. *New Statesman & Society,* 8 (345), S30.
> The authors outline the goal of public journalism and some of the specific possible benefits such as improved race relations, less crime, and better education.

Putnam, R. D. (1995, January). Bowling alone: America's declining social capital. *Journal of Democracy,* 6 (1).
> Often cited by advocates of public journalism, this article describes the growing disengagement of Americans from all aspects of public life.

Ray, G. (1995, January 2). `Public Journalism' is nothing new to most small papers. *Publisher's Auxiliary,* 131 (1), 5.
> Ray, a Colorado State University journalism professor, explains that most editors of small community papers "have missed the fireworks" over public journalism because their editors have been practicing it all along.

Rebeck, G. (1995, July-August). Making the news a 2-way street. *Utne Reader,* 70, 33.
> The author provides an overview of the public journalism concept and how it is being motivated by waning readership and low public opinion of newspapers.

Rieder, R. (1995, December). Public Journalism: Stop the shooting. *American Journalism Review,* 6.
> The *American Journalism Review* editor notes the common ground and benefits of traditional and the public journalism ideology. He says the real key to good journalism is good reporters. The positives of public journalism cannot make up for the decrease in news staffs.

Rosen, J. (1991). Making journalism more public. *Communication,* 12, 267-284.
> Using the *Columbus Ledger-Enquirer* as an example, Rosen of New York University presents different ways in which journalism might become "more public," which he says means "more supportive of a realm of meaningful public discussion."

Rosen, J. (1991, October). To be or not to be? *ASNE Bulletin,* 735, 16-19.
> Newspapers could be the last hope for recreating public life communities, the author says. He suggests that the solution is "to re-imagine the newspaper as a complex support system for public life."

Rosen, J. (1992, March). Community action: Sin or salvation? *Quill,* 80 (2), 30-33.
> Rosen looks at the *Columbus Ledger-Enquirer's* public journalism project, "Beyond 2000." He says they were biased, but in "a manner that we—we citizens, we journalists—ought to applaud."

Rosen, J. (1992, November-December). Discourse. *Columbia Journalism Review, 31* (4), 34-35.
Rosen explains that journalists should stop asking presidential candidates "tough" questions—often manipulated by campaign public relations staffs—and instead try uncovering issues that are pertinent to the American public.

Rosen, J. (1992, Winter). Forming and informing the public. *Kettering Review,* 60-70.
Rosen explains the public journalism project of the *Columbus Ledger-Enquirer.* The newspaper staff discovered there was a "political vacuum" in Columbus, and a town meeting was organized, which turned out to be a significant event because a number of task forces were eventually created. Rosen says once "a public is formed, it can then be informed about the issues it faces." His explains his assumption: "The newspaper can only remain valuable if public life remains viable."

Rosen, J. (1993, November-December). Public life and the press: Building a new house for journalism ethics. *Quill,* 27.
Rosen calls for journalism that encourages ordinary citizens to take part in shaping the political scene.

Rosen, J. (1993, November-December). Public life and the press: Building a new house for journalism ethics. *Quill, 81* (9), 27-28.
Rosen says that even though some journalists are worried the U.S. public is losing the will to tackle public issues such as health care, the media can still play a part in persuading citizens to get involved.

Rosen, J. (1993, Winter). Beyond objectivity. *Nieman Reports, 47* (4), 48-53.
Although objectivity has been viewed as the cornerstone of democratic journalism, Rosen advocates that journalists need to spark debate and participation from citizens—and accountability from politicians. He says that this seemingly violative journalism will do more to ensure democracy than will objective reporting.

Rosen, J. (1994, September-October). Journalism and the production of the present. *Tikkun, 9* (5), 13-18.
The author explains that journalism can be used as a tool by which people can develop a political perspective that allows them to separate themselves from news events.

Rosen, J. (1994, December). Making things more public: On the political responsibility of the media intellectual. *Critical Studies in Mass Communications, 11,* 363-388.
Rosen says that public journalism is one response to "the six alarm bells ringing for the press at the present": the electronic alarm, the technology alarm, the political alarm, the occupational alarm, the spiritual alarm, and the intellectual alarm. He also explores the problem of "the public," saying that in universities "the public" is successfully theorized, but theorized "one remove from the rest of society." He says academics need to contribute to the resolution or the common understanding of our current "complex and troubled" public life.

Rosen, J. (1995, May-June). Public journalism: A case for public scholarship. *Change, 27,* (3), 34-38.
Rosen explains public journalism and argues it is socially constructive. He says scholarly activities should integrate public service for the benefit the larger community.

Rosen, J. (1995, November-December). What should we be doing? *The IRE Journal,* 6-8.
Rosen says putting life first is essential to the survival of journalism, and that's what public journalism does best. He questions why investigative reporters are often not concerned with the positive prospect of politics, but focus on corruption. He advises comparative studies of communities to determine what works politically. Investigative reporters should also work on devising a civic barometer, he says.

Rosen, J. (1996). The propaganda of the present. *Tikkun, 11* (1), 19-24.
Public journalism guru Rosen reflects on civic identity in the media age.

Rosen, J. (1996, February 19). Take back the campaign. 1996 election campaign; media matters. *The Nation, 262* (7), 10.

Rosen says the success of the elite press ended because of tabloids, on-line media, C-SPAN and public journalism. He argues that editors should chose to practice public journalism in their 1996 election coverage for the benefit of the profession as well as the citizens.

Rosen, J. (1996, April 1). In the booth with the press. *The Nation*, 10.
Rosen examines *Washington Post* Executive Editor Leonard Downie's personal decision not to vote.

Rosenstiel, T. B. (1993, November 25). Reporters putting their own spin on news events. *Los Angeles Times*, A1.
Many papers are offering interpretation along with facts, Rosenstiel of the *Los Angeles Times* says, noting that this subjectivity may anger an already suspicious public. He explores the pros and cons of the loss of objectivity by interviewing several journalists and communications professors.

Rosenfeld, H. (1995, October 1). We regret to report that civic journalism is a bad idea. *The Times Union* (Albany, NY), E5.
The editor of *The Times Union* criticizes civic journalism because it encourages journalists to become participants in the events they cover. It thus prohibits objectivity, he argues. He also says that "newspapers are already inclined to reflect establishmentarian viewpoints."

Scannell, P. (1989). Public service broadcasting and modern public life. *Media, Culture and Society*, 11, 135-166.
Scannell of the School of Communication at Polytechnic of Central London argues for broadcasting as "a public good." He gives a brief, historical account of broadcasting in England and then looks at radio audiences and stresses the importance of "the public life of broadcasting."

Schneider, H. (1992, September). Are newspapers crossing a troubling line with efforts to lead their communities? Yes: That is not a newspaper's job. *ASNE Bulletin*, 743, 4, 6.
The author, the managing editor of *Newsday* in Long Island, New York, says that community connectedness is "a dangerous idea." He says this concept is often driven by newspaper chains that often have alienated communities by "musical chair management." He also says that attempts by journalists to organize the community may blur their newspaper's role but that the press needs to aggressively pursue electronic publishing and alternative ways of disseminating information—thus linking newsrooms to every home.

Schudson, M. S. (1995, Winter). The 1996 new news bias. *The Public Relations Strategist*, 1, 4, 37-41.
In his article, written to help public relations workers understand the press, Schudson warns that public journalism could result in boosterism. However, he adds that the press should be allowed to experiment.

Seals, L. (1995, Spring). Turning to readers to cover big stories. *Nieman Reports*, 12-13.
Seals, managing editor of *The Richmond (VA) Times-Dispatch*, writes about the importance and difficulty of focusing on readers' concerns. She advocates keeping a pulse on readers' opinions through various means—surveys, focus groups, reader calls and letters, and newsroom discussion. Each has its limitations, but all should still be used.

Shepard, A. C. (1994, September). The death of a pioneer. *American Journalism Review*, 16 (7), 35.
Some people blame the suicide of Jack Swift, the *Columbus (GA) Ledger-Enquirer* executive editor, on public journalism. Billy Winn, a newsroom employee, explains that the Swift-initiated "Columbus Beyond 2000: Agenda for Progress" series—and a subsequent task force—were necessary for Columbus. But the negative feedback for his participatory role bothered Swift and may have prompted his suicide.

Shepard, A. C. (1994, September). The gospel of public journalism. *American Journalism Review*, 16 (7), 28-34.
The author interviews advocates and nonbelievers of public journalism on the

ethics of the movement. The critics say that public journalism will hurt credibility by turning the media into players rather than chroniclers, while the advocates say news organizations have to listen more closely to their audiences and play more active roles in their communities.

Shepard, A. C. (1995, January-February). The real public journalism. *American Journalism Review*, 17 (1), 25.

The author explains that public journalism is not popular at *The Philadelphia Inquirer*, where editors and reporters don't believe that they should become part of the story; instead, they take complex issues and explain how they affect the reader.

Sheppard, J. (1995, May). Climbing down from the ivory tower. *American Journalism Review*, 17 (4), 18-22, 24-25.

Public journalism is spreading to editorial pages as editors "solicit reader contributions, offer contrasting views on an issue, and worry whether it's elitist to endorse candidates," the author says. She reports editors' differing views—from those who have positive things to say to those who say public journalism "dumbs down" the editorial pages.

Sheppard, J. (1995, May). Call-in columns: What's being said at the coffee shops. *American Journalism Review*, 17 (4), 23.

Some newspapers allow readers to call in their opinions anonymously; their opinions are then published on the editorial pages. Some editors worry about printing anonymous information, but some editors strongly support the idea.

Shriver, D. W. Jr. (1995, Summer). Journalists and the democratic memory. *Media Studies Journal*, 9 (3), 133-140.

The author says journalists and historians should redraft history to promote democratic culture. Journalists are obliged to remind readers of wartime incidents and other traumatic events.

Silverman, M. (1994, November-December). Journalists are getting closer to readers. *ASNE Bulletin*, 763, 12-14.

Gannet's NEWS 2000 program has succeeded in attracting new readers. The program strives to place greater emphasis on community news and national news in which the community is interested. The program has also involved getting feedback from readers through questionnaires.

Smith, S. A. (1991, Summer). Your vote counts: *The Wichita Eagle's* election project. *National Civic Review*, 80, 284-293.

Smith, managing editor of *The Wichita (KS) Eagle*, explains his newspaper's "Your Vote Counts" project, a 1990 election coverage plan built around community issues. Although the author reports that "it was not possible to demonstrate decisively that the project had increased voter turnout," he says the results were encouraging, and the paper plans to continue the project for the next election.

Spaid, E. L. (1994, March 4). New approach to election coverage wins fans. *Christian Science Monitor*, 1.

The author looks at several U.S. newspapers that are experimenting with public journalism; she presents the pros, not the cons, of the concept. She reports that during the 1994 elections a few newspapers will "let voters set the agenda on issues that they said mattered to them." Spaid interviews editor Davis Merritt of *The Wichita Eagle* and Jay Rosen, director of the Project on Public Life and the Press at New York University—both supporters of civic journalism.

Stavitsky, A. G. (1993, Summer). Ear on America. *Media Studies Journal*, 7 (3), 77-91.

University of Oregon professor Stavitsky presents evidence of "the universality, breadth, quality, and quirkiness of radio that serve all kinds of Americans every day" by profiling eight stations in eight U.S. states. His case studies highlight "the day-to-day value of radio, that `electronic wallpaper' that nearly all Americans make part of their lives."

Stavitsky, A. G. (1994, Winter). The changing conception of localism in U.S. public radio.

Journal of Broadcasting & Electronic Media, 38, 19-33.

Stavitsky addresses the changing conception of localism in U. S. public radio, "from a spatial emphasis—based on traditional geographic notions of community—to a social conception in which community is defined in terms of shared interests, tastes, and values." He explores serving a public through electronic communication.

Steffens, B. L. (1993, September). Must a watchdog always bite: Are we killing our future? *Quill*, 81 (7), 3.

Quill editor Steffens reports on journalists' growing interest in "reforming partnerships with both politics and the public." He mentions the Project on Public Life and the Press—created by the Knight and Kettering foundations and directed by New York University professor Jay Rosen in hopes of finding ways for the media to strengthen and improve public life.

Stein, M. L. (1992, August 29). More than just reporting: Editors want reporters who care about, connect with communities. *Editor & Publisher*, 125 (35), 22.

Speaking at the annual convention of the Association for Education in Journalism and Mass Communication in Montreal, news executives from the largest U.S. newspaper chains told educators that they want graduates who can connect with the communities.

Stein, M. L. (1994, October 15). A catalyst for public awareness? *Editor & Publisher*, 127 (42), 11, 41.

Editorial writers listen to New York University professor Jay Rosen, public journalism advocate, at the 1994 National Conference of Editorial Writers. They then explore the idea of newspapers reaching beyond their traditional role of providing only news.

Stein, M. L. (1994, November 12). In praise of public journalism. *Editor & Publisher*, 127 (46), 15, 45.

Newspaper executives who attended the 66th annual meeting of the Pacific Northwest Newspaper Association say public journalism programs are "off and running" at their newspapers.

Stein, M. L. (1995, May 6). Beware of public journalism. *Editor & Publisher*, 128 (18), 18-19.

Stein reports on William F. Woo's speech presented at the 30th annual *Riverside (CA) Press-Enterprise* lecture at the University of California, where the *St. Louis Post-Dispatch* editor praised some public journalism experiments but also raised ethical questions about the concept.

Stein, M. L. (1996, February 24). Suicidal course. *Editor & Publisher*, 14.

Stein reports that *The New York Times* Managing Editor Gene Roberts spoke at the annual *Riverside Press-Enterprise* lecture and criticized newspaper sponsorship of public meetings. Roberts said that the reason for dying newspaper readership is the declining news hole.

Stencel, S. (1996, September 20). Civic journalism: Can press reforms revitalize democracy? *CQ Researcher*, 6 (35), 817-840.

An entire issue devoted to civic/public journalism. The issue includes an extensive biography.

Stepp, C. (1996, May). Public journalism: Balancing the scales. *American Journalism Review*, 38-40.

Public journalism often has been presented as a "take-it-or-leave-it" package, but Stepp maintains it doesn't have to be that way.

Stoll, T., & Iverson, D. (1995, March). Still learning after all these years. *Civic Catalyst*, 1, 10-11.

Stoll, associate editor of the *Wisconsin State Journal*, and Iverson, the executive producer of Wisconsin Public Television in Madison, report on the lessons they learned from "We the People/Wisconsin," a civic journalism project created for coverage of the 1992 election campaign. The project remains alive.

Taylor, J. H. (1993, Fall). Can you be a catalyst without becoming a part of the story? *The Masthead*, 45 (3), 29-30.

Taylor, the editorial page editor of *The News Journal* in Wilmington, Delaware, argues that newspaper journalists—"particularly newspaper editorial staffs—can and should find ways to get involved in their communities." He presents the example of "The Delaware Agenda" and how his newspaper became involved in looking at the state's economic plans.

Tharp, M. (1996, March 18). The media's new fix. *U.S. News & World Report, 120,* 72, 74.
The author reports on the media's most recent ploy for regaining readers and viewers—public journalism. In general terms, the practice is defined and examples of its implementation are given. Tharp also touches on the arguments for and against this trend.

Thelen, G. (1993, November 21). The newspaper can help our community set its course. *The State* (Columbia, SC), D1.
Thelen, the executive editor of *The State* in Columbia, SC, explains the newspaper's interest in creating public spaces where citizens "can intelligently wrestle with the great issues of our day and come to public judgment." He says that the concept of public journalism energizes residents.

Theobald, W. (1996, March). Why can't we talk? *Quill,* 35.
Public journalism isn't the answer to all journalism's problems, the author says. But that doesn't mean its practices should be shunned. There is no one solution to reengaging the public in politics. Journalists should be prepared to accept what works with public journalism and toss out what doesn't.

Urenek, L. (1995, Spring). Empathy—path to a different world. *Nieman Reports, 49* (1), 19-21.
The author, editor of *The Portland (Maine) Press Herald,* says he thinks democracy means "the distilled experience of millions of regular people making judgments based on the witness of their individual lives." He suggests that reporters start reporting with empathy and thus start reconnecting with readers.

Walsh, J. (1994, January 15). Beyond the ballot box: Time for deliberative conversation. *The Cincinnati Post,* A8.
This editorial by Walsh, assistant editorial page editor of *The Post,* is based on a gathering held at the University of Cincinnati, where 200 residents came to hear Kettering Foundation President David Mathews speak on his book *Politics for People.* She reports that Mathews "figures that if the current citizen energy in this country is to be channeled beyond anger and cynicism into more constructive outlets, people need to start having more deliberative conversations." Walsh ponders whether a "citizens' revolution" might take place.

Walsh, J. (1994, July 16). We all have a responsibility to make our democracy work. *The Cincinnati Post,* A10.
This editorial is based on "the bizarre spectacle" of North Koreans mourning the death of their leader, who was no "Mr. Nice Guy," Walsh says. The author warns that democracy is "not necessarily an innate human value . . . if insufficiently nourished, democratic tradition can wither." Because the media often are blamed for this withering, she reports that several newspapers are experimenting with ways to try to reconnect readers to the democratic process.

Walsh, J. (1994, July 30). Public journalism has an attitude: We don't know everything. *The Cincinnati Post,* A10.
Walsh explains how *The Wichita (KS) Eagle* plans to cover the 1994 general election using the concept of public journalism. She says that although some journalists are not comfortable with the idea, the readers in Wichita seem to be embracing it.

Webb, W. (1995, June 10). Public interest journalism in the on-line era. *Editor & Publisher, 128* (23), 28.
On-line public interest journalism received overwhelming support by newspaper publishers at the Nieman Foundation's conference on "Public interest journalism: Winner or loser in the on-line era?" The new technology could give the public better access to information, supporters said. Critics fear the public may use the computing network more for entertainment than for news gathering.

Weaver, D. (1995, July/August). Public journalism: An editor and a scholar reflect on 'new journalism' at Indiana University's fifth annual Roy W. Howard public lecture. *Scripps Howard News*, 11-12.

> Weaver, a Roy W. Howard research professor, writes about the speeches made by scholar Jay Rosen and editor Davis "Buzz" Merritt at Indiana University. The speakers cited the victories of public journalism projects such as in Charlotte, NC, and Wichita, KS. Rosen also discussed the practice of teaming reporters to cover politics and government in a "more public" way.

Wharton, T. (1995, January 26). State of the Union reaction: Clinton has placed citizenship's decline on the public's table. *Norfolk (VA) Ledger Star*, A1.

> Clinton says in his State of the Union address that "our civil life is suffering." He asks that Americans give something back to their communities. "Opportunity and responsibility go hand-in-hand," he says. Comments about the speech from a variety of scholars—including Jay Rosen of the Project on Public Life and the Press at New York University—are included in the article.

Whitaker, B. (1995, August 27). Jay Rosen. *The Dallas Morning News*, 1J.

> Whitaker interviews public journalism leader Jay Rosen on his definition of public journalism and his hopes for it. She writes in a question-answer format.

Winn, B. (1992, September). In Columbus, GA, a report on the future led a newspaper to try to shape what would come. *ASNE Bulletin*, 743, 9-10.

> An upbeat article by the editorial page editor of the *Columbus (GA) Ledger-Enquirer* discusses the paper's "Beyond 2000" program, an early attempt at public journalism. He reports that a great deal was accomplished in Columbus due to the newspaper's efforts—from reopening racial dialogue to creating a new class of city leaders.

Winn, B. (1993, Winter). Public journalism: An early attempt. *Nieman Reports*, 47 (4), 54-56.

> The editorial page editor of the *Columbus Ledger-Enquirer* explains the paper's project "Beyond 2000," a program that involved the public in city planning; the project continues today—without the paper's stewardship.

Winship, T. (1995, April 1). Jim Batten and civic journalism. *Editor & Publisher*, 128 (13), 32, 37.

> Winship, the former editor of the *Boston Globe*, meets with *Miami Herald* CEO Jim Batten, and they chat about public journalism. Winship reports Batten is convinced that public journalism can rejuvenate the news business and briefly describes what civic journalism advocates throughout the country are doing.

Winship, T. (1995, October 7). Civic journalism: A steroid for the press. *Editor & Publisher*, 128 (40), 5.

> Civic journalism has caused such a stir in the journalism community that many skeptics of the movement refused to attend the Pew Center for Civic Journalism's symposium to debate it, according to Winship.

Woo, W. F. (1991, November 10). Journalists risk becoming disconnected. *St. Louis Post Dispatch*, B1.

> Woo reflects on the phenomenon of journalists and their disconnection with their readers. He says that "the greatest disconnective force of all is that which comes from not knowing about our readers, from not sharing in the lives of the people who buy the newspaper." He also explores the definition of "virtuous journalist."

Woo, W. F. (1992, April 19). Understanding our neighbors. *St. Louis Post Dispatch*, B1.

> The author bases his "Reflections" column on a Kiwanis Club morning prayer meeting, an event at which he spoke. He explains that the meeting was "a piece of the community fabric, revealing something about the people." He explains that no newspaper staff is big enough to cover all community meetings; however, when 300 people get up before dawn and pay $5 to gather and listen to a speech on media and ethics, newspapers must see this as significant—and a way of understanding their readers.

Woo, W. F. (1995, July-August). Should the press be an observer or an actor in public affairs? (William F. Woo speech). *St. Louis Journalism Review*, 25 (178), 10-12.

Woo calls for a return to objectivity in journalism, saying reporters have gotten too involved in the public affairs they are covering. This will require covering stories that may not be popular, but which may make journalism more relevant to the public.

Woo, W. F. (1995, Fall). Public journalism and the tradition of detachment. *The Masthead,* 47 (3), 15-20.

Woo concedes that reporters should listen more to readers, but questions how news organizations can be as proactive as public journalism prescribes and not become controllers of democracy. He also is concerned about where news and editorial decisions are made in the practice of public journalism.

Zang, B. (1994, March-April). The activist: The paper that really gets involved. *Columbia Journalism Review,* 32 (6), 12-13.

The author interviews Mike Phillips, editor of *The Sun* in Bremerton, Washington, about how his paper participates in the effort to solve community problems. Phillips believes newspapers should avoid partisan involvement and not become publicists for any group; however, he says they can still make a big difference by creating the right climate for community participation.

Reports/Presentations

Allen, D. S. (1995, August). *Theories of democracy and American journalism: Creating an active public.* Paper presented at the Civic Journalism Interest Group at the Association of Education in Journalism and Mass Communications annual meeting, Washington, DC.

Allen, of Illinois State University, illustrates how different practices within American journalism are connected to theories of democracy. His paper argues that although competitive and pluralist theories help lead to an informed public, deliberative and participatory theories strive to create an active public. Most conventional press practices are linked to an informed public, but the press should adopt policies to create an active public.

Aucoin, J. (1995, August). *Expanding the public conversation—or just sounding off? An appraisal of the newspaper call-in comment line.* Paper presented at the Civic Journalism Interest Group at the Association of Education in Journalism and Mass Communications annual meeting, Washington, DC.

Aucoin, a University of South Alabama professor, does a content analysis of six weeks of an urban daily's call-in column and its letters to the editor. Using the journalism-as-conversation model, Aucoin finds evidence that the columns expanded public dialogue. Nevertheless, editors should try to improve the conversation, he says.

Batten, J. K. (1990, February 8). *41st annual William Allen White speech at the University of Kansas—Newspapers and communities: The vital link.* Lawrence, KS: William Allen White Foundation.

Batten, chief executive officer and board chairman of Knight Ridder Inc., received the William Allen White Foundation National Citation of Journalistic Merit on February 8, 1990, at the University of Kansas, Lawrence. He speaks of "the sluggish state of civic health in many communities in the early 1990s" and notes that many newspapers are not positioned to improve this situation because "they themselves are basically disconnected from their communities." He suggests papers do what they can to retain staff.

Bhatia, P. (Ed.). (1994). *Public journalism: What it means, who is practicing it, and how it is done,* Associated Press Managing Editors Readership Committee report. Myrtle Beach, SC: APME.

The report begins with an interview with Jay Rosen of New York University, who explains the concept of public journalism. Thereafter, examples of what newspapers are trying are reported.

Christians, C. G. (1995, August). *The common good in a global setting.* Paper presented at the Civic Journalism Interest Group at the Association of Education in Journalism and Mass

Communications annual meeting, Washington, DC.

> The paper argues for a universal human good rooted in purposive nature. Civic journalism plays into this goal as it shifts emphasis from individual rights to community values. This leaves unanswered the question of norms by which local cultures are assessed.

Clark, R. P. (1992). *A call to leadership.* The Poynter Papers: No. 1. St. Petersburg, FL: The Poynter Institute for Media Studies.

> This booklet is "written at time of trouble for American journalism and the public it serves," says Clark, a Poynter Institute for Media Studies senior scholar. The document offers a blueprint for leadership and is a product of a Poynter seminar, "Ownership and Leadership: Imagining a Bright Future for Journalism," which convened in January, 1992.

Craig, D. A. (1995, August). *Communitarian journalism(s): Clearing the conceptual landscape.* Paper presented at the annual meeting of the Association for Education in Journalism and Mass Communications, Washington, DC.

> Craig's paper clarifies the contrasting ways the concept of communitarianism has been discussed by authors such as Altschull, Lambeth, and especially Christians, Ferré, and Fackler.

Demers, D. P. (1993, August). *Community attachment, social priming and newspaper reading.* Paper presented at the annual meeting of the Association for Education in Journalism and Mass Communications, Kansas City, MO.

> Demers reports that a study, which employed the community attachment model, hypothesized that the greater the attachments to a community, the greater the reading of the local newspaper. Data collected at a small midwest university support the hypotheses.

Dennis, E. E. (1993, April 15). *Fighting media illiteracy: What every American needs to know and why.* Speech presented at the fourth annual Roy W. Howard Lecture at Indiana University-Bloomington.

> Dennis, the executive director of the Freedom Forum Media Studies Center at Columbia University, talks about the importance of people being "media literate," or having an understanding of the media environment. He discusses ways to improve the relationship between the public and the media.

Dykers, C. R. (1995, August). *A critical review: Reconceptualizing the relation of 'democracy' to 'news.'* Paper presented at the Civic Journalism Interest Group at the Association of Education in Journalism and Mass Communications annual meeting, Washington, DC.

> Dykers said public journalists are forcing their profession to confront its basic value. The connection between democratic theory and journalistic practice conceals a debt to liberal democratic philosophy focusing on individual rights rather than communal interests. Because of that, it restricts practitioners' idea of news.

Ettema, J. S., & Peer, L. (1995, August). *Good news from a bad neighborhood: A theoretical and empirical approach to civic journalism.* Paper presented at the Civic Journalism Interest Group at the Association of Education in Journalism and Mass Communications annual meeting, Washington, DC.

> This paper encourages journalists to look for the positives in troubled neighborhoods rather than negatives. This conclusion is based on content analysis of two large metropolitan newspapers' coverage of a poor neighborhood.

Fallows, J., & Storin, M. V. (1996, May 14). Journalism: From citizens up. *Pew Center for Civic Journalism,* 1-20.

> In separate speeches at the Pew Center, Storin, editor of the *Boston Globe,* and Fallows, editor of *U.S. News and World Report,* give their takes on public journalism. Storin points out that public journalism has its pitfalls, but it's more of a solution to the survival of newspapers than a problem, he says. Fallows offers a three-part plan to further public journalism: people who support public journalism should be the first to complain when the label is misused, emphasize less the theory of the movement that its specifics, and recognize that the battle will be won when people stop

talking about "civic" or "public journalism."

Friedland, L. A. , Sotirovic, M., & Daily, K. (1995, August). *Public journalism and social capital: The case of Madison, Wisconsin.* Paper presented at the Civic Journalism Interest Group at the Association of Education in Journalism and Mass Communications annual meeting, Washington, DC.
> The authors write about the first results of a multi-method, multi-year study of the "We the People" public journalism project in Madison. The study is based on the concept of social capital and a community-wide survey.

Harwood, R. C., & the Harwood Group (1993). *A meaningful chaos: How people form relationships with public concerns.* Kettering Foundation.
> This seminal study in the literature on public journalism enumerates nine factors that contribute to the formation of "authentic" public opinion—that is, opinion that genuinely reflects people's enduring beliefs rather than their short-term manipulated views.

Huxman, S. S., & Iorio, S. H. (1993, November). *Helping newspapers become more responsive to community concerns.* Paper presented at the annual meeting of the Speech Communication Association, Miami Beach, FL.
> The authors conducted an in-depth interview research project with Sedgwick County, Kansas, residents, whom *The Wichita Eagle* newspaper serves. The paper wanted to uncover residents' concerns about politics and politicians. Two findings: The issues identified by residents were often part of much larger issues, and "how" people talk about issues was more meaningful than "what" was said about the issues.

MacLeod, J. M., Daily, K. A., Guo, Z., Eveland, W. P., Jr., Bayer, J., Yang, S., & Wang, Hsu. (1994, August). *Community integration, local media use and democratic processes.* Paper presented at the annual meeting of the Association of Education in Journalism and Mass Communications, Atlanta, GA.
> The paper examines "the multidimensionality of community integration, its relationship to local media use and proposes a set of criteria for citizen activity in democratic processes." The authors share the results of their research on this topic, explaining that there is evidence for "a clear, positive connection between the level of individual community integration and local democratic processes."

Miller, E. (1994). *Election 94: Newspapers, public radio cooperate on voter-driven election coverage.* Poynter Report/Special Report St. Petersburg, FL: The Poynter Institute.
> Miller of the Poynter Institute looks at election coverage for 1994 campaigns. A project involving NPR and newspapers in five cities is discussed as is the "Voices of Florida" project, which involved six Florida newspapers. A "poor editor's guide" to election coverage also is offered.

Miller, E., & Boyd, W. M., Jr. (1994). *Technology and journalism: Do they fit?* Poynter Report/Special Report, St. Petersburg, FL: The Poynter Institute, 2-4.
> The technological revolution is changing the relationship between journalism and its customers, and journalists need to understand the changing expectations of customers to survive. The authors explain how public journalism can be included in the changing relationship, for instance, by providing a way for public discourse.

Parisi, P. (1995, August). *Toward a 'philosophy of framing': Narrative strategy and public journalism.* Paper presented at the Civic Journalism Interest Group at the Association of Education in Journalism and Mass Communications annual meeting, Washington, DC.
> The City University of New York professor focuses on the use narrative form in public journalism. He argues that narrative can be the key to public journalism's success for it can provide readers with a more compassionate portrait of their community. By recognizing this, public journalists can draw on explanatory journalism, interpretive journalism, and conventions of objectivity.

Rosen, J. (1994). *Community connectedness: Passwords for public journalism.* The Poynter Papers: No. 3. St. Petersburg, FL: The Poynter Institute.

Public journalism advocate and New York University professor Rosen asks in his essay that journalists think of public life as "a work in progress." He reminds journalists "in a culture of public pessimism and journalistic cynicism . . . democracy is a system founded on hope."

Rosen, J., & Merritt, D. (1994). *Public journalism: Theory and practice.* Dayton, OH: Kettering Foundation.

This special report, written by two proponents of public journalism, is divided into two sections: The first, "Public Journalism: First Principles," is written by Jay Rosen of New York University and addresses public journalism as a philosophy and not as "a settled doctrine." The second essay, by Davis Merritt, editor of *The Wichita (KS) Eagle,* addresses the decline in journalism's role and the decline in public life; he explains how public journalism can help stop both of those declines.

Times Mirror Center for The People & The Press (1994, October). *The people, the press, and politics: The new political landscape.* Washington, DC: Times Mirror Center for the People & The Press.

The Times-Mirror Center research staff interviewed thousands of Americans during the summer of 1994 and found "no clear direction in the public's political thinking other than frustration with the current system and an eager responsiveness to alternative political solutions and appeals." The center's longitudinal survey shows there is less partisan self-identification and new economic realities have reshaped the electorate's center. Detailed results are given.

Weaver, D., & Wilhoit, G. C. (1992). *The American journalist in the 1990s.* Arlington, VA: The Freedom Forum.

The authors' study included interviews with more than 1,400 U.S. journalists. They present what they discovered about newspeoples' journalistic and political values; information about employment also is offered.

Woo, W. F. (1995, February 13). *As old gods falter: Public journalism and the tradition of detachment.* Paper presented at the Press-Enterprise Lecture Series, No. 30, University of California, Riverside.

Editor Woo of the *St. Louis Post Dispatch* says he is impressed by some examples of public journalism, yet he is unsettled by others. He explains, for instance, that during the 1994 election, journalists no longer served or informed the electorate—they became it. Woo wonders if a paper can objectively report on a community issue when a news staffer sits on a commission that is promoting a particular point of view. He fears journalists may be letting go too easily of traditions and values that they have held on to for a long time.

Zang, B. (1995, August). *Missing voices in the civic/public journalism debates: "I never thought a newspaper could ask 'what if?' " and other citizen-reader observations.* Paper presented at the Civic Journalism Interest Group at the Association of Education in Journalism and Mass Communications annual meeting, Washington, D.C.

Using a three-month field study, Zang explores what readers are saying about public journalism. Her findings are somewhat mixed. Readers want the newspaper to connect them with their community, but also want news to be "balanced."

Index